# Transnationalism, Education and Empowerment

*Transnationalism, Education and Empowerment* challenges the prevailing notion that transnationalism is concerned fundamentally with the process of enhanced global population movement that has been allied with modern globalisation. Instead, it argues that transnationalism is a state of mind, disassociated from the notion of 'place,' that can be observed equally in societies of the past. Drawing on the context of colonial Sri Lanka and the British Empire, the book discusses how education in the British Empire was the means by which some marginalised groups in colonised societies were able to activate their transnational dispositions. Far from being a universal oppressor of colonised people, as argued by postcolonial scholarship, colonial education was capable of creating pathways to life improvement that did not exist before the European colonial period, providing agency to those who did not possess it prior to colonial rule.

The book begins by exploring the meaning of transnationalism, arguing that it needs to be redefined to meet the realities of past and current global societies. It then moves on to examine the ways education was used within the period of 18th and 19th century European colonialism, with a particular emphasis on Sri Lanka and other parts of the former British Empire. Drawing from examples of his own family's ancestry, Casinader then discusses how some marginalised groups in parts of the British Empire were able to use education as the key to unlocking their pre-existing transnational dispositions in order to create pathways for more prosperous futures. Rather than being subjugated by colonial education, they harnessed the educational aspects of British colonial education for their own goals.

This book is one of the first to contest and critically evaluate the contemporary conceptualisation of transnationalism, particularly in the educational context. It will be of key interest to academics, researchers and postgraduate students in the fields of education, the history of education, imperial and colonial history, cultural studies and geography.

**Niranjan Casinader** is Senior Lecturer in Education (Curriculum and Assessment) in the Faculty of Education at Monash University, Australia. Originally trained as a geographer, he worked as a secondary school educator for many years before moving into academia. His research is focused on three related principal strands: the notion of transnationalism in education, particularly in relation to the impact of culture on curriculum, pedagogy and thinking; the teaching of Geography and other Humanities subjects in schools; and the role of education in British colonial policy and practice, with an especial focus on its relevance to contemporary society.

## Routledge Research in Education

For a full list of titles in this series, please visit https://www.routledge.com

**178 Children's Creative Music-Making with Reflexive Interactive Technology**
Adventures in Improvising and Composing
*Edited by Victoria Rowe, Angeliki Triantafyllaki and Francois Pachet*

**179 Community-based Media Pedagogies**
Relational Practices of Listening in the Commons
*Bronwen Low, Chloe Brushwood Rose, and Paula Salvio*

**180 Reclaiming Discipline for Education**
Knowledge, Relationships and the Birth of Community
*James MacAllister*

**181 The Politics of Differentiation in Schools**
*Martin Mills, Amanda Keddie, Peter Renshaw, and Sue Monk*

**182 Language, Race, and Power in Schools**
A Critical Discourse Analysis
*Edited by Pierre W. Orelus*

**183 Teacher Educators' Professional Learning in Communities**
*Linor L. Hadar and David L. Brody*

**184 Spirituality, Community, and Race Consciousness in Adult Higher Education**
Breaking the Cycle of Racialization
*Timothy Paul Westbrook*

**185 Multiracial Identity in Children's Literature**
*Amina Chaudhri*

**186 Transnationalism, Education and Empowerment**
The Latent Legacies of Empire
*Niranjan Casinader*

# Transnationalism, Education and Empowerment

## The Latent Legacies of Empire

Niranjan Casinader

Routledge
Taylor & Francis Group
LONDON AND NEW YORK

First published 2017
by Routledge

2 Park Square, Milton Park, Abingdon, Oxfordshire OX14 4RN
711 Third Avenue, New York, NY 10017

*Routledge is an imprint of the Taylor & Francis Group, an informa business*

First issued in paperback 2018



*British Library Cataloguing-in-Publication Data*
A catalogue record for this book is available from the British Library

*Library of Congress Cataloging-in-Publication Data*
A catalog record fot this book has been requested

ISBN: 978-1-138-91601-2 (hbk)
ISBN: 978-1-138-32579-1 (pbk)

Typeset in Galliard
by Apex CoVantage, LLC

For the trans-spatial family of my birth:

- Ranjitan Justin Tambimuttu Casinader
- Romanie Therese Wright Mulvaney
- Tarini Romanie Casinader
- Robin Romesh Casinader

# Contents

# Figures

# Foreword

Transnational encounters have been historically marked by power imbalances. In educational studies related to globalisation and transnationalism, very few scholars have focused on the complex and ambivalent relationships between the pulls of cultural continuity and modernity; between local and global hierarchies. In postcolonial studies, Gayatri Spivak and Homi Bhabha have highlighted some of the configurations of knowledge and desire that have constituted the complexities of the colonial encounter. Bhabha has focused on negotiations of cultural supremacy and the liminality of existence in-between spaces of incommensurability, whereas Spivak has focused on paradoxical 'enabling violences' where, for example, education and human rights imposed by colonial rule have enabled social groups to fight against local oppression and impediments to social mobility.

Following this strand of inquiry and attempting to complexify colonial relations, Niranjan Casinader examines transnationalism as a complex, trans-generational and multi-faceted space of negotiation of borders, of hierarchies, and of dreams, belongings and identities. He traces previous notions of transnationalism and their limitations in order to recast it as a transactional, transcultural and trans-spatial mind practice that transcends realities that are geographically fixed. Drawing attention to the dispositions of people that constantly cross North-South borders keeping connections with their originary places, Casinader explores the space where inter-generational, multi-sited narratives marked by cultural fluidity and hybridity emerge. He shows that these ambivalent narratives of origin and residence, of now and then, of here and there ground livelihoods of flow. Casinader invites us to consider whether a more holistic perception of the world and a more heightened level of transcultural understanding can be developed by those who have acquired a trans-spatial mindset, not constrained by fixed identities or geographic borders. He affirms that the recognition of trans-spatial mindsets as assets can contribute to the diversification of the teacher profession in schools.

As a migrant and mother of migrant children inhabiting multiple mind spaces, I can see how Casinader's proposition could support the educational system to validate the experiences of trans-spatial subjects and how these experiences in turn can enhance the understanding and advancement of transcultural practices in education. Most importantly, his argument challenges the conceptualization of trans-spatiality as deviance from a norm grounded in nationalist discourses based on ideas of sovereignty and ethno-homogeneity. As I read Casinader's final thoughts on the reconfigurations of power from nation-states to corporations and their implications on the mobilization of imaginaries of belonging, I was left with important questions, new insights and a sense of wonder in relation to the potential of trans-spatiality to disrupt the expansion and exploitative structure of global capital.

In my work with Indigenous communities who are trying to strike a balance between cultural continuity and flow, resisting the appeals of change driven by consumer mobility, I am constantly reminded that the very notion of the '21st century' is a culturally located social construction and that no attempt to cross or overcome borders is ever ideologically neutral. In this context, I wonder how trans-spatial mindsets can recognise the historical and systemic production of their privileged positions. Can trans-spatiality be self-reflexively oriented to identify complicity with the workings of trans-spatial global capital? Can trans-spatiality interrupt the single story of progress, development and human evolution? Can it be mobilised for solidarity with those who refuse a single notion of existence defined by access to social mobility? The greatest gift that this book offers in challenging taken for granted assumptions is the invitation for us to continue this important conversation.

Vanessa de Oliveira Andreotti, Associate Professor,
the University of British Columbia, Canada

# Preface

The origins of this book lie in the confluence of my academic research interests with a renewed consciousness of the globalised history of my family ancestry. As a geographer initially, and then as an educator, I have always maintained a personal and academic interest in the ways in which the character and quality of human societies have evolved over space and time, particularly through the lenses of development studies and culture. Several of my immediate family in current and preceding generations have had their working and personal lives indelibly associated with the growth of international development measures that emerged after World War II, especially in connection with multilateral organisations such as the United Nations and the Asian Development Bank, and my own childhood was immersed in the enaction of such themes as my family moved throughout countries that had just emerged out of the former British Empire.

It was inevitable, therefore, that the emergence of the phase of contemporary globalisation in the 1990s introduced a natural platform upon which to extend the scope of my own work, which places education, with an underlying geographic perspective, at its core. However, my growing awareness as to the ways in which my wider family has emerged through earlier historical phases of globalisation, and in particular, the British and other European Empires in the 16th – 19th centuries, established a number of intellectual disjunctures that demanded investigation and resolution. This book is the second in an intended trilogy, framed around the concept of transnationalism, which seeks to explore these issues.

My last book, *Culture, Transnational Education and Thinking: Case Studies in Global Schooling* (Routledge 2014), addressed the primary of these conundrums, the false assumptions that Euro-American ('Western') societies make in assuming the universality of culture in the exposition of thinking, and the subsequent influences on educational principles. It further argued that a more globalised life experience tends to lead to a transcultural disposition that facilitates working in a culturally diverse environment. This book is concerned with two other related themes: my position that the discourses are restricted in the ways in which transnational actions, including those in education, are being conceived and addressed, including its perceived linkage to 20th-century globalisation; and the persisting postcolonial generalisations as to the impact of colonial education on the lives of those who were colonised.

In the context of a family history that illustrates a multitude of gradations about transnational behaviour and the realities of colonial education, it was important to place some light on these disconnections. A more nuanced discussion of such themes has relevance for the direction of global society towards the second quarter of the 21st century, and also offers a more accurate assessment of the place of education as a feature of colonisation and through this, a deeper picture of the long-term impact of the development of local and global societies.

It is important to note that, whilst the content of this book has a large fundamental base in its exploration of the history of education and its impact, the nature of its themes are essentially transdisciplinary in character. Consequently, aside from education, the book draws on ideas from a diversity of disciplines and fields of learning, including imperial history, sociology, international politics, legal history, philosophy, cultural and development geography, among others. In this, it seeks to highlight that studies of education cannot be divorced from the influences of the nuances of society in which it functions. To do so may facilitate general comment and holistic understanding, but it is only by acknowledging and addressing the significances of those distinctions, however subtle they may be, that we can utilise our analysis of local, national or global dilemmas more effectively towards a more targeted purpose.

Whilst this book is a condensation of my own thoughts and deliberations, it would not have been possible without the opportunity to discuss, debate and dissect its ideas and propositions with others, and I am indebted to all of them for their help and support in the completion of this book.

First of all, I am eternally grateful for the willingness of many members of my immediate and wider family to be interviewed about their lives and our wider family history, as well as the connections to the theoretical themes within the book:

- my father, Ranji Casinader, and stepmother, Jennifer Casinader, who also supplied many written family history documents as well as a number of historical books on Sri Lanka's past and present;
- my mother, Romany Wright Mulvaney, whose personal memoir also provided many insights and possibilities for thought;
- my sister, Tarini Casinader, and brother, Robin;
- my youngest son, Simon;
- in the United Kingdom: my aunt and cousins, Suvendrini Jazeel, Riza Jazeel and Tariq Jazeel; and
- from Denmark, a cousin (now living in Australia), Marl Christiansen.

Secondly I am most appreciative of all those who have facilitated the clarification of ideas and logic through their willingness to be critical friends at various stages of the book's development, challenging me to look deeper into my intentions and notions: my oldest friends and companions in lives built on migration and philosophical discussion, Peter van Cuylenburg and Ron Kluvers; my many colleagues in the Faculty of Education at Monash, particularly Lucas Walsh, Gillian

Kidman, Jane Wilkinson, and Susan Webb; and mentors and colleagues beyond Monash, including Fazal Rizvi, Jeana Kriewaldt, Catherine Manathunga and Eeqbal Hassim.

I am especially appreciative for the mentoring and advice of Emeritus Professor Peter Gronn, who introduced me to Georgina Tsolidis and her insightful contributions on global culture and education. The readiness of Susan Webb, Lucas Walsh, Jane Wilkinson and Georgina Tsolidis to provide insightful observations on chapter drafts was much valued, and their comments played a major part in the formation of the final manuscript. In addition, I am particularly grateful to Vanessa de Oliveira Andreotti from the University of British Columbia, Canada, for our conversations on culture and education, and her kindness in agreeing to write the foreword to the book.

Special thanks are also due to Lee Godden (Melbourne Law School) and Roshan de Silva-Wijeyaratne (Griffith University): our ongoing interdisciplinary collaboration on the colonial legal history of Sri Lanka has been the foundation of many of the threads of thought within the book, and has been invaluable in developing my understanding of international law and archival research. In particular, I thank Lee for her assistance with the archival research conducted over three years at the Department of National Archives in Colombo, Sri Lanka, and the National Archives and British Library in London.

Finally, I am very grateful for the continuous, reliable and ever-gracious support from the team at Routledge, and especially my editor, Heidi Lowther, and editorial assistant, Thomas Storr. I could not have asked for a better team to work with in the production of this book.

Niranjan Casinader<br>
February 2017<br>
Melbourne, Australia

# Acknowledgements

Parts of Chapter 2 are derived from ideas first published in the following publication:

Casinader, N. (2016) Transnationalism in the Australian Curriculum: New horizons or destinations of the past? *Discourse: Studies in the Cultural Politics of Education, 37*(3), 327–340, doi:10.1080/01596306.2015.1023701

I also acknowledge the support of the Faculty of Education, Monash University, through their internal research grant schemes, for their contribution towards the cost of archival research in London and Sri Lanka.

# 1 Transnationalism

## Reconfigurations of past and present

### A The problematic of past and current intentions

In the modern academic age, the use of the term transnationalism has become almost ubiquitous, a chameleon whose identity has been claimed across multiple variations of use. Adopted by a diversity of disciplines, it has been embraced and interpreted from perspectives that range from the historical through the sociological into the economic and political, as well as the educational. Inevitably, such a variety of perspectives has meant that commonalities in its diverse interpretations have been slow to emerge. However, as this chapter will discuss, there has tended to be a coalescence of definition around several key aspects of transnationalism as a process – primarily, that it is a transactional practice founded on the movement of phenomena across national borders.

Aligned with these definitional parameters is a temporal association, in that the process or phenomenon of transnationalism is often judged as being a modern substantiation or descendant of contemporary globalisation. It is seen to embody and reflect the more complex and intense pattern of connections between places, a feature that has long been viewed as a key contemporary feature of the globalisation process (for example, see Burbules & Torres, 2000; Eckersley, 2007; Giddens, 2003). Consequently, transnationalism is seen as a phenomenon that has emerged as a result of the increased intensity of spatial connections across local, regional and global communities (Vertovec, 2009), fuelled by the more sophisticated and immediate technologies of 21st century communications.

These tightly controlled confines around transnationalism, both of definition and existence, are essentially problematic, because fundamentally they assume that extensive global movement across lines of sovereign control did not exist prior to the end of the 20th century. They also view the movement as being visible, observable and measurable, whether that shift be economic (such as in trade exchanges), social (as with migration) or multi-faceted (as with education). Consequently, the main underpinning contention of this book is that a new reconfiguration of transnationalism is required if we are to fully comprehend its impact on the nature of human society, and that education provides a strong context for the description, explanation and analysis of that conceptual transformation. To do so, however, requires a closer examination of these defining characteristics and the disconnections that they have created.

## B Globalisation and transnationalism: Mutual identities?

The reasons for the complexity surrounding the notion of transnationalism lie partly in the broad scope of the disciplines that have commandeered the concept, which range from business through sociology to history, but also in the diffuse nature of the idea itself, the compound and contested nature of which has provoked a high instance of debate. Portes, Guarnizo, and Landholt (1999) and Pries (2004) have all highlighted the fragmented nature of transnational research, along with its lack of analytical rigour and a well-defined theoretical framework, as one reason for the perceived uncertainty. Pries cautioned that, given the considerable growth in the field of transnational studies since the early 1990s, the challenge facing researchers in this field was no longer to establish the existence of the transnational phenomena, but to address the vague and indistinct uses of terms such as transnational and transnationalism with a targeted debate about the concept along with '. . . more explicit and closely defined empirical research . . . ' (Pries, 2008, p. 1).

In one of the more recent comprehensive classifications and treatments of transnationalism, Vertovec (2009) argued that the concept is more a product of the early 21st-century, and not the 1990s, reflecting a '. . . widespread interest in economic, social and political linkages between people, places and institutions crossing nation-state borders and spanning the world' (p. 1). He identified six types of framework within which the term has been used: social morphology, which focuses on the phenomena of migration, diasporas, and 'transnational communities' (Vertovec, 2009, p. 5); types of consciousness, or the range of experiences that enable individuals and groups to maintain identity and memory across multiple locations; as modes of cultural reproduction; as avenues of capital; as sites of political engagement; and in the context of a '(Re)Construction of 'place' or locality', in which he supports Appadurai's (1996) conception of transnationalism as reflecting a disconnect between place and personal identity.

One of the advantages of Vertovec's multi-faceted interpretation of transnationalism is that it takes into account the wider global socio-political changes that were taking place at the time when contemporary globalisation was beginning to emerge as a major economic and social process. The full impact of the decline and the disaggregation of the former Soviet Union had given rise to an impetus towards fully globalised economic activity based on the development of regional and worldwide trade agreements, in contrast to one that was confined to the ideological separations that had persisted for much of the 20th century. As part of this shift, there was a growing celebration as to the perceived success and 'superiority' of 'Western' economic principles over those of socialism and communism, leading to a surge in a widespread utopian belief in the capacity of the free market, the capitalist system and democratic institutions to become the global norm, using the universal power of the internet '. . . to mitigate inequality both within and across societies and to increase freedom, transparency, and good governance in even the poorest and most isolated countries' (Appadurai, 1996, p. 2). Whatever the case, 'transnational' became the most commonly used term in the

US academic world in the late 1980s and early 1990s, particularly in terms of its employment in relation to global flows in commerce and population movement, until 'transnationalism' superseded it around 1994 (Saunier, 2009).

Despite its associations with contemporary globalisation, the exact timing of the emergence of transnationalism as an idea within intellectual discourse is predictably nebulous. As Smith and Guarnizo (1998) observed, the phenomena that are often seen an representative of transnationalism are not particularly new, but it was the greater intensity of these activities at a global scale towards the end of the 20th century that saw the concept become more widely used across academic disciplines. Daswani and Quayson (2013) point to this period, and especially the early 1990s, as being the time when critiques of global development theories were growing; transnationalism offered a way forward, and that, therefore,

> . . . just as there are different ways of studying transnationalism (e.g., from above and below, at the borders), there are also multiple ways of being transnational, since transnationalism includes a multiplicity of historical trajectories or pathways that affect people in different ways.
>
> (Daswani & Quayson, 2013, p. 12)

Smith and Guarnizo (1998) suggested that this period also saw a growing convergence between the cultural studies approach – as reflected in the works of Appadurai (1996) and Bhabha (1994) – and the social sciences, such as the transmigration studies of Schiller, Basch, and Blanc-Szanton (1992). In a similar vein, Saunier, as part of a detailed study on the genesis and evolution of the term transnational, identified the rise of globalisation during the 1980s as being coincident with the emergence of terms such as transmigrants, transurbanism, translocality and transnations in the fields of cultural studies and anthropology, contained in new approaches that sought to '. . . qualify, observe, assess and prophesy a new multipolar and multicultural world in the makings in the 1990s . . . ' (2009, p. 1053); in other words, the advent of contemporary globalisation provided the foundations on which the intellectual transnationalist discourse could thrive.

## C The constants of interpretations

In spite of the contestation around the nature of transnationalism, there are several themes that can be continually identified, even if they are expressed in myriad ways: first, a persistent focus on the idea of the prefix 'trans-' in terms of movement; second, a tendency to frame ideas about transnationalism around the restricted parameters of economic activity and migration; and third, the growing association of the concept with the desirability of global citizenship.

### *1 Borders and State*

The centrality of sovereign States to both the actions and processes of transnationalism embodies a psychological anchor for the current interpretation of the concept. Across all its variations, the notion of transnationalism has tended to be viewed in a transactional, geographical sense; that is, it has generally been conceived as involving the movement of phenomena across defined borders from one region of national political control to another. The prefix 'trans-' is invariably perceived in literal terms, with transnationalism involving the shifting and movement of various singularities over these political borders, or the '. . . economic, social and political linkages between people, places and institutions crossing nation-state borders and spanning the world' (Vertovec, 2009, p. 1).

The difficulty with such a constricted perspective is not just confined to its innate contradiction of the element of cosmopolitanism that also imbues transnationalism, one that will be addressed later in this chapter. More importantly, it confines transnationalism to a limited realm, with a reduced emphasis, if any, on the wider social, cultural socio-political context in which these locational shifts occur. Specifically, transnationalism has been interpreted not so much as a concept, but as an actuality, invoking '. . . processes that transcend international borders' (Faist, 2010, p. 13), encompassing the act of people(s) crossing the political borders of sovereign States, both physically and through the avatars of human-induced activity (Papastergiadis, 2000; Pries, 2008; Vertovec, 2009). If these characteristics hold true, then transnationalism, as has been argued, is a phenomenon that, in its more common interpretation, can only have been observable since the emergence of the modern nation-State in late 19th-century Europe, when the significance of borders as spatial and psychological definers and maintainers of territorial authority gained more socio-economic and political significance. If this is the case, then it follows that transnationalism is a consequence that derived from the forces of Euro-American social, political and economic industrialised growth that was symbiotic with the evolution of the modern sovereign, nation-State. However, such a mono-dimensional interpretation of 'trans' both inhibits the intellectual power of transnationalism as an interpretive concept and ignores its inaccurate reflection of reality. With this conceptualisation, its underlying rationale is both limiting and restricted, necessitating a reconstruction of the definition of transnationalism into a form that is more reflective of its complex, multi-faceted nature.

## 2 *Migration and economy*

The second constant in the multiple interpretations of transnationalism is that it is centred fundamentally on the movements of people, along with their associated psychological and cognitive states, across defined national borders between regions under different political control. This transition gains a cultural centrality when migration patterns are involved. Transnationalism in this imaginary is framed around a series of re-locations across national borders that are irrevocably accompanied by transfers in cultural identity, capital and economic activity. The locational transfer of people acts also as a key driver in the spatial dissemination of economic activity that is symbiotic with both globalisation and Euro-American market principles (Casinader, 2015; King & McGrath, 2002; Luke & Luke, 2000), diffusing an ideology that highlights the significance of multinational and transnational entities in the organisation of economic production on a cross-border basis (Hoogvelt, 1997). Transnational activity is

> . . . characterised by an expansion and diversification of economic relations, the international population flows have become geographically far more diversified. They are no longer confined to the former channels carrying Europeans to the New World countries of immigration in Australasia and the Americas, nor earlier intra-regional movements in Asia and elsewhere. Many European countries have become receiving rather than sending countries.
>
> (Inglis, 2002, p. 182)

As enunciated by writers such as Inglis (2002), this focus on international spatial transfer arose through transnationalism's association with the period of the new postcolonial Age of Migration, initiated in the 1990s as part of the drive for globalisation, and through which transnationalism gained integrity as an academic concept. In this context, transnationalist movement is now identified by some (Inglis, 2002; Konno, 2010) as the more accurate and contemporary descriptor of global population shifts than the previous notion of 'diaspora' (Konno, 2010). Instead of the one-way demographic diffusion in response to push factors at the point of origin that is at the heart of diasporic shifting, transnationalism emphasises the continuing connection of the shifting individual between their place or location of emergence and their destination of hope. It incorporates the maintenance of this relationship through regular, if not frequent, temporary journeys back to the point of origin, a lifeline that is often observable in later generations, but one that can generate an internal disquiet about identity and belonging. For example, a multi-methods study of youths in New Zealand (Bartley & Spoonley, 2008) explored the experiences and strategies of one-and-a-half generation migrants from Asia in the context of contemporary transnationalism. This particular group, defined as migrant children between the ages of 6–18, were found to not only feel the sense of displacement and the difficulties of cultural adjustment common to all migrants, but also to experience complex layers of 'in-betweenness', often resulting in attitudes of ambivalence regarding their future aspirations in New Zealand.

Similarly, the transnational education experience of a second generation of Japanese immigrants in the 1930s was the focus of a multi-method study by Konno. Japanese migrants to the United States began arriving from the late 19th century. Many of these migrants considered it necessary for their children to temporarily return to Japan for a suitable Japanese education. In the language of Vertovec's typology of transnationalism (1999), Konno (2010) explored how the transnational consciousness of both the first and second generation Japanese was influential in pursuing second-generation education in Japan. This transnational consciousness was evident in the struggles the second generation experienced around their sense of identity and sense of belonging to two nations:

> These hardships served to intensify their ambiguous and transnational consciousness. Even before leaving for Japan, they had already held a degree of multiple self-identifications that linked them to different nations, either feeling proud of, or forced to cope with, their Japanese ancestry at the same time as being treated by other Americans as second-rate citizens. Once in Japan, however, they not only learned that they were foreign in their ancestors' land but also rediscovered their American selves in the process of tackling discrimination by the Japanese and trying to overcome cultural differences.
>
> (Konno, 2010, p. 110)

A common factor in the one-and-a-half generation migrants was the simultaneous tug-of-war between the country of origin, and that of residence. The complex and sometimes troubling ways the two are jostled in considerations of 'home', belonging, identity and fealty overshadowed other settlement factors (Bartley & Spoonley, 2008, p. 70). These transnational migrants, unlike their ancestral diaspora, are still embedded in their places of departure, maintaining roots that may extend to interests in property, commerce and even politics, as well as personal relationships. They '. . . may not have an either/or orientation, choosing to forego an assumed primacy of loyalty and attachment to one place or the other, and rather may simply be living simultaneously in both locations, neither absolutely here nor there, now or in the future' (Bartley & Spoonley, 2008, p. 64). Consequently, whilst the term 'diaspora' is now often used to refer to a community or group, transnationalism has become more employed in the context of more complex migration phenomena (Faist, 2010).

## 3 Global cosmopolitanism and cultural identity

The movement of people across national borders that is reflected in multifarious forms of migration is not a new global phenomenon, but one of the consequences of globalisation has been the increased capacity for greater numbers of people to relocate themselves in different parts of the world, either temporarily or permanently. It is the volume, rate and frequency of the current movement that differentiates it from previous eras of global migration. In addition, the major difference between diasporic movement and transnational shifting of people is that, whereas the former is more likely to be caused by centrifugal forces that have driven people away from a point of origin, transnational movement involves a greater degree of choice and attraction at the point of destination combined with a connection to the location of the past. The ability and capacity of individuals to ensconce this pattern of spatial and cultural renewal has been enabled by positive economic conditions that have provided people with the financial resources to build such movement into the mainstream of their life patterns, along with the developments in global transfer technologies that have made the costs of air travel within reach of a wider range of people from a broader socio-economic spectrum. The defining characteristic of these indentured connections is the ***dualisation*** of cultural identity within those who are shifting, maintaining and nurturing a constant and deep connection with both poles of cultural origin and destination through repeated movement back and forth. More significantly, though, the key aspect of the transnationalist experience is that it has taken on the singularity of inevitability, an unquestioned conception, one that has been taken on by people as an objective reality, an imaginary or '. . . social phenomenon that is tacit and unconscious, adhered to by a group of people in an un-reflexive manner' (Rizvi, 2011, p. 228).

The conception of who makes up this new transnational class, however, is less than absolute. For writers such as Igarishi and Saito (2014), there is no social stratification to those who are collectively engaged and are members of the process of transnationalism. Regardless of ethnicity, class or gender, '. . . transnationalism has become an umbrella term for global linkages and the diversity and contradictions of these exchanges' (Friedman & Schultermandl, 2011). For instance, the large number of people working in construction throughout the Middle East, having left their homes and families various parts of southeast Asia, including the Philippines, India and Sri Lanka, to take up employment opportunities in expanding economies that are very ready to take advantage of those who lack the power to assert their true employment value, are just as embedded in the transnational polity as highly paid professional experts who ply their trade as international consultants, moving around the globe in a perpetual state of geographical transition.

There is the contrary view, however, that some groups of people have a greater capacity for cosmopolitanism or global citizenship, and it is they who have the greater capacity to be more fully integrated into the transnational identity than others (Rizvi, 2008, 2009). This suggests that transnationalism encompasses a specific kind of lifestyle for those who possess '. . . more social, economic or political capital . . . ' (Igarishi & Saito, 2014, p. 224), their activities facilitated by an ability to use technology (Koehn & Rosenau, 2002) as the means by which they can shift their focus between disparate locations around the world, either physically or virtually. This centrality of human linkages between places contains the inherent element of a compound or merged emergent cultural identity that is born out of geographical movement, a state of positive cultural hybridity that I have referred to previously as being part of the notion of transculturalism (Casinader, 2014).

It is this particular condition of cultural flux or shifting that can be seen as part of the third common definitional facet of transnationalism. This association of transnationalism with the notion of culture has been present from very early on in the discourse, which might explain why, according to Saunier (2009), the term 'transnationalism' often has become used to represent not only a worldview, but also an ideology. It is perceived to be akin to a political project in which people were identified with a particular set of beliefs. In this case, the equivalent to that set of beliefs is the mindset of cosmopolitanism. The association established between transnationalism and globalisation also reinforced its links with cultural fluidity. One of the longstanding debates in globalisation has been centred on whether the process creates greater cultural homogeneity globally, or encourages a proactive reinforcement of cultural localisation. The reality is that both elements are possible and have been embedded in the process (Hannerz, 1990; Knight, 2004), reflecting the plurality of the cultural dimensions that globalisation, being composed of '. . . a world of flows' (Appadurai, 2006, p. 5), has encouraged.

As a result of this conflation, the notion of cosmopolitanism, which embodies a capacity for inter- and cross-cultural understanding, has become closely associated with the evolving conceptualisation of transnationalism, embedding a middle and upper class mentality within its overall form (Roudometof, 2005). For Rizvi (2011) and Andreotti (2011), the essence of cosmopolitanism is the embracing of global citizenship or global mindedness, which demands an acceptance of the part of the individual that cultural diversity is the natural condition. Igarashi and Saito are even more explicit, seeing cosmopolitanism as '. . . an orientation of openness to foreign others and cultures' (2014, p. 222). Similar thoughts have been expressed by Roudometof (2005), who saw transnationalism as the emergence of a new unidimensional reality of social life, where people opt to either develop an open (cosmopolitan) attitude, or a closed (local) disposition.

However, although the basic principle of this perspective is positive, it has limitations. First, there is a tendency for global cosmopolitans to be more welcoming and open to other cultures '. . . when it is associated with enjoyable experiences that cultivate one's identity (Skrbis & Woodward, 2007, p. 744) and not when '. . . an engagement with other cultures that is perceived to be threatening or challenging' (p. 745). The divisions and fears that have emerged about immigration from 'Others' in 'Western' countries such as the United States, the United Kingdom, France and Australia are testament to this dichotomy, where enjoyment of the diversity of cuisines of the 'Others' is frequently forgotten in the expression of the unknown.

A second difficulty with such the cosmopolitan perspective is that it fails to capture the sophistication in the complex and multi-dimensional nature of transnationalism (Olofsson & Öhman, 2007). For example, one important difference that distinguishes transnationalism from cosmopolitan or world theory concepts is its emphasis on the '. . . co-presence of universalising and particularising processes . . . ' (Faist 2010, p. 16). Local or national claims for political autonomy or the rights of culturally diverse groups are often made with reference to the global norms of the right to collective self-determination. In this context, transnationalism can be linked closely to the concept of 'glocalization', which highlights the mutual interdependence of activity at the local scale with human conceptualisations and behaviours in the globalised environment (Faist, 2010, p. 16).

## D The need for transition

The signs of such developments aside, the continued trend for transnationalism to be interpreted as essentially concerned with the transference of phenomena – whether people, goods, services or mental activity – across national boundaries ignores the complexity of the concept and its potential for deeper insight into the human condition. Such limitations are evident even within the thoughts of those who openly acknowledge the multi-dimensional nature of transnationalism. For example, despite his more inclusive conceptualisation based on the various strands of transnationalism, it is notable, and disconcerting, that Vertovec (2009) still places an emphasis on the phenomenon being based specifically on the movement across the borders of the nation-State. This is illustrated in his discussion of the different transnationalist frameworks that incorporate the literalist principle of movement across territorial borders, or delineated margins of political control. Social morphology is concerned with '... spanning borders ...', avenues of capital include flow of remittances back to countries of origin, and political engagement incorporates the notion of homeland politics being transported by global diasporas. Transnationalism is about '. . . sustained cross-*border* relationships, patterns of exchange, affiliations and social formations spanning nation-states' [author emphasis] (Vertovec, 2009, p. 5). It is this continued reliance on the existence of international political boundaries that is problematic.

The value of transnationalism as a means of interpreting and understanding the long-term impacts of the globalisation process is enhanced if the prefix is considered as representing the more liminal space of hybridity (Papastergiadis, 2000, p. 104) that results from the movement of people and ideas from one region to another; that is, 'trans-' as representing the merging of cultural identity or identities into a new form. Such a conceptualisation is, in fact, evident within Vertovec's classifications of transnationalism, but camouflaged as forms of consciousness and cultural reproduction. This fluidity in the creation of cultural identity is not a characteristic that is endemic to transnationalism or globalisation, for it is also a feature of the experience of any diaspora that, through the very act of moving from one place to another, is required to reshape its former cultural identity into something new. In the words of Stuart Hall, amongst others, the formation of identity is continuous, '. . . a matter of 'becoming' as well as of 'being'' (1990, p. 224). Said (1993) argued that cultures are inherently dynamic, regardless of whether migration is occurring or not. Consequently, within the context of the physical journeys that human beings undertaking the course of a transnationalist experience, that dynamism or fluidity of cultural identity is accentuated.

In the current era of enhanced globalisation, in which the permeability and porosity of national boundaries in respect of population movement is becoming increasingly highlighted the use of a definition of transnationalism that promotes both the symbolism and the actuality of those borders as phenomena of strength lacks long-term meaning and reason. In the middle of the first quarter of the 21st century, such a statement itself might seem to lack validity, given the multiple examples where sovereign States across Europe, North America and Australasia have taken action to re-establish the visibility of their power and control over national borders in response to the exponential growth in the numbers of people seeking asylum or refuge. Furthermore, these actions at the governmental level have been often translated into the fracturing of national populations along lines that are essentially demarcations of pro- and anti-transnationalist attitudes centred on controlling the movement of people and perceived cultural difference.

The success of the BREXIT campaign in the United Kingdom in June 2016, which resulted in the decision by the British polity to withdraw the country from the European Union, is one example of how this polarisation has been manifested. Others can be seen in the rise of populist and/or stridently conservative ideological movements such as the Tea Party and the successful 2016 Trump Presidential campaign in the United States, as well as the growth of the conservative, reactionary movements in France (Marine Le Pen and the National Front), the UK (Nigel Farage and UKIP, the UK Independence Party), and Australia (the right-wing elements within the Liberal-National Party coalition focused around politicians such as former Prime Minister Tony Abbott). It is also a phenomenon that is not confined to the Euro-American or 'Western' sphere of influence. The rise of Daesh or the Islamic State (ISIL), with its campaign on a variety of fronts to establish an anti-'Western' caliphate, can be considered to be a different, yet equally vociferous, statement of anti-transnationalism.

Regardless of origin, such reactions are essentially extreme manifestations of attempts by governments and peoples to reclaim a perceived national raison d'être in the face of the realities of modern globalisation. In themselves, however, they cannot, and do not, change the reality that the global human system has become one where national boundaries are increasingly amorphous. Transnationalism in its contemporary context, or, more precisely, anti-transnationalism, has been invoked by such forces in an attempt to cement the importance of international political boundaries and the underlying mosaic of nation-States in the maintenance of perceived nationalised cultural identities. Instead of doing so, these actions only serve to highlight the dominance that transnationalist behaviour and activity exert on global events, as well as the decreasing significance that national borders have in the imaginary of those who seek to cross them.

Tensions of conceptual structure such as these are exacerbated in the case of transnationalism because, despite its embodiment of human activity that transcends national borders, its very name indicates a foundation on the concept of a defined, delineated space; that is, a sovereign State. Whatever the particular perspective of transnationalism that is applied, one of the underlying current constants of the idea is a sense of the capability to override the limitations and existence of national boundaries, and yet its nomenclature is based on the existence reality of a specific region or 'place', the boundaries of which are considered to be highly managed and under the control of a governing authority. This paradox arises because of the conception of location and place as fixed entities, and yet such a notion of 'place' in a globalised society has long been challenged by geographers. Under the geographical interpretation of place, the fixity of boundaries that governments of nation-States desire – '. . . a site of an authenticity, as singular, fixed and unproblematic in its identity . . . ' (Massey, 1994, p. 5) – is a false illusion, for it relies on the assumption that any space on the Earth's surface is, in fact, unchanging. In reality, any 'place' is inherently transnational, the character or identity of which is being created continually by forces within and by its connections with phenomena or places beyond it; it is continually in the process of formation, not a completed and stable entity. The sovereign national boundaries on which the contemporary definition and utilisation of transnationalism depend are therefore themselves unfixed, evolving in location, nature and degree of porosity as a matter of course.

Such discontinuities are a strong argument for a reconfigured notion of transnationalism that is more reflective of a globalised and globalising world, one which also reconstitutes the concept as a human condition that is as much representative of the past as it is of the present and future. The starting point for this rebirth is the combination of ideas about transnationalism that are focused on its association with cultural identity, and more specifically, its connections to more hybrid and multi-faceted substantiations of personal identity.

## E New formations

### *Seeking a pathway*

In many ways, the contemporary vision of transnationalism as a transactional demographic concept is not unsurprising, given the extent to which it has been linked to modern globalisation. In its initial construction during the 1990s, globalisation was formulated as primarily an economic phenomenon, umbilically linked to the emerging neoliberal context (Burbules & Torres, 2000) that emphasised the value of freedom of economic thought and action – the transaction of commerce – across global spaces (Rizvi & Lingard, 2010). In this, the contemporary phase of globalisation was no different than earlier iterations, whether that was the Ancient Roman Empire, the naval ventures of 13th-century China or the Christian Crusades of medieval Europe (McGrew, 2007). However, one of the fundamental principles of the modern sovereign State is that it has control over activity within its defined territory, a power that it establishes and maintains through the maintenance of the geographical location and psychological integrity of its areal borders. In the economic form of globalisation, it is the power of global corporations to ignore or decrease the influence of sovereign governments to manage or oversee any operations that move across territorial borders that is at issue, the same borders that the conceptual existence of which is essential to the prevailing definition of transnationalism itself.

Consequently, the sovereign State has become now only important in terms of creating the international and political environment in which these geographical exchanges of economic activity can take place, accompanied also by movements in related necessities such as the workforce. As a result, transnational behaviour and action in its modern, limited idiom is best framed within the context of global corporate power, composed of a number of entities that have the capacity to transcend national boundaries. This power has resulted from the freedom given to them by the same sovereign States, either individually or through multilateral agreements brokered through organisations such as the United Nations or World Trade Organisation.

To confine transnationalism to such an imperfect perspective of the transactional, however, is to deny its capacity and power to describe and explain patterns of human behaviour and action in far more complex ways. The principal constraint on a wider conceptualisation of transnationalism is its intellectual umbilical cord to the modern age of globalisation. In doing so, the rationale or foundation of the argument that transnationalism is a process, and not a phenomenon in itself, depends ultimately on the degree to which the notion of the sovereign State – itself only a conception that is less than 200 years old – is confirmed or compromised. Consequently, any intellectual shift that can expand the potential of the term to contribute to a wider understanding of human experience depends ultimately on the negation, or at least a reduction, in the significance attributed to the notion of territorial 'borders' or 'boundaries'.

In this context, I am proposing that the notion of transnationalism as being primarily founded on the physicality of geographical movement across national boundaries ignores the holistic nature of such an approach to 'existence'. Instead, we need to both acknowledge and promote the view that transnationalism also incorporates a very distinct psychological, attitudinal belief in the power and the necessity of thinking beyond one's existing social/political/economic/national borders. In essence, transnationalism involves a subjective, universal sense, one that absorbs a disposition or state of mind to international movement and change that is present across all periods of time and space. It is not just a spatial movement between locations, the genesis of which is irretrievably associated with modernity in the form of 21st century globalised socio-economic activity. Such a renewed configuration is not, as some might suggest, better identified as a 'postcolonial cosmopolitanism', nor is it totally aligned with Arjun Appadurai's notion of transnationalism as comprising a 'post-national' force that counteracts 'territorial nationalism' (1996, p. 165). His concept of ideoscapes, incorporating the '. . . way some transnational forces have come to be configured in the imagination of residents . . . ' (1996, p. 60), still relies ultimately on the movements of people and identities between places, even if the 'de-territorialisation of culture' has diminished the significance of the boundaries associated with sovereign or nation-States. In my view, transnationalism is more of a pre-existing sensibility that is fundamentally disassociated from place, location and boundaries, one in which the notion of 'transculturalism' is an essential aspect.

## *A new direction*

As discussed earlier, the notion of 'trans-'in transnationalism embodies a more prominent emphasis on changes or shifts in personal identity or culture as a result of global mobility. Similar arguments can be found in the work of, for example, Papastergiadis (2000) and Rizvi (2011); indeed, for Papastergiadis, the key feature of transnationalism is its 'deterritorialization of culture', or

> . . . the ways in which people now feel they belong to various communities despite the fact they do not share a common territory with all the other

members. It also refers to the way the national or even the regional culture can no longer be conceived as reflecting a coherent and distinct identity.

(Papastergiadis, 2000, p. 115)

Cultures have moved on from '. . . being formed in particular territorial relationships with carefully established borders, separating one from another . . . ' (Papastergiadis, 2000, p. 104), founded on anthropological constructions that are based on a '. . . notion of culture as a visible set of manifestations of a way of life . . . ' (Casinader, 2014, p. 31) that is shared by its adherents. In concert with Vertovec (2009, p. 2), Rizvi (2011) and Alexander (2001), Papastergiadis argued that the increased degree and spatial extent in the movement of people and ideas between territories demanded an image of culture that was not '. . . a fixed script which actors are bound to follow . . . ' (2000, p. 109). Instead, culture needed to be viewed as a more dynamic entity, not located within the '. . . objective conditions of a society, or purely in the subjective consciousness of the individual, but [more in] the constantly mobile and transformative exchange between the two . . .' (p. 109). Transnationalism, then, is more accurately and comprehensively viewed as personifying the dynamic instability of transformative transition that occurs when people and ideas from different parts of the world meet and cross-pollinate dimensions of thought. These perspectives are also reflected in Ong's reminder that the increasingly rapid processes of cultural interconnectedness and mobility across space are inherently symbolic of transnationalism. Embedded in this term, she argues, are the concepts of trans denoting '. . . moving through space or across lines, as well as the changing nature of something . . . '. In addition to suggesting '. . . new relations between nation-states and capital . . . ' this term also '. . . alludes to the transversal, the transactional, the translational, and the transgressive aspects of contemporary behaviour and imagination that are incited, enabled, and regulated by the changing logics of states and capitalism.' (Ong, 1999, p. 4)

One of the more interesting, if frequently ignored, assumptions in the current dominance of the transactional view of transnationalism has been an almost universal conviction that the conceptualisation and enaction of thinking skills has been culturally neutral, the concomitant of which was that there can be no 'transcultural' way of thinking or reasoning. However, along with others such as Dahl (2010) and Singh (2013), in recent years I have argued that the notions of reasoning embedded in more industrially developed societies have been almost exclusively derived from Euro-American or 'Western' perspectives, a consequence of the globalisation and the geographical spread of 'Western' educational systems, which has facilitated the diffusion of such conceptions (Casinader, 2014). In themselves, the linear and abstract forms of critical thinking that underpin Euro-American systems of thought do not encourage a more inclusive notion of reasoning that derives from an acceptance that there are cultural variations in how thinking takes place, such as a priority being placed more on the value of contextual thinking and group problem solving than individual resolution. A transcultural disposition accepts the existence and natural validity of all the approaches, and generates the capacity to operate and function across multiple cultural contexts.

In a case of apparent paradox, this rejection of the universal dominance of one conception of culture sits beside a significant aspect of a wider conceptualisation of transnationalism; that is, the destabilisation of the link between culture and region. It is at this point, however, that opinions diverge. For instance, on the one side, Paspastergiadis (2000) argues that the very existence of transnationalism is a catalyst for the development of a global culture, as the phenomenon means that a '. . . national or even the regional culture can no longer be conceived as reflecting a coherent and distinct identity . . . ' (Papastergiadis, 2000, p. 115). This more specific identification of transnationalism with a global cultural identity links the concept with the wider discourse surrounding the globalisation of culture and educational practice, especially in relation to issues surrounding the formulation of a worldwide community.

However, these connections to the possible process of the creation of a global culture have been considered to be problematic. Even in his comprehensive summation of the facets of transnationalism, Vertovec (2009) tended to ignore the notion of global identity altogether, with little reference to any specific notions of global culture, global identity or global community. Papastergiadis was more forthcoming, if still cautious, arguing that there is no evidence the globalisation has led, or is leading, towards the actuality of a global culture '. . . which has developed . . . deep structures of belonging . . . ' (Papastergiadis, 2000, p. 112). He also mused on the implications of 'diasporised cultures' on the development on a universalised culture, especially in the context of globalisation often enhancing localised 'traditional' cultures (p. 104), whilst contributing to normative generalisations as to the character of national cultures attributed specifically to areas of space delineated by defined boundaries. Nevertheless, he still comes down on the side of cultural globality as the inevitable norm, because cultures have moved on from '. . . being formed in particular territorial relationships with carefully established borders, separating one from another . . . ' (Papastergiadis, 2000, p. 104), in which they are founded on anthropological constructions composed of '. . . systems of belief . . . that secured a homogeneous, coherent and continuous sense of affiliation . . . ' (2000, p. 104).

In contrast, others have argued that it is not axiomatic that the deterritorialization of culture leads to a universal culture. Rizvi argues specifically that the idea of a single global culture is incompatible with reality, and that cultural diversity should be acknowledged as an identifier of transnationalism:

> . . . diversity is best represented as an expression of transnationality, as well as a key driver of the processes through which people interpret the space in which they perform their cultures. Since always emergent, this space is never entirely transparent and coherent, but describes instead the messiness of living and acting in a world mediated by the work of global media, cultural diasporas and multinational corporations.
>
> (Rizvi, 2011, p. 184)

The opening up of cultural contact as a result of globalisation has not been mirrored in people's responses to dealing with cultural difference, as '. . . our modes of thinking about cultural diversity and managing interethnic relations [have] remain[ed] trapped within a national framework . . . ' (Rizvi, 2011, p.180). As Kenny expressed it:

> Transnational studies emphasise the interconnectivity of people as national boundaries continue to loosen and everyday experiences of people around the world place them within a simultaneous field of the local and the global. (2011, p. 12)

In part, this has derived from, as previously outlined, a conception of culture as an immutable construction that is seen as being clearly identifiable, despite the fact that the inevitable dynamism of cultures as entities over time and space has been part of the discourse for several decades (for example, Alexander, 2001; Bhabha, 1994; Casinader, 2014; Rizvi, 2011; Said, 1993). Instead of being a fixed representation of the stasis within a society at the moment in time, culture is a mobile and liquid entity that is continually evolving as result of the tensions between societal conditions and individual perceptions. Indeed, Papastergiadis argues that the commandeering of multiculturalism as the basis of national identity by some nation-States shows a lack of '. . . appreciation of the dynamic flux mobilised in all cultural identities . . . ' (2000, p. 113).

In my view, the line of thought that a global culture is a likely and essential component of transnationalism, is founded on more conventional and increasingly ill-fitting assumptions about culture and its supposed globality, and are an outcome of longstanding suppositions made as to the components of a culture; that is, whether it is defined in terms of anthropology, or a more mind-centred conception is based upon consciousness. In earlier writings, I have argued that transcultural dispositions of thinking, principally found amongst those who have been more exposed to globalising experiences (Casinader, 2014), enable individuals who have acquired the capacity to relate to and work in thinking approaches across cultural identities and spaces. Fundamental to this transcultural capacity is the perspective that cultural variation is endemic in human society, and that it is uniformity that is more 'unreal' than the 'problem' or 'anomaly' that cultural diversity is seen by some to represent(Casinader, 2016). It is possible, therefore, to conceive of transnationalism as embodying transcultural attitudes that are derived directly from the positive absorption of the cultural flux of globalisation, but ones that are not bound territorially.

In this framework, transnationalism becomes a far more sophisticated and long-reaching concept that extends beyond essentialised references to population movement; it is more inclusive of ideas of transferability that are able to incorporate notions of mutually inclusive cultural consciousnesses, which are themselves born out of globalised migrations of people, notions and perceptions. Consequently, as a phenomenon, transnationalism is more fully comprehended if viewed as personifying the dynamic instability of transformative transition that occurs when people and ideas from different parts of the world meet, cross-pollinating dimensions of thought in the process. It is a function of the rejection of prior and existing assumptions that have been asserted as to the definition of culture. Whether demarcated in terms of anthropology or a more mind-centred conception based upon consciousness, cultures are not necessarily nationalistic and co-existent with political territorial borders. Instead, a more holistic notion of transnationalism exists, promoting '. . . that the movement of people and cultures contributes to a Welbild (conception of the world) in which borders and boundaries of nation, culture, race, and gender need to be reconceptualised, blurred, challenged, and, potentially, eliminated' (Friedman & Schultermandl, 2011, p. 6). This more encompassing umbrella of transnationalism has, at its heart, a high degree of embedded transcultural understanding, the nature of which is characterised by acknowledgement and acceptance of difference as the norm. Cultural diversity is better characterised as a collective of cultural dispositions, rather than approached as a chess set of cultural pieces, existing side by side but in opposition to each other. The crucial feature here is the acceptance of cultural difference as the standard state of 'human culture', one that needs to be confronted and mediated with the aim of coexistence, rather than seeing difference as a boil that needs to be lanced with policies of homogenisation and assimilation. More significantly, the reality of globalisation demands that this shift in perspective take place, because it is '. . . [a paradox] of globalisation . . . that difference is becoming increasingly normative' (Suárez-Orozco & Baolian Qin-Hilliard, 2004, p. 3).

## F Transnationalism in the past

One consequence of seeing transnationalism as a disposition of the mind, rather than a transactional process, is that the umbilical connections that are frequently asserted between the phenomenon, modernity and globalisation cannot be sustained. In the context of historical discourse, transnationalism has been strongly associated with not only globalisation, but also the study of global history that has developed as '. . . a reaction to current unreal processes marked by a rapid changes in world order . . . ', raising '. . . questions of transnational and global governance, territoriality and sovereignty beyond, or as an extension of, the nation state' (Fuchs, 2014, p. 14). The concept's umbilical association with the existence, future and function of the sovereign or nation-State is used as a justification for the assertion that it cannot be relevant to societies that existed prior to the emergence of the modern State in the 18th and 19th centuries.

However, to limit the conception of transnationalism as being essentially a child of the contemporary phase of globalisation is to oversimplify its complexity of both nature and historical context, reducing its existence to a binary that is unmovably linked to the rise of Western capitalism from the 19th century onwards. The aggregation of territory under the dominant authority of one specific State or individual, which, in its simplest form, is the aim of empire-building during any historical age, incorporates changes in the meanings of boundaries between different regions as markers of social, economic and political influence.

The individuals and governments that drove the emergence and growth of empires such as those of Ancient Rome, Alexander the Great and Genghis Khan can all be conceived as being transnational in their determination to eradicate or, at the very least, reconfigure the existing boundaries of the territories that they incorporated through various forms of acquisition. Just like the later main Euro-American empires of Holland (the Netherlands), Portugal, Great Britain, France and the United States, the linkages that connected the various regions of each domain were based fundamentally on the principle of economic or societal growth through the establishment, management and control of trade, all characterised, to varying degrees, by the determination to bind these new territories to the originating centre through a number of measures designed to establish and promote economic, social and cultural cohesion.

The unique character of the current modern phase of transnationalism is identified both by the speed of its diffusion and the fact that its principal actors are neither individuals, nor organisations in government, but a wide range of non-governmental social and economic institutions. Nevertheless, all empires of history have been facilitated by their efficient and extensive maximisation of the communications technology available in their own times, and the collapse of those communications in the face of territorial expansion was invariably a factor in their demise. The decline of the Roman Empire was but one example of such a case. The very fact that empire-building *ipso facto* necessitates and embodies the demolition of existing territorial borders, whilst absorbing new limbs into the existing corpus, means that they are inherently 'transnational' under the existing interpretation of the term, which, as discussed earlier in this chapter, has been narrowed to one that is dependent upon the existence of sovereign States and their borders. In the context of the reconfigured conceptualisation of transnationalism that has been posited, however, the transnationality of empire encompasses far more than any geographical diffusion and transference of human beings; it incorporates also a mind-centred perspective that, arguably, has been as significant in influencing the true extent of the legacies of empire.

The following chapters will explore this reconfiguration of transnationalism through the context of the British Empire and the particular colony of Ceylon (Sri Lanka). Further justification for the use of these particular case studies will be provided throughout, especially in relation to their relevance to the broader themes of empire and British systems of colonial education. However, both elements are also central to my own family history of migration and transnational behaviour, and it is this that also comprises one of the key illustrative threads in this book's exploration of a new perspective on transnationalism.

## References

Alexander, R. (2001). *Culture and Pedagogy: International Comparisons in Primary Education.* Oxford: Blackwell Publishers.

Appadurai, A. (1996). *Modernity at Large: Cultural Dimensions of Globalization.* Minneapolis: University of Minnesota Press.

Appadurai, A. (2006). *Fear of Small Numbers: An Essay on the Geography of Anger*. Durham: Duke University Press.

Bartley, A., & Spoonley, P. (2008). Intergenerational Transnationalism: 1.5 Generation Asian Migrants in New Zealand. *International Migration, 46*(4), 63–84. doi:10.1111/j.1468-2435.2008.00472.x

Bhabha, H. (1994). *The Location of Culture*. London: Routledge.

Brydon, D. (2010). Critical Literacies for Globalizing Times. *Critical Literacy: Theories and Practices, 4*(2), 16–28.

Burbules, N. C., & Torres, C. A. (2000). Globalization and Education: An Introduction. In N. C. Burbules & C. A. Torres (Eds.), *Globalization and Education: Critical Perspectives* (pp. 1–26). London: Routledge.

Casinader, N. (2014). *Culture, Transnational Education and Thinking: Case Studies in Global Schooling*. Milton Park, Abingdon: Routledge.

Casinader, N. (2015). Culture and Thinking in Comparative Education: The Globalism of an Empirical Mutual Identity. In J. Zajda (Ed.), *Second International Handbook on Globalisation, Education and Policy Research* (pp. 337–352). Dordrecht: Springer.

Casinader, N. (2016). A Lost Conduit for Intercultural Education: School Geography and the Potential for Transformation in the Australian Curriculum. *Intercultural Education, 27*(3). doi:10.1080/14675986.2016.1150650

Dahl, M. (2010). *Failure to Thrive in Constructivism: A Cross-Cultural Malady*. Rotterdam: Sense.

Daswani, G., & Quayson, A. (2013). *A Companion to Diaspora and Transnationalism* (First ed.). Chichester, West Sussex: Wiley Blackwell.

de Oliveira Andreotti, V. (2011). The Political Economy of Global Citizenship Education. *Globalisation, Societies and Education, 9*(3–4), 307–310.

Eckersley, R. (2007). Teaching and Learning about Globalisation. *Ethos, 15*(1), 10–18.

Faist, T. (2010). Diaspora and Transnationalism. What Kind of Dance Partners? In T. Faist & R. Bauböck (Eds.), *Diaspora and Transnationalism: Concepts, Theories and Methods*. (pp. 9–34). Amsterdam: Amsterdam University Press.

Friedman, M., & Schultermandl, S. (2011). Introduction. In M. Friedman & S. Schultermandl (Eds.), *Growing Up Transnational: Identity and Kinship in a Global Era* (pp. 3–18). Toronto: University of Toronto Press.

Fuchs, E. (2014). History of Education beyond the Nation? Trends in Historical and Educational Scholarship. In B. Bagchi, E. Fuchs, & K. Rousmaniere (Eds.), *Connecting Histories of Education: Transnational and Cross-Cultural Exchanges in (Post-) Colonial Education* (pp. 11–26). London: Berghahn.

Giddens, A. (2003). *Runaway World*. New York: Routledge.

Hall, S. (1990). Cultural Identity and Diaspora. In J. Rutherford (Ed.), *Identity: Community, Cultture, Difference* (pp. 222–237). London: Lawrence & Wishart.

Hannerz, U. (1990). Cosmopolitans and Locals in World Culture. *Theory, Culture & Society, 7*(2), 237–251. doi:10.1177/026327690007002014

Hoogvelt, A. M. M. (1997). *Globalisation and the Postcolonial World: The New Political Economy of Development*. Basingstoke, UK: Macmillan.

Igarishi, H., & Saito, H. (2014). Cosmopolitanism as Cultural Capital: Exploring the Intersection of Globalization, Education and Stratification. *Cultural Sociology, 8*(3), 222–239.

Inglis, C. (2002). Transnationalism: An Australian Perspective. *The Brown Journal for World Affairs, 8*(2), 182–193.

Kenny, E. (2011). Identity, Bodies, and Second-Generation Returnees in West Africa. In M. Friedman & S. Schultermandl (Eds.), *Growing Up Transnational: Identity and Kinship in a Global Era* (pp. 119–139). Toronto: University of Toronto Press.

King, K., & McGrath, S. (2002). *Globalisation, Enterprise and Knowledge: Education, Training and Development in Africa.* Oxford: Symposium Books.

Knight, N. (2004). *Understanding Australia's Neighbours: An Introduction to East and Southeast Asia.* New York: Cambridge University Press.

Koehn, P. H., & Rosenau, J. N. (2002). Transnational Competence in an Emergent Epoch. *International Studies Perspectives, 3*(2), 105–127. doi:10.1111/1528-3577.00084

Konno, Y. (2010). Transnationalism in Education: The Backgrounds, Motives, and Experiences of Nisei Students in Japan before World War II. *The Journal of American and Canadian Studies, 27*, 81–113.

Luke, A., & Luke, C. (2000). A Situated Perspective on Cultural Globalization. In N. C. Burbules & C. A. Torres (Eds.), *Globalization and Education: Critical Perspectives* (pp. 275–297). London: Routledge.

Massey, D. (1994). *Space, Place, and Gender.* Minneapolis: University of Minnesota Press.

McGrew, A. (2007). Organized Violence in the Making (and Remaking) of Globalization. In D. Held & A. McGrew (Eds.), *Globalization Theory: Approaches and Controversies* (pp. 15–40). Cambridge: Polity Press.

Olofsson, A., & Öhman, S. (2007). Cosmopolitans and Locals: An Empirical Investigation of Transnationalism. *Cultural Sociology, 55*(6), 877–895. doi:10.1177/0011392107081991

Ong, A. (1999). *Flexible Citizenship: The Cultural Logics of Transnationality.* Durham, NC: Duke University Press.

Papastergiadis, N. (2000). *The Turbulence of Migration: Globalization, Deterritorialization and Hybridity.* Cambridge: Polity Press.

Portes, A., Guarnizo, L. E., & Landholt, P. (1999). The Study of Transnationalism: Pitfalls and Promise of an Emergent Research Field. *Ethnic and Racial Studies, 22*(2), 217–237. doi:10.1080/014198799329468

Pries, L. (2004). Transnationalism and Migration: New Challenges for the Social Sciences and Education. In S. Luchtenberg (Ed.), *Migration, Education and Change* (pp. 15–39). Milton Park, Abingdon: Routledge.

Pries, L. (2008). Transnational Societal Spaces: Which Units of Analysis, Reference, and Measurement? In L. Pries (Ed.), *Rethinking Transnationalism: The Meso-Link of Organisations* (pp. 1–20). Milton Park, Abingdon: Routledge.

Rizvi, F. (2008). Epistemic Virtues and Cosmopolitan Learning. *Australian Educational Researcher, 35*(1), 17–35.

Rizvi, F. (2009). Towards Cosmopolitan Learning. *Discourse: Studies in the Cultural Politics of Education, 30*(3), 253–268. doi:10.1080/01596300903036863

Rizvi, F. (2011). Beyond the Social Imaginary of 'Clash of Civilizations'? *Educational Philosophy and Theory, 43*(3), 225–235. doi:10.1111/j.1469-5812.2009.00593.x

Rizvi, F., & Lingard, B. (2010). *Globalizing Education Policy.* London: Routledge.

Roudometof, V. (2005). Transnationalism, Cosmopolitanism and Glocalization. *Cultural Sociology, 53*(1), 113–135. doi:10.1177/0011392105048291

Said, E. W. (1993). *Culture and Imperialism* (First Vintage Books Edition ed.). New York: Vintage Books.

Saunier, P.-Y. (2009). Transnationalism. In A. Irive & P.Y. Saunier (Eds.), *The Palgrave Dictionary of Transnational History* (pp. 1047–1055). Basingstoke: Palgrave MacMillan.

Schiller, N. G., Basch, L., & Blanc-Szanton, C. (1992). Transnationalism: A New Analytic Framework for Understanding Migration. *Annals of the New York Academy of Sciences, 645*(1), 1–24. doi:10.1111/j.1749-6632.1992.tb33484.x

Singh, M. (2013). Educational Practice in India and Its Foundations in Indian Heritage: A Synthesis of the East and West? *Comparative Education, 49*(1), 88–106. doi: 10.1080/03050068.2012.740222

Skrbis, Z., & Woodward, I. (2007). The Ambivalence of Ordinary Cosmopolitanism: Investigating the Limits of Cosmopolitan Openness. *The Sociological Review, 55*(4), 730–747. doi:10.1111/j.1467-954X.2007.00750.x

Smith, M. P., & Guarnizo, L. (1998). *Transnationalism from Below*. New Brunswick, NJ: Transaction Publishers.

Suárez-Orozco, M. M., & Baolian Qin-Hilliard, D. (2004). Globalization: Culture and Education in the New Millennium. In M. M. Suárez-Orozco & D. Baolian Qin-Hilliard (Eds.), *Globalization: Culture and Education in the New Millennium* (pp. 1–37). Berkeley and Los Angeles: University of California Press in association with the Ross Institute.

Vertovec, S. (1999). Conceiving and Researching Transnationalism. *Ethnic and Racial Studies, 22*(2), 447–462. doi:10.1080/014198799329558

Vertovec, S. (2009). *Transnationalism*. Milton Park, Abingdon: Routledge.

# 2 Education and transnationalism

## A An expanded relationship

In the contemporary phase of globalisation, the relationship between transnationalism and education has been highly restricted, aligned as it is with the utilitarian perspective, in which transnationalism has been seen primarily in the context of the international commodification of teaching and learning; the economic aspects of the globalising process have been very much in focus. The accent remains on the notion of 'trans-', reflecting the simple act of movement of phenomena across defined national boundaries, which is also at the foundation of transnationalism in the higher and school education context. Under the more expanded configuration as a disposition of the mind, however, the concept acquires much greater scope as a lens for interpretation of global movements, especially in the context of demographic shifting across the world, both temporary and permanent. The diversity of transnational priorities reflected in Vertovec's six-part classification of the phenomenon (2009) is not mirrored in the ways in which educators have connected with transnationalism, which have been being largely confined to the areas of 'social morphology' and 'avenues of capital'. In the main, the transactional nature of population movement across national borders has been overlain with the paradox of utilitarian individualism, focusing on either those who migrate to other countries, usually temporarily, for the sole purpose of obtaining qualifications, or on the delivery of education by an institution in a country outside that institution's home base.

In many ways, the current vision of transnationalism as a commercial concept in higher and school education, in which people move temporarily (at least, initially) from one State to another for the purposes of acquiring education for a paid fee, is not unsurprising. An interesting reflection of how different educational sectors are perceived by higher level policy makers can be observed in the greater application of transnationalist principles to higher education more than to school education, no better exemplified than by the definition of transnational education (TNE) adopted by the Council of Europe and UNESCO:

> All types of higher education study programmes, or sets of courses of study, or educational services (including those of distance education) in which the

> learners are located in a country different from the one where the awarding institution is based. Such programmes may belong to the education system of a State different from the State in which it operates, or may operate independently of any national education system . . . Transnational arrangements should be so elaborated, enforced and monitored as to and education widen the access to higher education studies . . .
>
> (Council of Europe, 2014)

The approach taken by higher education institutions to transnationalism is highly problematic as it is restricted to the economic configurations of globalisation (Foster, 2012), placing less emphasis on transnationalism's significance as a social phenomenon that is borne out of the globalising process; that is, the increasing mobility of people on a world scale. It also implies that the social aspects and consequences of this increased mobility are of less significance, notwithstanding analyses such as Martin and Rizvi (2014). Although higher education institutions do engage in other forms of 'transnational' activities such as international research collaborations and staff exchanges, I would argue that such operations can be regarded as being still part of the core 'business' of the higher education sector, and, at an institutional level at least, do not detract from the conclusion that the sector remains constrained within the narrower confines of a neoliberal economic perspective on transnationalism.

Regardless of this primary focus on the transactional aspects of educational transnationalism in higher education, educational researchers have shown an interest in other possible linkages between transnationalism and education. For example, Adick (2008) outlined three possible areas of research interest, including the aforementioned *transnational education*. The other avenues of connection comprised *transnational convergences in education*, which is concerned with global connections in terms of policy and practice, which have created a momentum towards international standardisation and comparative assessments in education, such as PISA and TIMMS, and *transnational education* **in** *transmigrant communities.* In this facet of the field, which was seen as being directly related to the school level of education, the approaches adopted have tended to be centred upon the work of sociologists working from the educational perspective, rather than on the implications for education itself; for example, Kenway and Fahey (2014); Kenway and Koh (2013); Koh and Kenway (2012); McCarthy and Kenway (2014). These works all flowed out of a project investigating the relevance of 'elite schools' in former British colonies in the contemporary age of globalisation. Such foci have persisted partly because of the tendency for educational research to regard migration in such a way so as to default to the '. . . classical notion on one-way migration processes, still centred on concepts of assimilation, integration, cultural identity, multicultural education, and so on, for migrant children and youths' (Adick, 2008, p. 128).

Although less developed than is the case in the Australian higher education context, the same principle of transactional transnationalism in the form of 'international education' has come to apply in the school sector. For instance, in locations such as Australia, international students have come to form key components of the enrolments of many schools (Fincher & Shaw, 2011), particularly in the independent or private school sector. Unlike the tertiary sphere, however, the use of the concept of 'transnationalism' in this context has not been a feature of school practice or academic reflections upon it. Although there has been discussion of the possible implications of transnational thinking for school education, such as by Fazal Rizvi (2000, 2009, 2011), this has been more concerned with the broader levels of policy development and the implications for school educational practice, rather than educational activity within schools themselves. One such example is Rizvi's highlighting of how increasing global population transnational mobility and resultant cultural diversity has resonances for teacher competencies in Australian schools:

> . . . If I were emigrating from India in 2011, I would bring to Australian schools many cultural resources and experiences of mobility that the schools could well take advantage of in internationalising their curriculum and pedagogy. At the same time, my teachers would need to better understand the rapidly changing world, associated with global forces, connections and imaginations, which I would inhabit in the 21st century.
>
> (2011, p. 21)

In terms of actual practice at the school and classroom level, however, there has been very little literary evidence of engagement by Australian schools and teachers with transnationalism as a specific concept, a pattern that is in line with the author's previous career experiences in secondary Australian schools over three decades. This dissonance between the concept of 'transnationalism' and the use within the institutions of school education is exemplified by its relative absence from current documentation related to the national Australian Curriculum, which has been introduced progressively since 2011 (Casinader, 2016).

There are indications, however, that educational researchers are finding new pathways into the transnationalist forest. For instance, there has been a more recent shift into transnationalism in the context of the history of education, a movement to which this monograph arguably belongs. In one recent example, McLeod and Wright draw on Foucauldian perspectives on genealogy and historical studies of transnationalism to examine the ideas about citizenship in 1930s Australia. Identifying the 1937 conference of the New Education Fellowship as a defining moment in Australian education history, the authors argue that the interwar years were '. . . more cosmopolitan and engaged in international discussions about citizenship and schooling than is usually remembered in the present' (McLeod & Wright, 2013, p. 170).

Overall, though, these deficits in a more comprehensive understanding of educational transnationalism are also reflected in arguments that suggest that, although not expressed in such terms, Spivak's notion of transnational literacy (1999) – a knowledge and understanding of how globalisation is affecting the nature of education and the national implications of international developments – is becoming a global imperative for educational leaders, and not just an optional extra. In one example, Brooks and Normore (2010) argue that a greater understanding of glocalisation – the notion that globalisation has re-energised the connections of individuals to their local place (Appadurai, 1996) – is becoming indispensable in the preparation and practice of education leaders in the 21st century. Noting the scarcity of literature on connecting glocalisation with educational leadership, they suggest nine literacies of glocalisation (which can be re-interpreted as a form of transnationalism) that are essential for leaders to promote if students are to educated for a transnationalist era: political; economic; cultural; moral; pedagogical; information; organisational; spiritual and religious; and temporal. All of these are expressed within a framework of a definition of literacy that incorporates new information and communication technologies, critical thinking, active citizenship and linguistic and cultural diversity. Since educational leaders are in positions to provide direction and exercise influence, the educational resources that they make available to their students and school systems need to be more reflective of the realities of their students' futures, countering current deficiencies in student literacies across these areas (Brooks & Normore, 2010).

## B Education, empowerment and historical transnationalism

### *The education – transnationalism nexus*

To understand the linkages between the posited reconfiguration of transnationalism as a concept (see Chapter 1) and education, it is necessary first to highlight the education-transnationalism nexus that emerged during the historical phase of globalisation that peaked in the 19th and 20th centuries, and its differences with its modern counterpart. Of particular interest are the implications of this development for the notion of education as an emancipator of individuals or groups who wished to actualise their own cultural priorities, rather than being empty vessels that succumbed to the colonising power as the dominant form.

The principle that formal education is the primary and most effective means towards personal liberation and self-improvement is, arguably, one of the more enduring aspects of Euro-American colonial philosophy. In the context of Age of Enlightenment in Europe, it is an intellectual precept that dates back to John Locke's assertion that, since all are born equal, the quality of the life that they will live depends upon how the mind is moulded by the quality of education that they receive. It is a principle that itself can be threaded back, in the 'Western' context, to the Socratic emphasis on reason as the highest form of human achievement on the one hand, as well as to the emphases placed on the search for truth through the focus of mind and spirit that are inherent in Eastern philosophies, including those in Hinduism and Buddhism. In this sense, the capacity of education to elevate individual lives can be presented as a universal truth, even though the form, organisation and accessibility of education has been, and remains, one of the most debatable aspects of human existence. Until the 19th century, education was reserved in civilisations throughout the millennia for those with economic and political power and for whom there was a perceived need, in the mould of Plato's philosopher kings. This book, however, is more concerned about the capacity of individuals to harness the powers of education when they have become accessible, as well as the relationship of education to the generation, existence and impact of transnationalism as a personal attribute, rather than a societal phenomenon.

## *Education and Empire: Past and present*

Throughout the Age of European imperialism, particularly in the 18th and 19th centuries, mass education acquired other aspects to its character and purpose, being progressively seen as a means of the creation and maintenance of a national identity (Hobsbawm, 1989), not only within the newly emerging European States, but also in the territories that were being acquired by those States as extensions of their central polity. This was particularly the case within the reaches on the British Empire, around which this monograph is centred. It was not only the cement that was the unifying force that bound people living within the boundaries of a defined State together, but also the net that could be used to haul in new and diffused 'bodies' of people into the cultural space defined and exhibited by the metropolitan power. It is therefore unsurprising that, since the end of the 19th century, writers and thinkers in the then newly emerging field of educational research surrounding the systems of mass education that had developed, were able to identify education as both the outward face and transmitter of societal culture in a particular region (Sadler, 1900/1979, and more recently, Foucault, 1972). This was certainly the case within the British Empire, where, despite the varieties of perspectives and meanings, there was a unifying psychological space occupied by those who were included within it, a mindset that encapsulated a 'Britishness'. The Empire was seen '. . . not as a piece of territory, or a framework of administration, but as a genuine community of people, tied together by common sentiments and traditions, a shared sense of purpose, and a collective memory . . . ' (Thompson, 2008, p. 8), around which British identity was woven.

Throughout the 19th century, and much of the 20th, the power of education to achieve societal improvement and raise the quality of life for all individuals was very much an undisputed concept. As has been long established in the discourse, there was little contestation as to the nature and direction that education needed to take in order to develop and enhance people's capabilities. The global socio-economic and political power wielded by the Euro-American territories in Europe and North America, and the ongoing success of both societies in achieving growth in living standards for a large cross-section of its peoples through the modernisation and industrialisation of society – albeit fractured, irregular and uneven – meant that it was perceived as self-evident that educational systems in 'less developed' regions and territories needed to follow the same policies and practices of the so-called 'developed' nations if they wished to achieve the same standards of socio-economic living. Whilst there were severe philosophical and political ruptures throughout the 20th century as to the means by which those socio-economic goals could be achieved, the place of education as a means of generating and enabling national goals was consistent across the width of the spectrum, encompassing both capitalist and communistic theories of development.

The period of the late 1960s and early 1970s marked a key stage in the emergence in terms of transnationalism as an intellectual concept. In global politics, amongst a deep morass of ideological confrontation and conflict, the years since the end of World War II had seen the final decline of the European imperial order established throughout the previous two centuries, with the decolonisation of former colonial possessions throughout Africa, Asia, South America and the Pacific. Consonant with this, there was also a shift occurring as to the perceived place of education as an element in colonial and national development constructs. Prior to this time, the prevailing view of education within the colonial period had been one generally of positivism, in which educational facilitation and establishment had been promoted as one of its more beneficial aspects. Such attitudes were mirrored in the contemporary phase after World War II, when the drive for internationalism as a philosophy of global action, conducted through such multilateral institutions as the newly-formed United Nations, was accompanied by national development programmes in the newly emerging ex-colonial States. The importance of education as a means of cementing national unity and building a future for all people within a State was seen as paramount (Lo Bianco, 2006; Stoer & Cortesão, 2000).

The basis of this educational imperative was the belief that national development and growth through economic mirroring of the Euro-American model of industrialised development, which itself had been fuelled and sustained by 19th- and 20th-century European colonialism, was the only means by which the welfare and future well-being of general populations could be advanced. It was therefore inevitable that educational systems in the newly independent States of the Global 'South' – seen by the 'West' as being 'backward' both economically and socially – were often comprised of economic and social constructions that emulated the systems in place in the 'developed, Western' world, or the Global 'North'. More often than not, these educational formulations were imported directly from the former colonial or metropolitan power. Given that the dominant empire of this period, at least in terms of geographical area, had been the British substantiation, the diffusion of British principles of educational philosophies of systems, structures, teaching and learning extended in all parts and all versions of the former Empire, from India and Sri Lanka (then called Ceylon) to regions such as East Africa (Kenya) and the Caribbean islands (Barbados). Perhaps inevitably, these newly independent systems of education were continuations of the systems established during colonial rule, and in that context, there was little disruption to the educational systems that had been in place previously, although changes in emphasis were not too far behind.

By the 1970s, however, driven in large part by the emerging critical mass of ideas and writings of thinkers from the so-called 'periphery' – see Brookfield (1975), Paolo Freire (1970/1996) and Franz Fanon (1967) – and later reinvigorated in the 1990s by Edward Said (1978, 1993) and others, the postcolonial perspective had begun to take root and establish itself as the dominant discourse (Carnoy, 1974). Instead of being seen as a means of liberation for local people, especially in the context of more recent successes in national independence, education was now seen as a means of not only social engineering and domination throughout the colonial period, but also as a pathway for former colonial powers to maintain their control over the periphery through neo-colonialist economic and social measures:

> colonialism . . . [was] not simply about extending informal political influence, establishing economic domination, or securing sovereignty, but it was a much broader set of asymmetrical relationships grounded in the desire of the colonizer to exert mastery over the colonized society, its natural and human resources, and its cultural forms.
>
> (Ballantyne, 2008, p. 177)

Educational control gave the colonial ruler power over the choice of knowledge to be taught, how it was represented and how it was delivered.

In this Foucauldian frame, cultural knowledge and identity was corralled, as was the dissemination and use of power, in favour of the colonial authority:

> Western formal education came to most countries as part of imperialist domination. It was consistent with the goals of imperialism: the economic and political control of the people in one country by the dominant class in another. The imperial powers contented, through schooling, to train the colonized for roles that suited the coloniser. Even within the dominant countries themselves, schooling did not offset social inequities. The educational system was no more just or equal than the economy and society itself-specifically, we argue, because schooling was organised to develop and maintain, in the imperial countries, and inherently in equitable and unjust organization of production and political power.
>
> (Carnoy, 1974, p. 3)

Consequently, the focus was now on a critical perspective that placed '. . . historically marginalised parts of the world at the centre, rather than at the periphery of the education and globalisation debate' (Tikly, 2001, p. 152). In the postcolonial frame, the reality of political independence had not been matched by economic and social replication. The imposition of mass education in the British mould in a form that met British interests, as the dominant, colonial power, was seen as de-empowering the cultural integrity and knowledge of those colonised (Said, 1993), removing pathways through which they might achieve any form of meaningful self-determination:

> For in destroying the authority of indigenous cultures, and imposing its own, [colonialism] wrecked the self-confidence and creative capacity of local elites and drove a deep wage between a collaborative minority seduced by the charms of imported ideas and the rest of society.
>
> (Darwin, 2012, p. 5)

The difficulty with the seeming simplicity of this deconstruction of colonialism, and the part played by education within it, is that it ignores the complexities of social and cultural constructs within sovereign States, as well as the complexity and multi-layered nature of the British Empire itself. For thinkers such as Mangan (1993), the sense of deliberate imposition of a power dynamic by the coloniser was reflected in their use of the word 'imperial' to denote its purpose. Thus, '[i]mperial education was very much about establishing the presence and absence of *confidence* in those controlling and those controlled' (1993, p. 6) However, to condemn colonial practices of education as being primarily one of general deficit, is to ignore the layers of social reality that existed in many ex-colonial states at the start of their newly independent existences. Whilst there is an argument that colonial education had a detrimental effect on the nationalist priorities of certain groups in specific regions, as enunciated by Sinhalese nationalist forces in Sri Lanka since independence in 1948, the educational systems introduced also provided pathways for other groups, or specific individuals, in the same society to attain a certain degree of community and personal sovereignty.

## *The forgotten side(s) of colonial education*

In large part, the opening up of these new opportunities was a direct result of the primary reasons for the development of mass education within British colonial societies, which were highly utilitarian in nature; that is, they were designed to fill a perceived gap in the commercial operations of the colony. The experience and attitudes of the East India Company in India was that their success in mercantilism would require a local indigenous, educated class who, led by their British – that is, white – managers, would be the foundation for efficient administration of the colony by the assigned governing authority. This workforce needed to be educated in a way that enabled them to possess the academic and cultural skills required to implement the British colonial vision (Ghosh, 1993). It was a new local professional class, working in administration, law, teaching, journalism and medicine, '. . . fluent in the language and cultural peculiarities of the white masterclass. . .', enabling this new group to '. . . communicate with each other, and with the larger world to which empire now linked them' (Darwin, 2012, p. 296). They were able to avail themselves of colonial structures and priorities, raising both their status and the quality of life within their home regions by acquiring the skills to participate in the new colonial economy, rather than being left to wallow in the margins.

It was these elements of colonial education, perceived in the postcolonial perspective to be oppressive of local intentions and the choices of individuals (Clignet, 1984; Fanon, 1967; Freire, 1970/1996) that also acted as the lines of deliverance that liberated others. The weakness of the postcolonial perspective in this regard is that it does not fully account for the reasoned desire by many of those colonised to *consciously* exercise choice and *actively* embrace the possibilities that education in the colonial form offered them (Ball, 1983; Taylor, 1984). In particular, it tends to treat education as introduced by the colonial power as a simplified binary, in which the imposed system reinforced existing socio-economic differences between the indigenous privileged – usually referred to as the 'elite' – and the mass of the population (Natsoulas & Natsoulas, 1993). However, the localised situations were often far more complex, as will be illustrated through the discussion in Chapters 4–6. It was possible that the opportunities that colonial education offered to those outside the elite enabled them to actualise their innate, dormant transnationalist dispositions and, in the process, assert a high degree of personal sovereignty over the direction of their future lives in an increasingly globalising economy.

To acknowledge these nuances of educational practice within British colonial territories is not to deny the negative impact that colonial policy did have on existing cultures and practices, including education, within the Empire. However, to acknowledge that such change did take place is not equivalent to the condemnation of all change as being deleterious and disruptive to the interests of the colonised peoples. Instead, it is recognition of the aforementioned condition of the Empire as a mosaic of applied British culture, '. . . [d]iverse in practice, fractured and ambiguous and meaning, local yet transnational' (Proudfoot & Roche, 2005, p. 1). The local conditions in each site of Empire meant that the nature of British intervention and the degree of impact varied considerably, even if the practices themselves were similar in nature and intent. Generalisations only serve to essentialise the character of both imperial ruler and colonial victim, without acknowledgement of the capability, potentiality or actuality of agency within colonised peoples to respond and adapt to changing circumstance. For example, the practicalities of imperial administration made it essential for the colonial authorities to work collaboratively with local leadership elites, '. . . and who[m] they worked hard to both to control and accommodate' (Levine, 2013, p. 125). Interaction was not always a foisted one-way street.

Furthermore, another aspect of this essentialised reaction to colonial administrative impact, often unacknowledged by both sides of the debate, is the assumption, based on contestable notions of cultural relativism, that existing cultures and societies in place prior to British colonialism were inviolate and deserving of preservation. In reality, existing societies and cultures were often feudal in nature, with highly stratified class divisions and employing brutal, fundamental systems of justice that are quite at odds with not only postcolonial assertions that cultural violence was a feature of colonial oppression, but also the context of contemporary conceptions of human rights and social justice. It also raises uncomfortable tensions, particularly in the current global context of international conflict policy and practices of the Islamic State, as to the degree of autonomy that should be ascribed to the cultural rights of the people to assert their beliefs and practices in the face of global attitudinal change.

To a degree, it also negates, ironically, one of the key statements of Edward Said (1993) in his observation that cultural change is inevitable. All cultures respond to shifts around them, and this continuous dynamism of culture is crucial for its long-term health and validity. On that basis, the abilities and successes of those colonised peoples who were able to appropriate certain colonial principles and attributes, utilising them to create a new future for themselves, founded on a re-manifestation of the existing culture in the search for '. . . group opportunity, spiritual promise and personal liberation . . . ' (Darwin, 2012, p. 268), needs to be recognised far more overtly than has been the case in the past and in the present.

I should reiterate here that I am not arguing that the imposition of colonial or Euro-American systems of education did not have any form of adverse impact upon the existing concepts of education within the societies that were being colonised, or that the act of educational supplantation was without criticism from the modern perspective. For instance, in the case of the British Empire, the notion of 'Britishness' as being the high point of civilisation followed the contemporary scientific and philosophical line that civilisation and intelligence were racially determined, which, in turn, meant that to be living in the British Empire did not automatically indicate that all were equal: '. . . . recognition was only ever extended to any non-white subjects of the empire in very tentative and precarious ways' (Howe, 2008, p. 163). Colonisation was the means by which 'civilisation' could be brought to the non-European world, enabling the transformation of those societies and peoples who were deemed to be more backward (Anghie, 2005). The identification of difference was crucial to the justification of the '. . . natural inequalities . . . ' that '. . . legitimated . . . the grounds that Britons were suited to conquest and settlement, and would bring the benefits of their superior civilization to others . . . ' (Hall, 2008, pp. 204–205).

Nevertheless, a total rejection of the British, 'Westernised' education system that was introduced as a result of Empire also implies that existing local and/or indigenous ways of life were without issues of contention. Judgement, of course, is a subjective process, in the sense that it is formulated on the basis of the values promulgated by the society in making the evaluation, but to now see local ways of life that existed in pre-European times as largely immune from criticism, and therefore argue that they had a moral priority to be retained, is merely to replicate the simplifications of Rousseau's 'noble savage' thesis; it also consolidates a picture of non-European cultures as 'exotics' that need preservation, regardless of what exists.

Furthermore, the nuances of cultural discourse being as they are, it is inevitable that the old adage of 'the past being always greener' has tended to sublimate some of the darker sides of indigenous life and society prior to the imperial period, whilst ignoring the cohesive capacities of education to maintain stability and security within pre-colonial societies which had the potential, often actuated since independence, to fracture along ethnic lines. The reductionist tendencies of pure postcolonial thought tend to label education as a simple binary equation; that the receipt of colonialised education automatically leads to colonisation of the mind and the rejection of the local and past (for example, Joseph, 2008). However, cultural transmission through education is not the same as cultural acquisition (Quist, 2001), and the individuality of learners makes it inevitable that the process of colonisation through schooling had differential effects depending upon discrete circumstances. The ultimate efficacy of British imperial governance as a means of unifying difference was, nevertheless, in large part, due to the power of education; a means by which the colonial power could establish social sovereignty (which is not to be confused with cultural sovereignty) in a territory that it had formally claimed previously in a political framework. Moreover, within this flux, there were instances where education in the imperial sphere was able to create an atmosphere or condition of instability, in which local people could thrive. Within such parameters, it provided a catalyst for those whose drive was founded on self-improvement and socio-economic security, and whose identity was essentially bound up with transnationalism and less tied to the specifics of place.

## C Transnationalism as an activator of rights

One of the fundamental intellectual bases of the postcolonial view is that imperial education was a destructive force because it denied the right of local people to actualise their own traditions of education and knowledge in a way that reflected their own way of life. As discussed previously, these philosophical reactions to colonial policy and practices, especially from writers based in the Euro-American sphere, can be seen as being part of a wider historical shift away from a global belief in the principles of internationalism, founded on a conception of the world divided into autonomous sovereign States, to a situation where a less territorialised notion of transnationalism has been emerging as a modern socio-political phenomenon. In the same period of change, the notion of individual human rights was also undergoing a transformation.

Prior to this time, in concert with the emphasis placed on the sovereign state as the base unit of global economic, social and political organisation, the notion of rights pertaining to an individual in society was very much incorporated with the principle of citizenship, an individual belonging to, and being part of, the society contained within the defined territorial borders of recognised sovereign State; individuals were a '. . . part of the authority of the [S]tate, not invoked to transcend it' (Moyn, 2010, p. 7). From the 1970s, however, the same forces that were mobilising in response to the growing influence and impact of globalisation were contributing to a reconfiguration of human rights as universal entitlements that were both inalienable and unconditional. These rights were not specifically linked to a person's identity as a citizen of a specific State, but to their very existence as a human being, and were being actuated through such multilateral conventions as the United Nations Declaration of Human Rights, which, significantly, in the context of this discussion, includes the right to determine and practice one's own cultural identity: '. . . cultural rights indispensable for his[sic] dignity and the free development of his[sic] personality' (United Nations, 1948, Article 22). Interestingly, and somewhat paradoxically, the same set of rights also cements the right of all individuals to belong to one nation-State, and through that "nationality', practise their entitlements to participate in the effective civic life of that territorial unit (Article 15).

In terms of the increasing shift into a global stasis of transnationalism, including its inherent inclusion of a transcultural way of thinking (Casinader, 2014,

2016) that goes beyond its relevance within a specific range of cultural environments, the right to an individual's culture, and for the right of that individual to practise that culture, as facets of a universal right can be problematic. In the first place, in the case of a nation-State, where there is a presumption of a greater homogeneity of culture as compared to a less culturally defined sovereign State, there is a concomitant assumption that all people within that culture perceive it to embody and enact a certain set of common beliefs and principles. Such generalisations deny the natural state of diversity that is a more accurate representation and reflection of the complexity of human society and existence. The many variations of global faith that exist, and how they are practised, ranging through the branches of Christianity, Islam, Hinduism and Buddhism, are themselves salient examples of this. Second, there is also the underlying assumption that the culture, even if there is agreement as to its major elements, is static and readily determinable. Yet, as Edward Said and others have highlighted, all cultures are organic entities that are constantly shifting. They cannot afford to be unchanging; a living culture must be responding to variations in shifts in the environments within which it operates if it is to maintain a relevance and attraction. And third, and perhaps more importantly, the United Declaration of Human Rights, regardless of its more observable focus on eradicating discrimination, does not highlight the specific right of someone from within a particular group to reform their cultural identity as they see fit into a way that benefits them, even though it might put pressure on the cultural context of their fellow citizens or existing neighbours. There can be a great tension, therefore, between the assertions of cultural integrity and universal rights, especially in relation to the right of all individuals to choose how and where they should live.

In the colonial context, when the European powers introduced their systems of education into the colonial territories, the variations extended not only to the different educational priorities of the various metropolitan powers, but also to how educational systems were applied within varying territories controlled by the same power. For example, France, the colonial power in French West Africa and Indochina, implemented systems of learning in both regions in the first half of the 20th century that reflected completely different approaches to the treatment of local pre-European systems of society and education (Kelly, 1984). In Indochina, a full system of primary and secondary education that led to university was put in place by the French administration, and teaching in the first three years of schooling was provided in the vernacular languages of Vietnamese, Lao, Khmer, Rhade and Meo, with written resources supplied in each. Although all post-elementary education was then conducted in French, such an approach was in stark contrast with French West Africa, where no education of any sort in the indigenous languages was provided.

In a striking exemplification of the class structures that were sometimes embedded in colonial education, the variance existed because of the difference in the audience for whom colonial education was designed in each locale; the local elite or the public at large. Education in French West Africa was aimed at the leadership group, who were deemed to be in more need of French as the future leadership class, whereas Indochina's system was focused on the population at large (Kelly, 1984). Similarly, in the British India of 1817, a group of Baptist missionaries or, as they came to be known, the Serampore Three, promoted the importance of producing books of learning in the vernacular languages if effective learning was to take place. This was in direct contradiction of the views of Thomas Babington Macauley, who, as a member of the Supreme Council of India, was instrumental in reinforcing the mantra of British culture and values within British India by persuading the Governor General to mandate English being the language of instruction in Indian schools from 1835 (Hilton, 2014). In colonial Sri Lanka, the British adopted a variation on the same approach, with English being prescribed as the language of administration, partly as a means of economic efficiency, as well as cultural reformation. Whether purposely or not, it also served the purpose of providing a plane of unity for the island where there were, at the very least, three existing sets of languages between the Sinhalese, Tamils and Muslims who comprised the population of the island prior to British rule, along with Dutch and Portuguese.

There were other viable reasons for the colonial imposition of an educational system, however. Rightly or wrongly, within the British Empire, education was the means by which the colonial power considered that it could extend the rights of citizenship – the mark of civilisation according to 'Western' thought – to all the peoples that were now included within the arms of the Empire. The contemporary system of 'universal' human rights is founded on the principle that there are certain aspects of life and existence to which all human beings have an inalienable entitlement regardless of the context of their existence, and their substantiation in thought and legal enabling is generally attributed in large part to their emergence after the sobering global realisation of the Holocaust after World War II (for example, Moyn, 2010), They are, in that sense, a reaction to historical events, '. . . strong ethical pronouncements of as to what should be done' (Sen, 2009, p. 357).

Such a viewpoint was not the case in the mid-19th century, when the concept of human rights was very much tied to the notion of the State, and the rights pertaining to a citizen of that State. In Britain itself, citizenship itself was highly prescribed: women could not vote, regardless of class or status, and the right to vote was linked to property ownership. Colonial identities were influenced by gender and class, as well as ethnicity, and what was absent was as important as what was evident: '. . . effeminacy signalled an incapacity for independence and for self-government associated with the subaltern position in the world' (Hall, 2008, p. 203). The principles embedded in British education, the values of which were deemed to embody 'civilised' citizenship, were coincident with those practised by the British populace and a function of their time. Although modern commentary often condemns such colonial educational practices as the embodiment of European arrogance, it is not so far removed from situations in the contemporary world. The demands that educational systems should be supporters and disseminators of government policy in respect of nationalistic conceptions of citizenship are being increasingly promulgated by ruling authorities in regions as diverse as the United States, Australia, Japan, China, and areas currently under the rule of groups such as Daesh (Islamic State). Within the British Empire, there were those ethnic and cultural groups who saw their own rights as being non-existent under the pre-European societal structures. The development of a liberal existence, along with the promotion of the rights pertaining to citizenship and human beings that were embedded within British educational systems, offered a facility that could be used by those groups to improve what they saw as their formal reality.

As an illustration of this transnationalism-education pathway, Chapters 4, 5 and 6 will be centred upon the use of the educational system in colonial Sri Lanka by minority groups. Further explanation of the value of this particular case study will be provided throughout, but suffice to say, at this point, that one of the key features of British rule in colonial Ceylon was the way in which marginalised minority ethno-cultural groups such as the Ceylon Tamil, Muslims and Burghers were able to use the system of equity created by colonial education as an administrative framework to generate new directions of life and fulfil longstanding aspirations. For many, it freed up their inability to shift status, lifestyle and social position, activated in the process by a previously dormant sense of transnationalism that was later translated into a mind-centred disposition, a change guided by principles of self-improvement and security, and not necessarily an attachment to place, as assumed in the current interpretation of transnationalism. For groups such as the Ceylon Tamils and Burghers of colonial Sri Lanka, colonial education was the way in which a renewed cultural integrity within the community was able to be born out of the colonial experience. The introduction of mass education helped to open up lines for improvement and lessen the socio-economic gap between the elite and the general population (Hobsbawm, 1989), providing the means by which these groups and individuals could activate their drive for freedom from existing socio-political structures. It was the means by which they could choose to enforce their own rights to emancipation from socio-economic constraint, assisted by a capacity for transnationalism of the spirit and mind, as part of which personal, spiritual, social and economic advancement and security were more important than attachment to any particular location or cultural home.

## References

Adick, C. (2008). Transnational Organisations in Education. In L. Pries (Ed.), *Rethinking Transnationalism: The Meso-Link of Organisations* (pp. 126–154). London: Routledge.

Anghie, A. (2005). *Imperialism, Sovereignty and the Making of International Law* (Electronic Book ed.). New York: Cambridge University Press.

Appadurai, A. (1996). *Modernity at Large: Cultural Dimensions of Globalization.* Minneapolis: University of Minnesota Press.

Ball, S. J. (1983). Imperialism, Social Control and the Colonial Curriculum in Africa. *Journal of Curriculum Studies, 15*(3), 237–263. doi:10.1080/0022027830150302

Ballantyne, T. (2008). Colonial Knowledge. In S. Stockwell (Ed.), *The British Empire: Themes and Perspectives* (pp. 177–198). Oxford: Blackwell Publishing.

Brookfield, H. (1975). *Interdependent Development*. London: Methuen & Co Ltd.
Brooks, J. S., & Normore, A. H. (2010). Educational Leadership and Globalization: Literacy for a Glocal Perspective. *Educational Policy, 24*(1), 52–82.
Carnoy, M. (1974). *Education as Cultural Imperialism*. New York: David McKay Company Inc.
Casinader, N. (2014). *Culture, Transnational Education and Thinking: case studies in global schooling*. Milton Park, Abingdon: Routledge.
Casinader, N. (2016). Transnationalism in the Australian Curriculum: New Horizons or Destinations of the Past? *Discourse: Studies in the Cultural Politics of Education, 37*(3), 327–340. doi:10.1080/01596306.2015.1023701
Clignet, R. (1984). Damned If You Do, Damned If You Don't: The Dilemmas of Colonizer-Colonized Relations. In P. G. Altbach & G. P. Kelly (Eds.), *Education and the Colonial Experience* (Second Revised ed., pp. 77–95). New Brunswick, NJ: Transaction Books.
Council of Europe. (2014). Code of Good Practice in the Provision of Transnational Education. Retrieved from http://www.coe.int/t/dg4/highereducation/recognition/Codeofgoodpractice_EN.asp
Darwin, J. (2012). *Unfinished Empire: The Global Expansion of Britain*. London: Penguin.
Fanon, F. (1967). *Black Skin, White Masks* (C. L. Markmann, Trans.). New York: Grove Press Inc.
Fincher, R., & Shaw, K. (2011). Enacting Separate Social Worlds: 'International' and 'Local' Students in Public Space in Central Melbourne. *Geoforum, 42*(5), 539–545.
Foster, G. (2012). The Impact of International Students on Measured Learning and Standards in Australian Higher Education. *Economics of Education Review, 31*(5), 587–600.
Foucault, M. (1972). *The Archaeology of Knowledge and the Discourse on Language* (A. M. Sheridan-Smith, Trans.). New York: Pantheon Books.
Freire, P. (1970/1996). *Pedagogy of the Oppressed* (M. Bergman Ramos, Trans., New Revised ed.). London: Penguin Books.
Ghosh, S. C. (1993). 'English in Taste, in Opinion, in Words and Intellect': Indoctrinating the Indian through Textbook, Curriculum and Education. In J. A. Mangan (Ed.), *The Imperial Curriculum: Racial Images and Education in the British Colonial Experience* (pp. 175–193). London: Routledge.
Hall, C. (2008). Culture and Identity in Imperial Britain. In S. Stockwell (Ed.), *The British Empire: Themes and Perspectives* (pp. 199–217). Oxford: Blackwell Publishing.
Hilton, M. (2014). A Transcultural Transaction: William Carey's Baptist Mission, the Monitorial Method and the Bengali Renaissance. In B. Bagchi, E. Fuchs, & Rousmaniere (Eds.), *Connecting Histories of Education: Transnational and Cross-Cultural Exchanges in (Post-) Colonial Education* (pp. 85–104). London: Berghahn.
Hobsbawm, E. J. (1989). *The Age of Empire 1875–1914* (First Vintage Books ed.). New York: Vintage Books.
Howe, S. (2008). Empire and Ideology. In S. Stockwell (Ed.), *The British Empire: Themes and Perspectives* (pp. 157–176). Oxford: Blackwell Publishing.
Joseph, C. (2008). Difference, Subjectivities and Power: (De)Colonizing Practices in Internationalizing the Curriculum. *Intercultural Education, 19*(1), 29–39.
Kelly, G. P. (1984). Colonialism, Indigenous Society, and School Practices: French West Africa and Indochina, 1918–1938. In P. G. Altbach & G. P. Kelly (Eds.),

*Education and the Colonial Experience* (Second Revised ed., pp. 9–32). New Brunswick, NJ: Transaction Books.

Kenway, J., & Fahey, J. (2014). Staying Ahead of the Game: The Globalising Practices of Elite Schools. *Globalisation, Societies and Education, 12*(2), 177–195. doi:10.1080/14767724.2014.890885

Kenway, J., & Koh, A. (2013). The Elite School as 'Cognitive Machine' and 'Social Paradise': Developing Transnational Capitals for the National 'Field of Power'. *Journal of Sociology, 49*(2–3), 272–290. doi:10.1177/1440783313481525

Koh, A., & Kenway, J. (2012). Cultivating National Leaders in an Elite School: Deploying the Transnational in the National Interest. *International Studies in Sociology of Education, 22*(4), 333–351. doi:10.1080/09620214.2012.745342

Levine, P. (2013). *The British Empire: Sunrise To Set* (Second ed.). Milton Park, Abingdon: Routledge.

Lo Bianco, J. (2006). Educating for Citizenship in a Global Community: World Kids, World Citizens and Global Education. In J. Campbell, N. Baikaloff, & C. Power (Eds.), *Towards a Global Community: Educating for Tomorrow's World* (pp. 209–226). Dordrecht, The Netherlands: Springer.

Mangan, J. A. (Ed.). (1993). *The Imperial Curriculum: Racial Images and Education in the British Colonial Experience*. London: Routledge.

Martin, F., & Rizvi, F. (2014). Making Melbourne: Digital Connectivity and International Students' Experience of Locality. *Media, Culture & Society, 36*(7), 1016–1031. doi:10.1177/0163443714541223

McCarthy, C., & Kenway, J. (2014). Introduction: Understanding the Re-Articulations of Privilege Over Time and Space. *Globalisation, Societies and Education, 12*(2), 165–176. doi:10.1080/14767724.2014.893188

McLeod, J., & Wright, K. (2013). Education for Citizenship: Transnational Expertise, Curriculum Reform and Psychological Knowledge in 1930s Australia. *History of Education Review, 42*(2), 170–184. doi:10.1108/HER-09-2012-0029

Moyn, S. (2010). *The Last Utopia: Human Rights in History*. Cambridge, MA: Belknap/Harvard.

Natsoulas, A., & Natsoulas, T. (1993). Racism, the School and African Education in Colonial Kenya. In J. A. Mangan (Ed.), *The Imperial Curriculum: Racial Images and Education in the British Colonial Experience* (pp. 108–134). London: Routledge.

Proudfoot, L., & Roche, M. (2005). Introduction: Place, Network, and the Geographies of Empire. In L. J. Proudfoot & M. M. Roche (Eds.), *(Dis)PLacing Empire: Renegotiating British Colonial Geographies* (pp. 1–11). Aldershot: Ashgate.

Quist, H. O. (2001). Cultural Issues in Secondary Education Development in West Africa: Away from Colonial Survivals, towards Neocolonial Influences? *Comparative Education, 37*(3), 297–314. doi:10.1080/03050060120067794

Rizvi, F. (2000). International Education and the Production of Global Imagination. In N. C. Burbules & C. A. Torres (Eds.), *Globalization and Education: Critical Perspectives* (pp. 205–225). London: Routledge.

Rizvi, F. (2009). Global Mobility and the Challenges of Educational Research and Policy. *Yearbook of the National Society for the Study of Education, 108*(2), 268–289. doi:10.1111/j.1744-7984.2009.01172.x

Rizvi, F. (2011). Experiences of Cultural Diversity in the Context of an Emergent Transnationalism. *European Educational Research Journal, 10*(2), 180–188. doi:http://dx.doi.org.ezproxy.lib.monash.edu.au/10.2304/eerj.2011.10.2.180

Sadler, M. S. (1900/1979). How far can we learn anything of practical value from the study of foreign systems of education?, Address, Guildford Educational Conference, October 20th, 1900. In J. Higginson (Ed.), *Selections from Michael Sadler: Studies in World Citizenship* (pp. 48–51). Liverpool, Merseyside: Dejail & Meyorre International Publishers.

Said, E. W. (1978). *Orientalism* (25th Anniversary ed.). New York: Vintage Books.

Said, E. W. (1993). *Culture and Imperialism* (First Vintage Books ed.). New York: Vintage Books.

Sen, A. (2009). *The Idea of Justice*. Cambridge, MA: The Belnap Press/Harvard University Press.

Spivak, G. C. (1999). *A Critique of Postcolonial Reason: Toward a History of the Vanishing Present*. Cambridge, MA: London: Harvard University Press.

Stoer, S. R., & Cortesão, L. (2000). Multiculturalism and Educational Policy in a Global Context (European Perspectives). In N. C. Burbules & C. A. Torres (Eds.), *Globalization and Education: Critical Perspectives* (pp. 253–274). London: Routledge.

Taylor, J. (1984). Education, Colonialism, and Feminism: An Indonesian Case Study. In P. G. Altbach & G. P. Kelly (Eds.), *Education and the Colonial Experience* (Second Revised ed., pp. 137–151). New Brunswick, NJ: Transaction Books.

Thompson, A. (2008). Britain's Empires. In S. Stockwell (Ed.), *Empire and the British State* (pp. 39–62). Oxford: Blackwell Publishing.

Tikly, L. (2001). Globalisation and Education in the Postcolonial World: Towards a Conceptual Framework. *Comparative Education, 37*(2), 151–171.

United Nations. (1948). *United Nations Declaration of Human Rights*. New York: United Nations. Retrieved from http://www.un.org/en/universal-declaration-human-rights/

# 3 The British Empire

## An imaginary of dualities and contradictions

### A The duality of empire

Compared to previous ages of world history, one of the singular features of the European period of imperialism, especially in the 18th and 19th centuries, was its symbiosis with the emergence of the sovereign State as the foundation of societal governance in the modern age (Benton, 2012, p. 1098). Concomitant with this relationship was the development of international law as a means of organising, or perhaps, more accurately, justifying actions of the more powerful and imperial of those nation-States (Koskenniemi, 2002). The historical and legal discourses have long agreed that European colonisation was a major driver and conduit in the creation of international law, which itself was utilised to justify the extension of European sovereignty over the external territories that each nation-state acquired (Anghie, 2005). In the postcolonial construction (for example, see Spivak, 1999), the process of extending the power of sovereignty that emanated from the metropole to lands and peoples that have been 'acquired' in the course of colonial expansion resulted in the creation of the imaginary of 'civilisation', in which colonisation had its embedded justification; the transport and distribution of Euro-American or 'Western' ideas about the construction and operation of human society to people and lands whose knowledge and understanding about the world lacked validity because of the very absence of European ideals: '. . . the work of civilization acquired direct rule and effective sovereignty for the European coloniser . . . ' (Koskenniemi, 2002, p. 113). In establishing this imperial imaginary, the British Empire was no different from many of its contemporaries and predecessors across time and place. Alongside 19th-century European imperial powers such as France and Germany, the purpose of its imperial ambition had its initial roots in economic drivers, such as the acquisition of resources and the generation of trade (Cote-Meek, 2014; Said, 1993), or in strategic imperatives such as establishing a perceived secure and protected homeland centre. However, the long-term stability of imperial annexations depended ultimately on the transformation of minds, the regeneration of an existing society in a way that reinforced its new point of origin and encouraged a sense of imperial belonging:

> An empire was more than simply dominion over territory and people; it was an exercise (literally) in creating a world and controlling its meaning. It is not necessary for creating a world that the whole world is territorially within it.

> The territories outside the realm of empire were de jure within it, whatever the de facto limitations on the exercise of power.
>
> (Mehta, 2011, p. 148)

At the heart of this dominant framework of Euro-American or 'Western' civilisation was, and is, Christianity. It is this connection that theological Christian philosophers such as Christopher Dawson have argued is not only synonymous with 'civilisation', but is also fundamental to the underpinning structures and belief systems of 'Western' culture itself (Dawson, 1998). For the postcolonial perspective, the key to the creation of this Christian, 'Westernised' modernity within the colonised populace is seen as being centralised control over the dissemination of knowledge throughout the colonised society and the role of education, which saw '. . . concentration of knowledge production functions in the European metropolis and use of education as an instrument of cultural hegemony' (Bhattacharya, 2014, p. 31).

Liberation from colonial domination in the decades immediately after World War II, therefore, was not just viewed by many as not just composed of independence from political external control, but also emancipation from Euro-American culture in all its aspects, especially in terms of belief. One purpose of this book, however, is to put the argument that not only was national liberation from colonial sovereignty not always aligned with personal liberation, but that such a logical construction is itself founded in notions of 'Western'-centric 'assumptions' about the holistic and linear nature of cultural and political authority. In the case of the British Empire, the transnationalist mindset present within some minority groups in colonised populations was set 'free' by British colonial education systems, a means by which personal, and therefore far more significant, emancipation from established ways of and perceived pathways in life was achieved. These constrictive ways of life were often ones that had been in existence prior to European colonisation. For some, therefore, 'Western' culture and the introduction of a colonial imaginary was far from being a disabler of personal identity; it was, instead, an enabler of personal self-determination.

It is this theme that will be explored through a case study throughout Chapters 4, 5 and 6, using the context of Ceylon (colonial Sri Lanka) and the British Empire, as well as the employment of the author's family histories and ancestry to illustrate key analytical themes. Amongst others, it will be argued that the impact of this component of the 'informal' aspects of empire has been, and continues to be, more lasting than any facet of 'formal' empire growth, and is no better demonstrated by the two centuries of British imperial reach. In the Ceylonese Colony, minority groups were able to utilise the educational capacities of the British Empire to engage their innate transnationalist dispositions in transforming and transcending the limits of their lives beyond the physical and psychological boundaries of colonial Sri Lanka.

## B The nuances of the British Empire

The evolution of the British Empire, which reached its peak during the 19th and early 20th centuries, has tended to be viewed from two main lines of thought, both of which reflect conflicting interpretations of, in the first instance, the nature and strategy of the imperial growth, and second, the morality and character of the impact of the colonial period on the participants. On the one hand, it has been characterised by many as a deliberate, transnational act that was the logical and planned outcome of a focused national policy of economic and political expansion. Aligned with this particular trope is the view that, as exemplified by the postcolonial discourse, Empire was built on the foundations of deliberate racism and emasculation of the knowledge, political and cultural power of the colonised (Ballantyne, 2008; Fanon, 1967; Freire, 1970/1996; Said, 1993) leading to an oppression of subaltern history (Spivak, 1999), the collective stories of the voices of those whose access to political power had not been 'sanctioned' under Empire (Darwin, 2012, p. 4) The power structures that existed within these colonised societies were inevitably weighted in favour of the dominant colonial power, meaning that, no matter what actions individuals might take to climb out of the suppressive hole, the colonised only had a choice of inferiority or dependence (Fanon, 1967); the only avenues that were open to them were those that were permitted by the hierarchy of imperial power.

In the contrasting perspective, the growth of Empire is conceived as being more organic, the consequence of a series of erratic, cumulative happenings as opposed to a deliberate strategy of acquisition. From this standpoint, the legacies of Empire were invariably positive, with the Empire bestowing the benefits of 'civilisation' upon those that were brought into its ambit. Behind both these diametrics is the debate as to whether colonialism hastened the modernisation of the colonised territories, or merely reinforced the traditionalism of the 'periphery' for the ends of the metropolitan power; in other words, whether 'Empire' revolves more around the relationship between economics and power, or knowledge and power (Howe, 2008).

As is inevitably the case, the reality is situated more in the middle of these two extremes. The difficulty with the more intense examples that the postcolonial perspective produces is that, implicitly or not, it relies on the assumption that British imperial strategy was a rational, organised process, delivered consistently by a sequence of monarchs and governments of very diverse socio-political philosophical standpoints over 300 years. The collective body of imperial action and evidence across the geographical mosaic of the British colonial territories does not suggest any organised, deliberate scientific approach, nor any degree of **consistent** purposeful intent, on the part of the British governments (Howe, 2008). Furthermore, to focus on a perspective that emphasises the perceived 'evils' of colonialism being perpetrated by a metropolitan 'monster' is to negate or underplay the resilience of colonised peoples to determine their own paths to emancipation from the perceived 'colonial yoke':

> . . . the colonised cannot continue to be conceived as victims of a triumphant Englishness imposing its rule and civility on its radical other; on the contrary, the colonial space was to reconstitute itself in response to the imposition of Englishness; in inventing itself, the colonial space would also reinvent the

structure and meaning of the court terms of Englishness, including Shakespeare and cricket.

(Gikandi, 1996, p. xviii)

The postcolonial critique of European colonialism tends to reflect language that embodies the inherent violence that underpins the character given to the act of colonisation. Freire, for instance, referred to the colonising powers as the '. . . oppressors, to oppress, exploit or rape by virtue of their power . . .' (1970/1996, p. 26), and Fanon refers to the colonised as '. . . people in whose soul and inferiority complex has been created by the death and burial of its local cultural originality . . . ' (1967, p. 19). What is problematic about the depth of this assertion of power differential as a totally one-sided negative force is the generalised cloak that it dons about all imperial regimes, with no room for complexity or nuancing of the comparative picture. In the case of the European empires of the 19th century, the differences in the attitudinal imperial approaches of France, Belgium, Germany and Great Britain cannot be ignored, and even within the parameters of these colonial philosophies, suggest that there was a great deal more variation between the territories of an individual empire than the postcolonial perspective highlights.

Of all these European empires, the British context was the largest in terms of area as well as geographical extent from the metropole, and it was those very dimensions that encouraged and permitted a far more diverse pattern of colonialism than is generally acknowledged. Whilst the colonial structures may have been constructed by the dominant power, the ways in which those structures were utilised and enacted did not necessarily follow the intentions of their designer. The capacity of the colonised to use such structures for their own designs in order to circumvent any power framework, to employ implicit strategies to defuse the more explicit expressions of that power structure, to proclaim their subaltern voice in less strident, but no less effective ways, deserves a higher profile in the discourse. The pushback, as discreet as it may have been at times, was as much a key part of the colonisation story as the imposition of colonial rule itself.

## C The notion of British Empire: Building an imaginary

### *A multiplicity of visions*

Contrary to popular impression – as was exemplified through the popular media in literature (Rudyard Kipling) and music (Noel Coward) – the British Empire was not a consistently and uniformly identifiable entity, and neither did it possess or reflect a unified sense of purpose and direction that permeated the actions and decisions of those people and organisations that, over time, guided and administered its evolution and decay. Instead, the Empire was a mass of contradictions, a bubbling cauldron of constant change that gave rise to more variations in intentions, practice and possibilities that have been allowed by many of its critics, particularly from the postcolonial perspective. It was '. . . an empire of hybrid components, conflicting traditions, and unsettled boundaries between races and people: a source of constant unease as well as extra ordinary energy' (Darwin, 2012, p. xii), a creation that only gained its full, transnational character and purpose at the tipping point just prior to its slow 20th-century disintegration and decline.

In actuality, it has been argued that there were several British Empires (Stockwell, 2008), separated by geography, time and imperial character. The original version was the Atlantic Empire, centred on the triangular slave trade of the 1600s-1800s between West Africa, the colonies of North America, and the Caribbean. Later followed the Empire of the East, centred on India, as well as the settler colonies of Australia, Canada and Southern Africa; and in its last phase, the Empire of the Middle East. There was, in fact, limited opportunity for centralised rule of the Empire, and so the trope of a unified strategy of imperial growth and oppression is difficult to sustain in fact and practice. The sheer distances between the limits of the Empire and the British Government in London, combined with the comparative slowness of communications in line with contemporary technologies, almost demanded that variations in colonial practice would occur, regardless of the universal imperial policies the British did apply at various stages in different locations with mixed degrees of success.

The reasons for this multiplicity of dimensions are essentially twofold. In the first instance, reflecting the fact that the '. . the story of empire is really hybridity one of than a essentialism . . . ' (Proudfoot & Roche, 2005, p. 205), the Empire represented and presented different ideas and possibilities to the different groups and institutions within British society. Darwin (2012) summarised these as being the Empire of conquest, the Empire of enlightened officialdom, and the Empire of free trade. The first saw imperial growth as the means by which colonised territories and their peoples could be socially, economically and culturally improved, and thus can be seen to represent the heart of postcolonial objections to the notion of colonialism. The second focused more on the '. . . construction of an ideal society by . . . systematic application . . . ', based on the Benthamite solution of utilitarianism and '. . . administered by expatriate officials recruited in Britain and taught to command' (Darwin, 2012, p. 27)] The final imperial variant expounded the virtues of a free trade system that enabled colonial economies to be linked directly with the commercial and cultural centre that was Britain, and through the economic association, gain the benefits of the acquisition of the fundamentals of British culture.

What did unite these disparate elements in British imperial thought, however, was a sense of the essentiality of the British way of life to a valuable and purposeful existence, with all its inherent values and practices. Given the nature of such an overriding imperative, it is possible to understand that it was seen to be both natural and indubitable that 'Britishness' should be 'granted' and taught to peoples that came under the ambit of the British Empire. The 'rightness' of such a purpose was consolidated and reinforced by the strength of Christianity as an underlying presence and foundation of British society during the creation and maintenance of the 'Age of Empire' (Hobsbawm, 1989) and acts of imperial endeavour. By its very existence, the Empire was seen to reaffirm and reiterate the perceived superiority of the British race and civilisation, and it was the duty of the British people, therefore, to ensure that its principles be adopted and accepted. The advantages of the British way of life were never questioned; the possibility that these offerings may not be accepted by others as being advantageous, never considered.

The second main reason for the multiple realities of the British Empire was that the growth of British imperial ambition in the 18th and 19th centuries was, from the perspective of the national government, one of accident and seized opportunities, rather than one of deliberate and planned intent. No British government was inclined to spend the considerable funds required to establish colonies in far-off lands purely on the speculation of possible future economic success. The deliberate colonisation of an overseas territory was invariably conducted and maintained through the establishment, provision and maintenance of an armed force, both in obtaining territories, or in maintaining and protecting them afterwards. As is the case in the current age, such ventures were major drains on national budgets. Government still accepted, however, that the acquisition of overseas territories was crucial to the future economic expansion of the new, burgeoning industrialised economy, but it was much more preferable to encourage private enterprise to take the risk, with the government creating and monitoring the conditions under which such imperial expansion could take place.

Consequently, the initial stages of British imperial expansion into various territories were undertaken by private mercantile concerns that had been provided with a charter or authority to develop and conduct business in the relevant region on behalf of the Crown. These included the first settlements in Virginia during the late 1500s, the development of the trade centres in West Africa as part of the Atlantic Empire, and the later colonisation of the Caribbean islands. In the same vein, the newly established East India Company was the agent through which British economic links with India were first established as the process of territorial acquisition commenced. The bond that united both government and business was that the two parties agreed that the purpose of imperial expansion was national prosperity, or to increase the wealth on Britain as a nation.

Alongside this economic imperative, however, set a more strategic purpose that acquired more significance as the Empire entered its 19th-century phase. Up to this point, the Empire had grown in two distinct phases that were, on the whole, geographically defined. (Darwin, 2008, 2012). The Atlantic Empire, which was centred on the triangular slave trade between Britain, West Africa and the colonies of the Caribbean and the east coast of North America, was based upon entrepôt imperialism. Within this parameter, the function of the colonies was to produce primary goods – which, in the moral distortion of Christianity that prevailed at the time, included slaves as well as more prosaic items such as sugar – goods that were sent back to Great Britain, in order to be transformed into new commodities that were then sold back to their regions of origin. In time, this group of 'settler colonies' was joined by its equivalents in Australia and New Zealand, both geographically anomalous, but very much located within the same colonising imaginary. This was an empire based on settlement by British citizens, who maintained control on every stage of the commercial network, protected by British maritime power, transforming the societies that they had subsumed in the process.

On the other hand, the eastern part of the Empire, which had grown up around the core of India, had taken on a very different character by the 19th century. Unlike its Atlantic equivalent, which had been largely moulded and controlled by British interests from the start, the Empire of the East had materialised in an atmosphere of far more intense and contended flux. At the beginning of the 1800s, it was a region that had been already controlled in parts and at different times by the main European imperial powers, such as the Dutch, Portuguese and French, as well as the British. Maritime power between these imperial forces was highly contested and never dominant. The work of the East India Company was structured around linkages with local rulers and social structures, through which economic trade took place, '. . . an empire of conquest and rule, but far more dependent on local agents and allies, and far less attractive to British settlers and migrants' (Darwin, 2012, p. 35). Geographically, India was far more isolated from the British motherland in comparison with the Caribbean component, which made direct control from the European centre far more problematic; consequently, local centres of government gained much greater significance and a degree of local autonomy. It was not until the economic and political base of the East India company began to decline in the mid-19th century – a time that culminated in the Indian War of Independence or the Indian Mutiny, depending upon one's perspective – that the British government itself took over direct control of its territories in India and therefore assumed the financial burden of Empire. It was also at this time, however, that the competing interests of the different European powers in the region, to be joined in the last half of the 19th century by the imperial ambitions of developing European nation-states such as the newly created state of Germany, had the effect of giving physical – and therefore military – control of regions much greater significance than had previously been the case. Since India was now the Jewel in the Crown, and both the economic, social and political symbol of the British Empire, any possibility of political weakness that might have been exploited by other European powers in the Asian region needed to be snubbed out before they could be utilised against British interests.

## *The forgotten balustrade: Ceylon and the 'Jewel in the Crown'*

To see this shift in the approach of the British government to the Empire centred around India as being purely one linked to the mid-19th century, however, is to downplay the importance of a long 50-year history over which the British Government had progressively wound back the powers of the East India Company to act as an autonomous agent on behalf of the British Crown. There is also evidence to suggest that the strategic importance of India, and therefore the possibility that the British government might assume authority from the East India

Company at some stage, had long been recognised and acted upon with far more stealth by the British Government in the years just prior to the 'long eighteenth century' than has been discussed in the relevant historical discourses.

In the late 1700s, the decline of the Dutch presence in Southeast Asia had ended with France and Britain remaining as the two European powers competing for dominant regional influence. Maritime power and technology was still crucial to the maintenance of economic and political control in the region, as shipping was the dominant – indeed, the only viable – form of communication between the region and Europe. Although, at the time, the East India Company was still firmly in control of British affairs in India, it did not possess the military maritime forces to safeguard its authority over the regions under its control by securing its oceanic surroundings.

It is here that the island of Ceylon, so central to the history of my family and its connections with Empire and education (see Chapters 5 and 6) becomes a key part of the British imperial story, although the significance of its relevance has been rarely addressed in the mainstream discourse. Instead, academic attention has been more focused on the imperial narrative of India (Seth, 2007, for example). A more comprehensive reading of British imperial developments on the Indian sub-continent highlights not only the importance of Ceylon to wider aspects of colonial activity around Central and Southeast Asia, but also the multifarious ways in which colonial governance and administration on the island pre-empted and guided actions and events in other parts of the British Empire (see Godden & Casinader, 2013). This includes the ways in which education became central to the systems of governmentality established within the Crown Colony of Ceylon.

In the 1790s, the British were in negotiations with the Dutch and French over the division of their respective colonial territories. It was a period of substantial colonial realignments, following a succession of major changes, including the British loss of its American colonies following the War of Independence, the first steps in the European invasion and settlement in what became the modern state of Australia, the French Revolution, and the Dutch loss of its mercantile and imperial territories in Southeast Asia. After the impact of the American War of Independence, and the loss of its American colonies, the colonisation of Australasia as part of the eastern half of the British Empire was primarily fuelled by the desire and need to find a new destination for convict transportations, in order to relieve pressure in the overcrowded prisoners and prison hulks that consumed British justice prior to the development of a more rehabilitatory penal system. The development of a colony that would have reciprocal beneficial economic relationship with the home country was not high on the agenda. These imperatives notwithstanding, the negotiations over what became the Treaty of Amiens in 1802 were very protracted, but throughout the process, the British Government placed great significance on retaining possession of the island of Ceylon at the expense of other possible territories.

The significance of the island was not so much in its important role in the spice trade as a source of cinnamon and other spices, but that on its northeast coast was the port of Trincomalee, generally acknowledged to be the best deep-water harbour in the region. Consequently, the British saw the island as an essential component in the strategic network required to maintain maritime power in the Indian region over the French, who also recognised the military significance of Ceylon. The island, therefore, was seen as a key possession in maintaining the security of the real 'Jewel in the Crown', that of India. This acknowledgement of the greater political and strategic attribution to Ceylon's value as a colonial territory, as opposed to its pure mercantile significance, was not confined to the British. It had been central also to the Dutch for the same set of reasons, a situation well-known to British colonial administrators such as Sir James Emerson Tennant, who was Colonial Secretary of Ceylon between 1845–50:

> . . .[the Dutch] possession of the island was a military tenure, not a civil colonisation in the ordinary sense of the term. Strategically its occupation was of infant moment for the defence of their factories on the continent of India; and for the interests of their commerce, its position (intermediate between Java and Malabar) rendered it of value as an entrepôt.
>
> (Tennent, 1859, p. 59)

Equally significant, though, was that the British government established the island as a Crown Colony in 1802, controlled directly from the Colonial Office, and not through the East India Company, who had administered the territory between 1796–1802. This was some 50 years before the East India Company was nationalised and the Government assumed direct control of its Indian possessions. In 1796, impasses in negotiations with the Dutch and French regarding the Dutch East Indies had led to consideration of direct rule from that point, but, in the end, a compromise was reached with joint administration by the Crown and the East India Company, with the latter guaranteed a trade monopoly, the most valuable component of which was the cinnamon trade. The strategic importance of Ceylon was deemed to be far more important than commercial interests, despite the considerable benefits that such activities brought. Ultimately, then, both India and Ceylon were 'accidental' colonies, only brought into the direct purview of the British Government as official Crown Colonies when there was the distinct possibility that British long-term and regional interests were under direct threat.

The implications for this dualised or hemispherical character of British imperialism for transnational thought and notions of identity were profound. Within the Atlantic Empire, there was a strong unity in the deeply embedded British character of the colonised societies that had developed. The plantation communities in North America and the Caribbean had evolved from the establishment of a society based on an imported elite of British families, and not just a temporary trader population. Built on a foundation of rejection and diminution of indigenous people and culture, and a utilitarian justification of the moral dilemma surrounding the international slave trade that was the foundation of the plantation economy, the 'whiteness' of British colonial society in the Atlantic Empire shared participation in a representative democracy, a common obligation to the British Parliament and Crown (Darwin, 2012), and the maintenance of a cultural identity was merely an extension from what was found in Britain itself. Its insularity from global influences outside existing British norms and attitudes meant that the possibility of developing a transnational perspective that went beyond the borders of the British Empire was substantially diminished.

The boundaries that did exist between Britain and its territories on either side of the Atlantic were more of geographical reality in the existence of coasts, seas and oceans, and not an exclusion based on the integrity of political borders. The people of the Atlantic Empire, at least those of British European origin, could not be transnational even under the contemporary perspective that has emerged from modern patterns of migration. They were not migrants into a different cultural milieu who merged into the new, whilst maintaining consistent links with the society in the region of their origin; instead, they were biological and cultural citizens of Britain who had transported their worldview into different geographical territory, but into an extension of the same psychological, monocultural space, in which local peoples of a different colour could not equate.

On the other hand, the Empire of the East, based on India, had been built essentially on a community of male traders working within the context of a commercial enterprise, depending upon interactions with local societies through their leadership elites to obtain desired goods of commerce. In turn, there was greater interaction between the agents of the East India Company and the aspects of local society in which they worked, negotiating relationships in both the professional and personal sphere, and thereby encouraging, whether intentionally or not, a two-way flow in cultural ideas and habits of life. The lack of a familial society base as existed in the Empire of the Atlantic mitigated against the desirability and practicality of maintaining cultural insularity, and it is in this context that the emergence of transnational dispositions of thought can be observed. Cultural identity was much more amorphous, more open to interpretation and more receptive to new ideas. It was not until the British government assumed direct control of its Indian possessions in 1857 that the insularity of the cultural tent of British society descended, when the separation between British administrators, along with their families, and local society, became acute in the same mould of the Atlantic imperial communities, and the emerging conduits of transnational thought disappeared.

It was at this stage of the 19th century that belief in the scientific stratification of civilisation based on race and colour became intensified (Howe, 2008), and separation of peoples and cultures became the dominant practice. The actions of the past, when many of the East India company men had openly adopted Indian customs, dress and food habits (and which they had later transported back to Britain on their return), were forcefully rejected in all its forms. The die, however, had already been cast, for the process of cultural hybridity had already begun with the interactions of the Company agents with the local Indian population, leaving the door open for future development and implementation of transnational dispositions.

This maintenance of 'Britishness' in the face of large-scale cultural difference, although variable in degree and character between imperial territories, was one of the defining aspects of Empire, whatever form that imperial existence represented for the individual. The exact nature of the societal transformation that took place in any specific part of the empire depended ultimately on the concepts of 'Britishness' held and emphasised by the particular British cohorts who relocated to the region in question, although Ferguson has outlined nine general features which characterised British colonisation of a place. Aside from the English language, these include English systems of land tenure, banking systems, the Common Law, Christianity in the form of Protestantism, representative government, and the notion of liberty (Ferguson, 2003, p. xxxiii) Over 10 million Britons left the 'home country' for other parts of the Empire between 1815–1913, with nearly five million alone to the settler colonies of Australia, New Zealand, Canada and South Africa (Thompson, 2008). The resolution to be connected to whatever was defined as British culture extended to the long-term maintenance of connections back to Britain '. . . through correspondence, return journeys and remittances, British migrants forged tightly personalised networks, stretching from their place of settlement all the way back to their place of origin' (Thompson, 2008, p. 49). In other words, they exemplified the type of transnational migrants that are seen as being an outcome of the migration patterns generated by modern globalisation. The difference, however, was in the exercise of power; as colonisers, there was an imperative to establish control of one State over the lands of another people; for today's migrants, it is a matter of personal, not political sovereignty.

The dominance, or, as some might describe it, the oppression, engendered by the sense of Britishness and culture is a sign that there was a fourth vision of Empire, or, at least, a fourth layer to its constituency. It is another reflection of culture being essentially more of a mind- centred entity (Casinader, 2014; Geertz, 1973) rather than one centrally defined by its symptoms of artefacts, language or organised belief. Consequently, it is possible to see British culture as a psychological disposition, or a mentally constructed and maintained entity, that was essentially transnational, not confined by territorial boundaries of the regions consumed by colonialism. Instead, 'British culture', or as it was more interpreted during the imperial period, British civilisation, was defined by where the British *were*, and not only where they had originated *from*. The colonial enterprise included the transplantation of 'Britishness' into new territories, to be maintained by those who had left Britain to undertake the 'adventure', and transmitted to those who had been brought into the fold, although the actions of those who chose to shift their imaginaries in the reverse direction were not approved of so readily. The British cloak of identity was, in this trope, less defined by place itself, but more as by being a distinctive cultural imaginary that could *transcend* place. One of the key dimensions of Empire in the British mould was that it was

> . . . a matter of minds . . . It projected a moral and cultural authority, the implication of which was that British values, beliefs, institutions and habits were the norm against which all others should be measured-and usually

found wanting. The deeper implication was that the colonial regime or British connection, far from inflicting oppression or the denial of freedom, was liberating, empowering . . . and progressive . . . Those who opposed it was not just a nuisance, they were backward, foolish and ignorant. Their civilisations were at a standstill, if not in actual regression. Worse still, 'history' was against them: their failure was certain.

(Darwin, 2012, pp. 265–266)

## References

Anghie, A. (2005). *Imperialism, Sovereignty and the Making of International Law* (Electronic Book ed.). New York: Cambridge University Press.

Ballantyne, T. (2008). Colonial Knowledge. In S. Stockwell (Ed.), *The British Empire: Themes and Perspectives* (pp. 177–198). Oxford: Blackwell Publishing.

Benton, L. (2012). Law and Empire in Global Perspective: Introduction. *American Historical Review, 117*(4), 1092–1110.

Bhattacharya, S. (2014). Towards a Global History of Education: Alternative Strategies. In B. Bagchi, E. Fuchs, & Rousmaniere (Eds.), *Connecting Histories of Education: Transnational and Cross-Cultural Exchanges in (Post-) Colonial Education* (pp. 27–40). London: Berghahn.

Casinader, N. (2014). *Culture, Transnational Education and Thinking: Case Studies in Global Schooling.* Milton Park, Abingdon: Routledge.

Cote-Meek, S. (2014). *Colonised Classrooms.* Halifax & Winnipeg: Fernwood Publishing.

Darwin, J. (2008). Britain's Empires. In S. Stockwell (Ed.), *The British Empire: Themes and Perspectives* (pp. 1–20). Oxford: Blackwell Publishing.

Darwin, J. (2012). *Unfinished Empire: The Global Expansion of Britain.* London: Penguin.

Dawson, C. (1998). *Christianity and European Culture: Selections from the Work of Chrsiotopher Dawson* (G. J. Rusello, Ed.). Washington DC: Catholic University of America Press.

Fanon, F. (1967). *Black Skin, White Masks* (C. L. Markmann, Trans.). New York: Grove Press Inc.

Ferguson, N. (2003). *Empire: How Britain Made the Modern World.* London: Penguin.

Freire, P. (1970/1996). *Pedagogy of the Oppressed* (M. Bergman Ramos, Trans. New Revised ed.). London: Penguin Books.

Geertz, C. (1973). *The Interpretation of Cultures.* New York: Basic Books Inc.

Gikandi, S. (1996). *Maps of Englishness: Writing Identity in the Culture of Colonialism.* New York: Cambridge University Press.

Godden, L., & Casinader, N. (2013). The Kandyan Convention 1815: Consolidating the British Empire in Colonial Ceylon. *Comparative Legal History, 1*(2), 211–242. doi:10.5235/2049677X.1.2.211

Hobsbawm, E. J. (1989). *The Age of Empire 1875–1914* (First Vintage Books ed.). New York: Vintage Books.

Howe, S. (2008). Empire and Ideology. In S. Stockwell (Ed.), *The British Empire: Themes and Perspectives* (pp. 157–176). Carlton, Victoria: Blackwell Publishing.

Koskenniemi, M. (2002). *The Gentle Civilizer of Nations: The Rise and Fall of International Law 1870–1960.* New York: Cambridge University Press.

Mehta, B. P. (2011). After Colonialism: The Impossibility of Self-Determination. In J. T. Levy & with Iris Marion Young (Eds.), *Colonialism and Its Legacies* (pp. 147–169). Plymouth: Lexington Books.

Proudfoot, L., & Roche, M. (2005). Displacement. In L. J. Proudfoot & M. M. Roche (Eds.), *(Dis)PLacing Empire: Renegotiating British Colonial Geographies* (pp. 201–206). Aldershot: Ashgate.

Said, E. W. (1993). *Culture and Imperialism* (First Vintage Books Edition ed.). New York: Vintage Books.

Seth, S. (2007). *Subject Lessons: The Western Education of Colonial India.* Durham and London: Duke University Press.

Spivak, G. C. (1999). *A Critique of Postcolonial Reason: Toward a History of the Vanishing Present.* Cambridge, MA: London: Harvard University Press.

Stockwell, S. (2008). Ends of Empire. In S. Stockwell (Ed.), *The British Empire: Themes and Perspectives* (pp. 245–268). Oxford: Blackwell Publishing.

Tennent, J. E., Sir. (1859). *Ceylon: An Account of the Island Physical, Historical, and Topographical with Notices of Its Natural History, Antiquities and Productions* (Second ed., Vol. 2.). London: Longman, Green, Longman, and Roberts.

Thompson, A. (2008). Britain's Empires. In S. Stockwell (Ed.), *Empire and the British State* (pp. 39–62). Oxford: Blackwell Publishing.

# 4 Education n pre-colonial Sri Lank ions and Pre-cons suppo

## nsnationalism and personal sovereignty

the doctrine of sovereignty has a very precise meaning, being
A to the point in time when a ruling authority is deemed by inter-
in control of a defined territory. However, within that field, the
ception of State sovereignty has been under considerable contes-
years. At its most fundamental level, it refers to '. . . a functional
d by a ruler or a government to rule a population for its own good'
2011, p. 63). Over the last decade or so, the very concept of sov-
een challenged by a discourse that has been centred on the future
ne sovereign State itself in the face of increased globalisation. The
onstellations of authority and community which transcend the divide
the domestic and the international spheres' (Bartelson, 2006, p. 463)
put increasing limitations on the ability of the State to exercise that authority
n a situation where sovereign States have '. . . almost fully given up their decisionmaking powers in some area – economic or energy policy for example – to an international organization' (Koskenniemi, 2011, p. 63)

Nevertheless, in spite of the debate on its contemporary relevance, the concept of sovereignty remains an important element in the study of colonialism from the historical legal perspective, marking, as it does, the specific time and place in which political autonomy over a particular region has been established, or has changed. However, the very instability and variation of Empire meant that the nature of sovereignty was itself reflected and substantiated in different ways. The age of colonisation itself was the means by which the foundations of modern international law were laid, as different colonial powers negotiated mutual agreements to cement acknowledgement of the respective imperial possessions (Anghie, 2005; Koskenniemi, 2002). Distances between colonial territories and the metropole were barriers to formal exercising of sovereignty over imperial additions as experienced in continental Europe itself; instead, with the delegation of legal authority or sovereignty to mercantile interests such as the East India Company, local indigenous leaders were a necessity rather than an option (Benton, 2010).

During the period of European colonialism, the emergence of the accepted principles of international law – or, to be more precise, the principles as defined, accepted and promoted by the European imperial powers – stated that acquisition of colonial territory could be achieved in one of three ways: by treaty, by cession or annexation by conquest (Anghie, 2005, [illegible]). A key part of that principle of sovereignty, however, is the recognition by the European states of the existence of that control, and hence the need for an ag[illegible] of acceptance. Economic activity, the foundation and underlying princip[illegible] [illegible]al expansion, could not take place without the stability that an acceptan[illegible] [illegible]tribute of sovereignty engenders.

Although, within the relevant discourses, the definition of s[illegible] primarily expressed in legal terms as referring to political and a[illegible] trol, the point when claimed sovereignty is actually enacted beco[illegible] [illegible]been of a study of colonial experience. Acknowledged political contro[illegible] does not guarantee that the ruling authority has actionable power o[illegible] live within that region; that is a matter of reality, if not theory. Ac[illegible] the people of the political authority, or what might be termed social s[illegible] becomes a key factor in the consideration of when the veracity of sove[illegible] validated within a region, as opposed to the legal point of origin.

Whatever the initial intentions of various British colonial administrators i[illegible] implementations of imperial education in their own part of the Empire, in h[illegible] sight, the educational system was a key tool of establishing a more complete a[illegible] comprehensive *social* sovereignty over a region. Certainly, whatever its ultima[illegible] benefits, education, whether it was in a limited or mass form, was not introduced by ruling authorities purely for altruistic reasons. As will be developed throughout this chapter, the notion of education was far from the minds of the British administrators in Ceylon when they signed the Kandyan Convention in 1815, the instrument by which Britain gained control of the Kandyan Kingdom in the central part of the island of Ceylon, as it was then known, and through it, acquired control over the whole island. In common with other parts of the British Empire, including Australia and India, the first installations of any educational offerings were through the ministrations of religious authorities and missionaries, operating to the limits of the degree to which they were allowed within the colonised territory by the new colonial leadership. For the ruling authority, whether the local colonial administrators or the Colonial Office back in London, the introduction of government-organised education became relevant only when it became necessary in terms of growth of the local economy or strategic advantage, such as the need to develop a cadre of locally educated administrative workers to enable the economic activities of the colony to both be maintained and flourish.

The diversities in local colonial situations also saw a variety in the ways that education was constructed, implemented and administered across the Empire, even if there was some form of unified or common intention. In Australia, the beginnings of education in the new colony of New South Wales were largely influenced by the fact that it was, at the time, perceived as Terra Nullius. Sovereignty was declared under the principle of Acquisition and the Doctrine of Recognition rather than treaties of cession or conquest. Since, from the beginning, chaplains were included as members of the governmental force administering the v colony, it was they who were given responsibility for organising schooling ıin the new territory. What eventuated over time was a series of schools that run by private individuals with government assistance, some of whom were onaries. Education in the new colony of New South Wales was a means of ıting a European societal imaginary amongst a group of diverse individuals, l as further consolidating the cultural principles of the centre of Empire bell & Proctor, 2014, pp. 10–12).

dia, education took on a different narrative. The introduction of an edu- system, initially for the elite of local society (1835), and later on in a iversal manner (1854), was accompanied by a much more strident asser- the main goal of the new policy was the prioritisation, dissemination ıotion of European society, with all its incorporated knowledge and ding, as the civilising force over local systems of thought and practice. 'cist' victory of Thomas Macaulay's administrative goal over the prac- ups like William Carey's Baptist missionaries, who championed the cular languages as the language of instruction, extended not only to breadth of knowledge that was the subject of instruction, but also ogic practices that were used to teach and disseminate it (Hilton, 007).

l authorities to attain a more complete or comprehensive sover- er, they had to develop a more personal 'independence', or an political sovereignty, within the people that were now in their r for that to occur, the local populace needed to find a reason ven promote and celebrate, the existence of the presence of the ather than perceiving it as an intrusion that was designed to erase ces. It is in this context that education can be seen as being the the ruling British imperial authority was able to gain personal its newly acquired 'citizens', and thereby obtain and maintain eration.

be seen as supporting the view that education was the means lonial governments were ultimately able to impose their cul- ıe local populace, using the diffusion of an educational system edge systems, values and priorities of the governing power or her, and, in the process, consuming the indigenous cultural eople towards its own ends. However, the possibility that orm might also provide a skylight opportunity for increased rt of the local population (Taylor, 1984) was also beyond dministrators, in part because of the contemporary percep- our were significant indicators of intelligence and intellec- there was an assumption of incapacity on the part of the sense of self-determination for themselves, and that there the intestinal fortitude and intellectual character to seize path towards their own ends; in other words, those who t – the provision of education not as a road to disillu- on, but as a highway to advancement and emancipation.

The essential nature of 'agency', with both its cognitive and action components (Wilson, 2000) could only be actuated by an educational system that provided the colonised with the capacity to think critically, to problem solve in a persistent manner until an appropriate action plan had been devised. Paulo Freire, despite his critical stance on the influence of colonialism of indigenous free will, had identified such a capacity as being essential if colonised people were to have the opportunity to break out of their societal shackles (Freire, 1970/1996). Paradoxically, however, it is those very same characteristics that were, and remain, an inherent part of a Euro-American approach to education (Casinader, 2014), and its existence meant that colonial education in some parts of the British Empire provided local people with the opportunity of an intellectual ladder to escape over the wall of colonial fiefdom.

Consequently, education became the means by which personal sovereignty could be activated by individuals or groups across the local populations across the Empire, utilised to develop a sense of purpose. Cultural integrity was being defined in terms of personal agency, and if that meant adopting the beliefs and customs of the dominant power in order to achieve as personal ends of advancement, then the goal was seen to justify the means. Whether local peoples also recognised that the very educational system that they were using to generate their ow capacity for self-agency was also the means by which they themselves absorbed ar imparted many colonised values and attitudes is debatable. In many ways, the capacity to utilise the educational system to personal advantage was engender by the very skills and attitudes that they had acquired through their participati in the education defined by the coloniser, not the colonised. To deny the valid of their actions, however, is to question their capacity for self-actualisation.

## B The Sri Lankan point of difference

### *False assumptions and generalisations*

Under the dominant postcolonial interpretation of colonial education, the vision of learning for the local populations was a profoundly negative ex ence, the implementation of a policy of deliberate inculcation in the cu dominance of the new governing power (Carnoy, 1974). In the case of the ish Empire, education was the means by which the British social, economi political imaginary could be projected and perpetuated. Only the upper of the indigenous social system – usually characterised as the 'elite' – had through this avenue to participation in the new socio-economic order colonised state, with all the socio-economic advantages that accompani virtue of class leadership. The 'elite' had a vested interest in supporting th nial policies and practices of the coloniser, because it enabled them to m the social and material status that they had possessed prior to the assump colonial control (Mangan, 1993). For the bulk of the colonised populatior ever, their educational opportunities were limited to the portholes affo them by the colonial administration, who were interested primarily in pro workforce supportive of, and trained in, the British imaginary for the lower ranks of the local civil service, but not creating positions of high leadership to which the majority could aspire.

The difficulty with such a broad evaluation is that it treats all colonial powers and all colonised territories as if they are homogenous in character, with the same set of influences and local conditions, and subject to the same sets of colonial ambitions. In the case of the British Empire, such generalisations are highly problematic. As discussed in Chapter 2, the more common view amongst imperial historians is that the Empire had different faces and depth of meaning for diverse groups of people and various locations within the Empire, but even here, the discourse tends to be highly localised. Historical dissembling and discourse on the nature of the British Empire (see, for example, Darwin, 2008, 2012; Ferguson, 2003; Stockwell, 2008) tends to be dominated by discussion of certain touchstones, as if they presented accurate reflections of the Empire as it existed. Such 'pillars of imperiality' include the settler colonies of Australia, Canada and New Zealand – a grouping of colonies that may reflect common examples of Anglo settlement or invasion, but otherwise exhibit some strong contrasts in the origin, structure and outcome of the colonisation process – India, elements of the Caribbean, the Middle East and parts of East Africa. Colonies such as Burma, Ceylon and Malaya tend to be treated, if not as afterthoughts, then certainly more in the context of being conjoined with the touchstone territories, as if they existed only to help reinforce important facets of imperial practice in the 'more significant' parts of the British Empire. Examples of this territorial hierarchy in imperial studies can be seen in the indices of accounts ranging from the seminal work of Hobsbawm (1989), which makes little or no mention of the colonial territories of Ceylon, Malaya or Burma, to the work of James (1998) and Levine (2013), both of whom give short accounts for British Empire in Burma and Malaya, but make only passing references to Ceylon, particularly in the context of decolonisation.

In this minimalised context, many of the fine nuances of imperial history can become lost or ignored, even though they tend to challenge and disrupt the logic and thinking behind the postcolonial imprimatur. In accounts of the British Empire, Ceylon (to use the last of its colonial nomenclatures) is often associated with the experience in India, not regarded as being significantly different enough to justify acknowledgement of its existence, or treated as a minor example that further reinforces trends in other parts of the Empire. The reality, however, is that there are a number of singularities about the Ceylonese colonial experience that stand prominent and demand that it be seen in its own light. A closer consideration of Ceylon's colonial history highlights that events in this part of the Empire predated and pre-empted policies and decisions which were made in other parts of the Empire at a much later date (see, for example, Godden & Casinader, 2013; Scott, 1999). In large part, it is arguable that the hidden significance of Ceylon within the overall construction of the British Empire has been much underestimated by both historians and other development researchers, and it is this difference that is the foundation for many of the nuanced variations between the assumed and actual reality of colonial education within Ceylon and its developing impact.

### *The phases of education in pre-independent Ceylon*

Contrary to the prevailing discourse on colonial education in the British context, the remainder of this chapter, in conjunction with Chapter 5, will argue that significant differences in the wider context of the Ceylon colonial experience meant that the role of education was far more positive and significant for the local population than more conventional postcolonial thought allows. Indeed, the long-term significance of the educational aspects of British colonial practice were such that it was not until the British colonial government in Ceylon instituted a comprehensive and policy system of educational provision that British sovereignty over the island can be said to have been actuated in practice, and not just international law.

The reasons for this assertion fall into four main areas, each of which will be discussed in turn. The rest of this chapter questions the accuracy of the assumptions that have been made as to the nature of education in Ceylon before European colonisation. Chapter 5 will address the issues that are directly related to the introduction of European colonial education: the inference within the postcolonial viewpoint that the introduction of Christianity was a totally negative force at the expense of local traditions; the debate as to whether the introduction and management of educational services was part of a deliberate policy on the part of colonial government; and the view that the introduction of colonial education was a universally destructive element in terms of local cultures and their opportunities for growth and self-determination.

## C Pre-European times: Education in the indigenous past

One of the key moralities underlying the postcolonial critique of European colonial education was that it was the primary means by which indigenous faiths and religions were displaced by Christianity, which the imperial powers justified with the logic that the mark of civilisation and the level of human achievement was defined by the character of society as exemplified by European nation-States (Anghie, 2005). The bases of this ideal society were ascribed to reasons of ethnic group – or, in other words, the whiteness of skin colour – and the philosophical, legal and governmental traditions derived from Christianity, as interpreted by the variety of European powers. In the case of Ceylon, such generalisations are less tenable because of the incorrect assumptions made about the nature of indigenous faiths and religions on the island prior to the colonial experience, and the timing of the introduction of Christianity into that mix.

At the end of the colonial rule in 1948, the composition of the newly independent Ceylon (the country was not re-named Sri Lanka until its republican rebirth in 1972) was complex and diverse. The population had four main ethnic groups, who, whilst nominally attached to a specific religion, were far from discrete. The Sinhalese, who were predominantly Buddhist, were the majority, comprising 70% of the population (Ceylon Department of Census and Statistics, 1953). The Tamils were divided into two groups: the Ceylon Tamils (approximately 11%), descended from those who had migrated to the island centuries earlier; and the Indian Tamils (~12%), brought over from India by the British in the mid-19th century to work tea estates or plantations, but denied rights of citizenship and acknowledgement by all others, including the Ceylon Tamils. The last two main groups comprised the Burghers (0.5%), the descendants of Portuguese, Dutch and other Europeans who had married into the local Sinhalese population; and the Muslim or Moor community (6%), descendants of Arab traders who had been visiting and living in Ceylon since around the ninth century.

These supposed divisions, however, were far from defined. As shall be discussed later, many Tamils, Sinhalese and Moors had converted to both Catholicism and Protestantism in response to the waves of European infiltration that had commenced with the Portuguese in the early 16th century, and which then continued with the Dutch in the mid-17th century and the British in the early 1800s. There was some geographical association with ethnic-cultural groups, with the Ceylon Tamils being concentrated in the northern province around Jaffna and eastern coast around Batticaloa, the Sinhalese mainly in the central and western regions, the Burgher community around Kandy and Colombo, and the Muslim community north of the colonial capital (see Figure 4.1).

However, in many ways such areal associations were nominal in a country that is no bigger than the island state of Tasmania in Australia; there was a large Ceylon Tamil population in Colombo itself, for instance. Reinforced by the succession of strongly nationalistic Sri Lankan governments since independence in 1948, the prevailing political standpoint has been dominated by a pro-Sinhalese modernity (de Silva-Wijeyaratne, 2014), in which the island was, and is, a Buddhist society first and foremost, a haven for the faith in relation to the Hindu-dominated Indian sub-continent to its north and in other parts of Islamic Southeast Asia.

Under this tenet, Ceylon (and modern Sri Lanka) was and is perceived by some to be a Sinhalese-Buddhist nation-State, akin to Israel and Judaism. The Ceylon Tamils, along with other smaller ethnic groups such as the Islamic Moors, were, and are still in the eyes of many Sinhalese, essentially guests in a Buddhist land. It was a mantra that was used to pointed effect in the attainment and exercise of extreme Sinhalese nationalists like Mahinda Rajapaksa. As President of the country in 2005–15, he was seen as a hero by many Sinhalese for ending the long civil war with the Tamil paramilitary force, the self-proclaimed 'Tamil Tigers', but was also accused and condemned at home and abroad for disregard for human rights, especially in respect of the Tamils and media critics, as well as enabling nepotism and family corruption. However, a different perspective to the Sinhalese nationalist construction is that, for a number of centuries *prior* to the first of the colonial European powers assuming political control in the last decade of the 16th century, Ceylon saw a number of ethnic and societal shifts, which suggest that the island was a far more diverse cultural polity than has been postulated previously, with considerable fluidity and merging between different ethnic groups. This

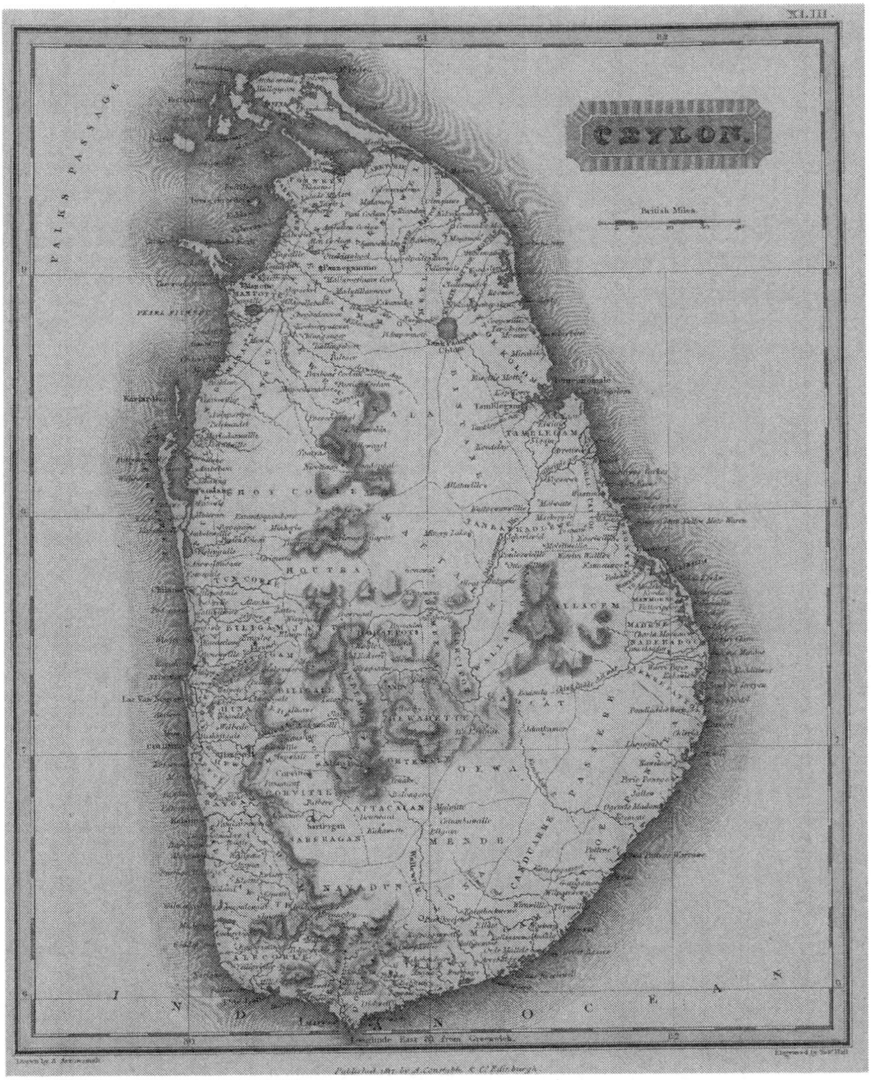


*Figure 4.1* Ceylon in colonial times

perpetual dynamism in ethnic and cultural changeability was actualised with a pre-European society that was a paradox of separateness and interweaving, with far more interaction between different ethnic and cultural groups than either the postcolonialist perspective or post-independence Sinhalese nationalism allow.

It is not the purpose of this monograph to detail a comprehensive cultural history of Sri Lanka up to the European colonial period, but it is necessary to provide a broad outline in order to place its central arguments within a relevant context. The scholarly literature tends to concur that the Sinhalese, who derived from Indo-Aryan groups in what is now northern India, were the first group to colonise the island in circa 480 BC, displacing the original indigenous inhabitants, the Veddah or Vadda. Buddhism, however, was not established until about 400 years later, although the writing of the Pali Chronicles by Buddhist priests or Bhikkhus contrived to present the arrival of the Sinhalese and Buddhism as being entwined (De Silva, 2005). It was this written connection that has been highlighted regularly as proof of the continuing contention that Sri Lanka is a Sinhalese, Buddhist society above all else.

Politically, at this stage of its history, Sri Lanka was divided into a number of Sinhalese kingdoms, with no unified government over the island. These kingdoms, although essentially feudal in character and governance, were not fixed entities. Roshan de Silva-Wijeyeratne (2014) has argued that these regions of Sinhalese polity, as represented by the longest-existing example, the Kandyan Kingdom, were essentially 'mandala States', in which centralised government was diffused in impact and character from the centre. Those who lived on the outer edges of the kingdom were more bonded to the local headman than the central king, who in turn gave his allegiance to a daisy chain of climbing allegiances.

Given the geographical proximity of Ceylon to southern India, especially at the northern tip, which is only 30 km away from the Indian coastline, it was inevitable that there has been a continuous history of two-way migrational movement in this part of the sub-continent, evidence of which emerges around AD 800. The way in which modern Sri Lankan historians have characterised these steady migration waves of Malabar or Tamil people from South India is revealing, and tends to mirror the arguments put by de Silva-Wijeyaratne (2014) that post-independence governments in Sri Lanka have appropriated the pre-European imaginary of the island as a pure and divine haven for Buddhism in a region dominated by Hinduism. For instance, in his comprehensive historical account, De Silva (2005) refers to the 'invasion' of the island by Tamils at the time of what he perceives as part of the height of Sinhalese civilisation in the northern part of the island.

The nuances of such language provide a different context for the analysis of the Tamil presence in Sri Lanka in its pre-European times. The argument is put, along with scholarly comment, that there was little evidence that the Tamils who first arrived were traders or settlers. Instead, they were soldiers and mercenaries of fortune, used by various Sinhalese kings to acquire, maintain and defend their kingdoms. De Silva argues that the earliest signs of a Tamil settlement in the very north of the country do not appear until close to AD 1000, indicating that these buildings were constructed more for Tamil military forces serving Sinhalese masters than any independent Tamil settlement. The inference that one of the attractions for Tamils to invade was the contemporary success of the irrigation kingdoms around Anuradhapura is very strong (see De Silva, 2005, p. 27 onwards). Perhaps even more revealingly, the book index contains no reference to specific Tamil kingdoms or governance during the pre-European era. Whilst reference is made to the Jaffna Kingdom, such a treatment tends to de-emphasise the argument that Tamils have an equal right to a role in modern Sri Lanka.

What such contestation does highlight, however, is the multicultural nature of Sri Lankan society well before the European era of colonisation, and that, given the hybrid nature of its margins, with intermarriage between Sinhalese and Malabar (Tamil) or Moor (Muslim) not uncommon, it had elements of a more integrated or intercultural society. Consequently, it is not possible to sustain the postcolonial principle that European colonisation, in the case of Ceylon, 'invaded' an existing and defined indigenous society. The advents of Portuguese, Dutch and British rule were simply new additions to the list and sequence of those who have migrated or moved to the island over the centuries, all of whom had imprinted their mark on the character of historical Sri Lankan society. The shifting mix between Tamil and Sinhalese in the kingdoms of the North eventually even resulted in the rise of a Malabar (Tamil) king as the last ruler of the Sinhalese kingdom that came to symbolise, and in some ways reify, the nationalist conception of pre-European Sinhalese society. The Kandyan Kingdom in the centre of the island was the last region to fall under colonial control, despite the best efforts of both the Portuguese and Dutch colonial authorities to bring the region under its wing. In 1815, when the British colonial authorities under Governor Robert Brownrigg took advantage of internal politics within the Kandyan kingdom to assume control of the region, and as a result, the whole of the island, for the very first time, it was the Malabar (Tamil) Sri Vikrama Rajasingha who was removed from the Kandyan throne (Godden & Casinader, 2013).

Within this pre-European cultural amalgam, education was linked umbilically to Buddhism, which was, some have argued (Jayasekera, 1969) the most significant influence on social order at this stage of Sri Lankan history. In that context, education was seen as a fundamental preparation for entry to the life of the Buddhist priests, or *bhikkhus*, similar to the way the clergy were the centre of educational delivery in medieval Europe. Education began in the village school in the home of the teacher, before students moved to live and study in the temple school. As described in the context of the Kandyan kingdom, it was an extensive, staged process, culminating in an examination before an assembly of a number of priests that was then ratified by the individual receiving Royal approval (Davy, 1821/1983, pp. 162–163). Moreover, it was very much a male preserve, in which female members were seen as the exception rather than the rule:

> . . . apart from royalty and nobility, girls from ordinary stations in life received an education of a domestic and vocational nature, if at all they received an education. There may have been exceptions, but the early society may have considered the woman's rightful place to be the home, and consequently were prepared for it by the parents, perhaps especially by the mother.
>
> (Jayasekera, 1969, p. 171)

What tends to be lost in the historical accounts and studies of Sri Lanka, however, was that education was not only respected as a noble quality within Buddhist, and therefore Sinhalese, society. Within traditional Hindu culture, to which Tamils from South India ascribed, and essentially the religion of the original Sinhalese who had migrated to the island in the years BC (a point often forgotten in the arguments of Sinhalese nationalism), a similar priority was placed upon the value of education for its own sake. It reflected a divine duty and self-obligation, part of the desire for self-realisation and fulfilment, and essential if a person were to be released from the two bottom edges of karma and rebirth (Jayasekera, 1969). But like Buddhism, traditional Hinduism saw education as a class-based privilege and confined to the leadership classes; it was not for the enlightenment of the general populace.

In such a context, postcolonial arguments as to the inherent 'rightness' of indigenous systems of education are not entirely tenable. In the case of Ceylon, both the main existing cultures placed importance on education, but confined its relevance in social terms. Compared to the British system of education that was to be introduced later, the indigenous system of Buddhist education (Ruberu, 1962) was highly restricted in terms of class and gender, limited to the clergy and king (Tennent, 1859). For both Sinhalese and Tamil, just as it was for the future European systems of education, the main purpose of schooling was the continuation and dissemination of the respective religion, and was, therefore, in reality, an instrumental characteristic rather than an ideological principle.

As far as the British colonial period of Ceylon is concerned, postcolonial arguments relating to the negation of an indigenous society are even more tenuous, as the island that the British 'acquired' in 1796 was one that, apart from the Kandyan Kingdom itself, had been largely colonised and transformed by both the Portuguese and Dutch. As outlined earlier in this chapter, the society that the British inherited had already been overlain with layers of Portuguese and Dutch influence, both of which, it can be argued, had added more complexity to the existing base of an already multi-faceted Sinhalese-Tamil social context, thereby adding to the existing society rather than totally transforming it. It was the British, however, who were able to build on this foundation of constructed society. Instead of imposing British societal structures and values on an indigenous population, the impact of the British colonial period was more of an evolution of the mutable society that already existed at the time of their arrival.

## References


Anghie, A. (2005). *Imperialism, Sovereignty and the Making of International Law* (Electronic Book ed.). New York: Cambridge University Press.

Bartelson, J. (2006). The Concept of Sovereignty Revisited. *The European Journal of International Law, 17*(2), 463–474. doi:10.1093/ejil/chl006

Benton, L. (2010). *A Search for Sovereignty: Law and Geography in European Empires, 1400–1900.* New York: Cambridge University Press.

Campbell, C., & Proctor, H. (2014). *A History of Australian Schooling.* Crows Nest: Allen and Unwin.

Carnoy, M. (1974). *Education as Cultural Imperialism.* New York: David McKay Company Inc.

Casinader, N. (2014). *Culture, Transnational Education and Thinking: Case Studies in Global Schooling*. Milton Park, Abingdon: Routledge.

Ceylon Department of Census and Statistics. (1953). *Census of Ceylon*. Colombo: Department of Census and Statistics.

Darwin, J. (2008). Britain's Empires. In S. Stockwell (Ed.), *The British Empire: Themes and Perspectives* (pp. 1–20). Oxford: Blackwell Publishing.

Darwin, J. (2012). *Unfinished Empire: The Global Expansion of Britain*. London: Penguin.

Davy, J. (1821/1983). *An Account of the Interior of Ceylon and Its Inhabitants with Travels in that Island*. Dehiwala, Sri Lanka: Tissa Prakaasakayo.

De Silva, K. M. (2005). *A History of Sri Lanka*. Colombo: Vijitha Yapa/Penguin.

de Silva-Wijeyaratne, R. (2014). *Nation, Constitutionalism and Buddhism*. Milton Park, Abingdon: Routledge.

Ferguson, N. (2003). *Empire: How Britain Made the Modern World*. London: Penguin.

Freire, P. (1970/1996). *Pedagogy of the Oppressed* (M. Bergman Ramos, Trans., New Revised ed.). London: Penguin Books.

Godden, L., & Casinader, N. (2013). The Kandyan Convention 1815: Consolidating the British Empire in Colonial Ceylon. *Comparative Legal History, 1*(2), 211–242. doi:10.5235/2049677X.1.2.211

Hilton, M. (2014). A Transcultural Transaction: William Carey's Baptist Mission, the Monitorial Method and the Bengali Renaissance. In B. Bagchi, E. Fuchs, & K. Rousmaniere (Eds.), *Connecting Histories of Education: Transnational and Cross-Cultural Exchanges in (Post-) Colonial Education* (pp. 85–104). London: Berghahn.

Hobsbawm, E. J. (1989). *The Age of Empire 1875–1914* (First Vintage Books ed.). New York: Vintage Books.

James, L. (1998). *The Rise and Fall of the British Empire*. London: Abacus.

Jayasekera, U. D. (1969). *Early History of Education in Ceylon: From Earliest Times Up to Maha ̄sena*. Colombo: Ceylon Department of Cultural Affairs.

Koskenniemi, M. (2002). *The Gentle Civilizer of Nations: The Rise and Fall of International Law 1870–1960*. New York: Cambridge University Press.

Koskenniemi, M. (2011). What Use for Sovereignty Today? *Asian Journal of International Law, 1*(01), 61–70. doi:10.1017/S2044251310000044

Levine, P. (2013). *The British Empire: Sunrise To Set* (Second ed.). Milton Park, Abingdon: Routledge.

Mangan, J. A. (Ed.) (1993). *The Imperial Curriculum: Racial Images and Education in the British Colonial Experience*. London: Routledge.

Ruberu, T. R. (1962). *Education in Colonial Ceylon*. Kandy: The Kandy Printers.

Scott, D. (1999). Colonial Governmentality. In D. Scott (Ed.), *Refashioning Futures: Criticism After Postcoloniality* (pp. 23–52). Princeton: Princeton University Press.

Seth, S. (2007). *Subject Lessons: The Western Education of Colonial India*. Durham and London: Duke University Press.

Stockwell, S. (2008). Ends of Empire. In S. Stockwell (Ed.), *The British Empire: Themes and Perspectives* (pp. 269–293). Oxford: Blackwell Publishing.

Taylor, J. (1984). Education, Colonialism, and Feminism: An Indonesian Case Study. In P. G. Altbach & G. P. Kelly (Eds.), *Education and the Colonial Experience* (Second Revised ed., pp. 137–151). New Brunswick, NJy: Transaction Books.

Tennent, J. E., Sir. (1859). *Ceylon: An Account of the Island Physical, Historical, and Topographical with Notices of Its Natural History, Antiquities and Productions* (Second ed., Vol. 1). London: Longman, Green, Longman, and Roberts.

Wilson, K. (2000). Citizenship, Empire, and Modernity in the English Provinces, c. 1720–90. In C. Hall (Ed.), *Cultures of Empire: Colonizers in Britain and the Empire in the Nineteenth and Twentieth Centuries* (pp. 157–186). New York: Routledge.

# 5 Colonial Sri Lanka

## Religion, sovereignty and the education of Empire

### A Education, Ceylon and Empire: Competing conceptions

As discussed in Chapters 2, 3 and 4, one of the underpinning principles of post-colonial thought is that education was the means by which colonising power imposed its values and way of life upon the people that it had come to rule, particularly in terms of religious conversion. However, whilst the evidence clearly illustrates the racial superiority that the European colonisers held towards those that they had colonised, to treat such a process as universal and all-encompassing denies both the nuances of human thought and endeavour, as well as to repudiate the capacity of the colonised to have any degree of individual agency to change, as well as ignoring the extent of cultural change within the shifts of European history itself. Is there any difference, for instance, between the effect of colonisation of ancient Britain by the Anglo-Saxons in the fifth century AD, or its later invasion and colonisation by the Normans in the 11th century, and the impact of European empires on colonial territories in different parts of the world in more recent times? All these events had dramatic impacts on the socio-economic structures of the lands that were colonised, including shifts in religious thought, and yet, in the modern age, there is relatively little debate as to the morality of such transitions in the European context. Instead, we tend to rejoice in the societal complexities that are part of today's age.

As outlined in the previous chapter, the Buddhist system of education that existed in pre-European times was essentially exclusive in terms of both class and gender, and was designed primarily as means of serving and continuing the dominant religion. Hinduism, practised by the Tamils or Malabars, had similar structures. Consequently, although the intensity of the Christian proselytization by all three European colonisers of Ceylon was very evident, there were a number of distinct differences in the way the interaction between education and religion was implemented. Neither was it the case that all the measures taken and adopted to convert local people to the new faith were antagonistic and harshly implemented; the process was far more nuanced than the broad sweep of history tends to suggest.

It is also possible to argue that there was, to some degree, a great deal of self-agency employed by the local people in adopting the new faith. In the first instance, the depth of spirituality in personal reflection that underpins both Buddhism and Hinduism encourages a high degree of internal cognitive debate within the individual, and the ability of some Ceylonese to be persuaded intellectually by the theological base of the new religion cannot be discounted. To assume that they were empty vessels who could be easily persuaded is its own form of imperial demonization. Moreover, it can also be argued that conditions under the British were more supportive of freedom of religion, despite the Christian emphasis, and that within the more liberal societal context, the capacity of Ceylonese to use faith and education as the means to personal advancement was enhanced.

As described by Seth (2007), a similar instrumental duality of purpose was evident in India. Colonial authorities in the 1840s were confounded by the apparent willingness of Indians to practise traditional forms of worship in their own language whilst, at the same time, being willing to study Christianity in a language that was foreign to them. The reality was the Indians saw the learning of English and the practice of Christianity as a means of achieving the kind of employment that would provide them and their families the life that they wished. It was not a case of mindless conversion, but the deliberate adoption and practice of the skill that would enhance their own lives.

The promulgation of Christianity aside, between the Portuguese in the 16th century and the advent of the British in the late 18th and early 19th centuries, lay a steady progression from an educational system based on dogma to one that, although centred on Christianity, was set in the context of a liberal democracy and the encouragement of free thought. The most substantial difference between the British system of education and its European predecessors in Ceylon was its societal place in comparison to existing religions, and in particular, Buddhism. At its most basic level, whereas the Portuguese openly condemned any other faith as being heathenism and not to be tolerated, the British encouraged freedom of religion and the right of peoples to practise their own faith, even though, until the late 1800s, learning about Christianity and conversion to the faith was still the core of government educational policy (Jayasuriya, 1976). Ironically, it was under the more enlightened colonial rule of the British that education finally became the pathway to self-improvement, available to people of all ethnic origins within the country, and not just confined to the traditional Sinhalese leadership elite. In common with all three periods of European colonial rule, however, was the fact that education – and therefore religious instruction – was left very much in the hands of non-government intermediaries.

To the Portuguese, education was not the concern of government or the ruling authority, but was rightfully left to the religious (Jayasuriya, 1969). For the Dutch, unlike their colonial predecessors, education and religious conversion was very much the duty of government, and so was regulated. Only Protestant ministers could be teachers, for instance. Under the Portuguese, the way in which education was conducted depended very much on the order to which a particular group of monks belonged. The Jesuits, who already had experience of missionary work in India, were determined to teach local people in their own language, as they had done in the sub-continent, unlike the Franciscans or Dominicans.

Having knowledge of the Tamil language from their missionary work in South India gave an advantage. There was also a great emphasis on ensuring that the children of Portuguese and Sri Lankan women were brought up in the Catholic faith. Although the dominant pedagogical tool was the use of the catechism – some Jesuit leaders such as Francis Xavier had a poor opinion as to the cognitive abilities of the Ceylonese – the Jesuits were also able to incorporate cultural strengths into their teaching to great effect. The use of the Sinhalese aptitude for the visual was employed in the construction of biblical scenes, and there was a great focus on conversion by attraction rather than condemnation, which '. . . made teaching more simple and less mechanical . . . [and] attracted Sinhalese to church by love rather than by fear' (Wyndham, 1933, p. 19). In spite of Xavier's judgement of the intelligence of the Ceylonese that he met, other Jesuit priests found the local population faster and more effective learners of Latin, philosophy and other sciences than Europeans of their experience (Ludowyk, 1966).

Regardless of any moral dilemmas pertaining to the principle of missionary conversion, there is no doubting the success of the Portuguese clergy in achieving their aims. By 1641, there were over 27,602 Catholic Christians, 3,981 catechumens, and 608 schoolchildren in Colombo, with nearly 25,000 converted Tamils, 4,260 catechumens and 609 schoolchildren in Jaffnapatam (Jaffna). Although most of the schoolchildren were Burghers, born out of relationships between the Portuguese and local women, some priests had been successful in persuading elite Sinhalese families to educate their children in the same environs (Wyndham, 1933, p. 20).

In contrast, unlike the Portuguese, and later on, the British during of the first half of the 19th century, the Dutch saw education as very much a government responsibility.

> From the very inception of its overlordship, the [VOC] endeavoured to commit the indigenous people to it through measures such as conversion to Protestantism, the spread of the Dutch language, and a fair administration. A common religion would strengthen the bond between the European rulers and the conquered subjects. The introduction of the Dutch language proved to be a failure. The propagation of the Protestant faith, on the other hand, appeared initially to meet with more success.
>
> (van Goor, 1978, p. 1)

From the Dutch perspective, the major problem that they faced from the outset was that the Christian converts to date had been in the Catholic Faith, and not the Protestant, and that, consequently, all existing Bibles and written material were written in Portuguese. The missionaries that were imported by the Vereenidge Oost-Indische Campagnie (VOC) to undertake both the religious and educational work complicated the situation further by insisting that education, and therefore instruction in the Protestant faith, took place in Dutch, rather than in Portuguese or either of the local languages of Sinhalese and Tamil. Such Dutch expressions of cultural superiority were not new; in the Dutch East Indies, missionaries had refused to learn Portuguese or Malay, with the result that conversion rates were extremely low there, also. Between 1642 to 1725, only four of the 97 Dutch ministers who practised in Ceylon could speak Sinhalese, and only four could speak Tamil.

These attitudes of the Dutch clergy towards Ceylonese traditions of education, whether Sinhalese or Tamil, reflected a general disdain for local peoples and customs. Francois Valentijn, who spent an unspectacular period in Ceylon as a Dutch Reformed minister in the early 18th century, saw the Sinhalese as having no '. . . learned men . . . ' or schools, as well as being superstitious, '. . . cunning, crafty and very clever at discovering loopholes so that one should not believe them whatever promise they may make' (Arasaratnam, 1978, p. 160). It became very clear to local authorities that '. . . [e]ducation had of necessity to be in the vernacular, as only native schoolmasters and teachers were available' " (Wyndham, 1933, p. 24).

The failures of the Dutch educational efforts in conversion were also hindered by class sizes, as groups of 200 were not considered to be extreme, a situation exacerbated by the lack of Protestant local teachers and willing missionaries. Pedagogical techniques were invariably confined to the memorisation of catechisms, even though the Dutch government itself in Amsterdam suggested that explanation was important and that excessive memory work would be deleterious. Nevertheless, the Dutch constructed a system of three school commissions based on Colombo, Galle, and Jaffna, with two specific seminaries at Colombo and Jaffna. The schools were heavily regulated, had annual inspections by a minister and a layman, and particular attention was paid to those children who would leave school early and parents who wanted their children baptised. As the Dutch period of colonialism progressed, closer attention was paid to the customs and preferences of the local people, with a view of respecting them in the course of teaching about Christianity. The government covered the cost of training respectable 'natives' to join the seminaries and be educated so that they could take on the position of administrators and educational leadership. The success of the Dutch system of education, regardless of one's opinion as to the missionary aspect of its goal, was reflected in the fact that by the end of the Dutch colonial period, there were 70,000 students in schools,(Wyndham, 1933) a figure not reached again until 1879 when the British finally committed resources to the development of an educational system within the island.

## B Economic sovereignty: The Portuguese and Dutch

The notion of sovereignty in the scholarship of legal history is a complex and oft-debated concept, and it is not my intention to explore and attenuate that particular discourse within this book. My principal concern is the role of education in determining the degree and nature of sovereignty that a particular government has over the region of territory; consequently, in that context, sovereignty is being considered as being achieved when the ruling body is recognised by other sovereign states as being in control of a territory – and, therefore, the population of that territory – that is delineated by defined borders. Under that construction, it is arguable that the island of Sri Lanka *per se* had never been sovereign territory in its history before the British wave of colonisation. The island had, prior to that time, being composed of a shifting set of kingdoms, the rulers of which depended upon military strength and relational loyalty for the maintenance of their control and rule, but there had never been a situation where one particular kingdom and or king had exercised control and rule over the whole island. The coming of the Portuguese in 1505, and later the Dutch in 1685, did little to change that political reality. One of the other difficulties with the anti-colonial rhetoric in the case of Ceylon is the validity of the argument that the European presence on the island was essentially a one-sided affair, in which the European metropolitan powers asserted their own terms and for their own purposes. To a degree, this assertion has some merit, as it is possible to view both the Portuguese and Dutch periods of colonial rule as being essentially ones concerned with economic sovereignty, and not total political sovereignty.

There are several reasons to support this contention. In the first instance, its strategic value notwithstanding, the Portuguese and Dutch were very much attracted by the spice wealth of the island, and in particular, that of cinnamon, the very resources that had drawn Muslim traders from what is now the Arabian Peninsula since about AD 800. Consequently, neither of these powers was interested in colonisation through settlement by free citizens. The Portuguese influx was essentially military, with little attempt to bring even the families of those who occupied the military establishments. It was not the Dutch government that drove the push by Holland in the 17th century, but the merchants and investors who operated through the Vereenidge Oost-Indische Campagnie (VOC), the Dutch equivalent of the British East India Company, which itself formed the *de facto* British government of India until the mid-19th century. Although some of the Dutch officials brought over their families, the temporary migration was confined to the VOC cadre. Their time of residence in 'Zeylan' (the Dutch name for the island, and the original of its English derivation) was always seen as a short-term affair; a return to Holland, even after many years, was seen as the natural course of action.

In the second instance, neither colonial power ever had direct control over the island as a whole, or even indirect control over the entire territory. In addition, the Portuguese and Dutch had never become involved in the growing of spices itself. Both obtained their goods through arrangements made with the rulers of the coastal kingdoms, using the established trading networks within the relevant kingdom to bring the desired spices to the coastal trading centres on the western and southwestern coasts. The port of Colombo was essentially a colonial creation because, as a port – albeit a poor natural harbour compared with others – it faced the Indian Ocean and the sea route back to Europe. A similar situation existed with the port of Galle, just to the south of Colombo. The line of Portuguese and Dutch forts along the western coast can be seen today as a reminder of the extent of this trade. The area of Portuguese control, compared with that of the Dutch, was more confined to the wetter southwest, which was, and remains, the core of

Sri Lankan agriculture, along with the central highlands. Nevertheless, the Portuguese also maintained a presence on the northern coast in Jaffna, which enabled them to control the sea trade routes between the island and South India, and undertook a relationship with the Kandyan Kingdom in central Ceylon.

The Dutch, for reasons that will be discussed shortly, were able to extend their control of the coastal kingdom to the entire coastline, but were thwarted by a succession of rulers of the central Kandyan Kingdom in their attempts to negotiate an agreement of trade cooperation. Attempts at a military solution by a takeover of the Kingdom also failed, largely due to the Dutch failure to cope with a military campaign played out in very un-European expectations of warfare: oppressive heat, mountainous terrain where the Kandyans held the local advantage, and the use of guerrilla tactics by a force well-practised in this localised example of jungle warfare. It was not until 1815 that the British were able to establish unified control of the whole island under one administration.

The third reason lies in a re-interpretation of the degree of resistance to European colonial activity by the rulers of the littoral Sinhalese kingdoms. The traditional rulers of these internal territories were not beyond using the perceived military strength and support of the European newcomers to assist them in defending their domains against adjacent kingdoms and leaders. When the Portuguese landed in 1505, the King of Kotte, the region surrounding present-day Colombo, saw an opportunity to cement his authority by co-operating with the strangers, although his popularity as a ruler seems to have suffered as a result. The line of kings in the central Kandyan Kingdom was particularly inclined at employing alliances with each successive European power, starting with the Portuguese in the 1540s, when they accepted the status of a Portuguese satellite in order to stave off the encroachment from the Sitavaka Kingdom on its southwestern border (De Silva, 2005, p. 149)

Consequently, the act of colonisation on the part of the Portuguese and Dutch was not one of immediate conquest, but more of an incremental acquisition of the territory deemed necessary for the conduct of mercantile trade. As a result, their concern with the creation of socio-legal structures was confined to the establishment of those parameters that were required to conduct and meet their trade priorities. For the Portuguese, whose colonial policy was based, not on the acquisition of territory, but on the control of strategic locations that enabled them to control the regional spice trade through naval power, there was minimal interest in the establishment of any local supporting structures. This was one reason why their territorial focus in Ceylon included the northern Jaffna peninsula, as it gave them control of the lucrative trade route from the northern tip of the island to the southern coast of India. For the large part, and with two major exceptions that will be discussed shortly, their general preference was to maintain a separate existence from the local community, dealing predominantly with the leadership elite and rarely interacting with the local populace.

The Dutch approach, although more extensive, was still designed to facilitate the long-term existence and expansion of their control of trade on the island, with minimal official interaction with the local communities beyond the leadership groups. In order to facilitate their own operations, the Dutch instituted systems of laws and justice, a land tenure system, and a schooling system designed to meet the needs of the VOC families who had accompanied some of the company officials to Ceylon. However, they were also not averse to using existing local systems of social structures for their own purposes. For example, in order to meet some of the costs of colonial venture, Dutch used the traditional feudal structures of Sinhalese kingdoms to their advantage, employing the traditional obligation of servility to ruler in order to extract taxes in-kind from the low-country Sinhalese farmers in the coastal or maritime provinces.

For both the Portuguese and Dutch, then, the priority for economic sovereignty meant that they were more concerned with peaceful coexistence then territorial conquest. That is not to say that they were not averse to military campaigns to achieve their aims if the desired cooperation from the Sri Lankan leadership was not forthcoming, but the aim remained control and expansion of trade, rather than control and governance of the land and resources. The nature of the relationships of both European colonial powers with the Kandyan Kingdom in the centre of the island was a good example of this pragmatic colonisation. Although high-value spices such as cinnamon grew in the lowland, western coastal kingdoms of the island, which is where the sovereignty of both Portugal and the Dutch was centred, the Kandyan Kingdom was also the source of areca, pepper and cardamom, all of which formed an important part of the traditional trade between the Kandyan Kingdom and the South Indian coast, and which was of great attraction to the Europeans. The Kandyan rulers, the only Sinhalese authority on the island by the early 18th century that was politically independent of the European colonisers, did not accept the total trade monopoly claimed by both Portugal and the Dutch, but needed the salt and textiles that were part of the trade networks between the lowland and highland kingdoms. As a result, both sides were keen not to generate an all-out conflict. The Dutch, in particular, were eager to have their authority over the lands that they had acquired from the Portuguese acknowledged by the Kandyan leadership, and this reinforced their determination to maintain civil relations and, where possible, to develop official agreements with the Kandyan monarch.

There were two major exceptions to this principle of minimised interaction, however, both of which have had long-lasting impacts in the nature of Sri Lankan society. First, the male-dominated composition of both the Portuguese and Dutch colonial operations led inevitably to personal relationships being established between some Europeans and the island peoples, principally the Sinhalese. The offspring of these relationships, who were predominantly, along with their mothers, left on the island when the European fathers finished their time in Ceylon and returned to Europe, formed the beginnings of what became known as the Burgher group within Sri Lankan society, and the one that came to be most closely associated to European colonialism in the eyes of post-independent Sinhalese nationalists.

Second, both the Portuguese and Dutch introduced Christianity onto the island, albeit with very different ontological principles. Both saw conversion through education as a central goal of their administration, although their strategies were quite different. In building their trade empire, one of the major priorities of Portugal as a society was the dissemination of Christianity and the Catholic faith. Members of the clergy accompanied every trading expedition with the expressed intention of converting as many local people as possible, a 'manifest destiny' that was intense in its commitment and implementation. Such was the case in Ceylon, and it was therefore no surprise that the area around the kingdom of Kotte (Colombo) became one of the centres of Catholicism on the island by the end of the Portuguese colonial period, one that persists to this day. The conversions covered both main ethnic groups, Sinhalese and Tamil, as well as minority groups such as those living in the Muslim enclave around Mannar on the northwest coast. Similar priorities existed with the Dutch, but their greater consideration with the creation of social structures to support their mercantile purpose was reflected in the priority that was placed in government providing specific opportunities for conversion, unlike the Portuguese, who left the religious venture to the clergy. Moreover, as will be discussed later, the systems of education left by both colonial powers were to be a major influence, direct and indirect, on the place of education in the British era.

## C Political sovereignty: The British

The replacement of the Dutch by the British as the colonial power in 1795 marked, in my view, a distinct shift in the nature of colonialism by the metropolitan power, and as a result, determined a gradual shift in the role of education as an imperial instrumental regulator of colonial life. The difference lies in the degree and type of significance that Ceylon played in the overall structure of each country's colonial empire. As has been previously argued (see Chapters 2 and 3), the primary motivation for both the Portuguese and Dutch was one of commerce, a desire to exploit the commercial parameters of the island as far as possible. In the case of Britain, however, I contend that Ceylon's value was essentially strategic; a combination in which location, relative to both the islands of the East Indies, India itself, and the Cape of Good Hope on the other side of the Indian Ocean, made Ceylon an imperative component in the British Empire of the late 18th and early 19th centuries in assuring the survival and growth of its Indian possessions as the 'Jewel in the Crown'.

In general terms, British imperial historical accounts, even when they acknowledge the existence of the colony (see, for example Ferguson, 2003; Hobsbawm, 1989; James, 1998), tend to treat the importance of Ceylon to the region's successive European colonial colonisers (Portuguese, Dutch, French and British) as being primarily one of economics; that is, its significance as a source of cinnamon and other goods within the general context of the spice trade within southeast Asia. What appears to have been ignored, however, is the island's significance in terms of global navigation and strategic naval power. At this stage of historical globalisation, the primary criterion for the claims of a global superpower was its control of the seas, for it was maritime transport that was the broadband

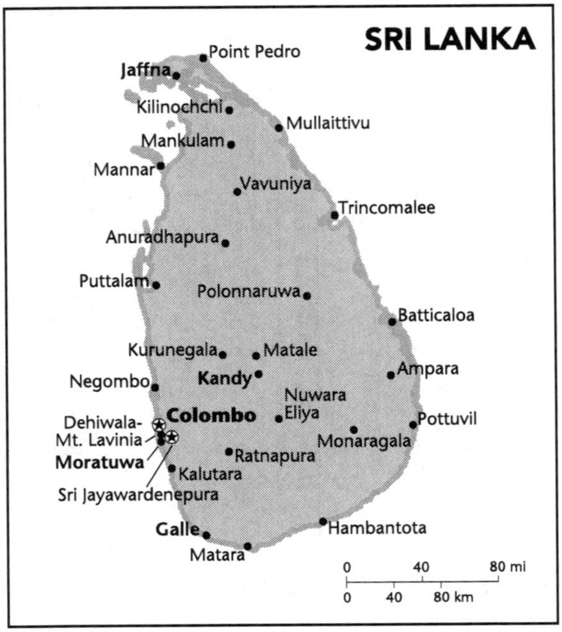


*Figure 5.1* Sri Lanka (Ceylon): Major towns and cities

network of global trade and population movements. With the port of Trincomalee, located on its northeast coast, Ceylon possessed, and possesses, one of the best deep-water harbours in Asia (see Figure 5.1). The island was also a natural staging point for ships sailing between the Cape of Good Hope at the southern tip of South Africa and the Spice Islands of the East Indies. Moreover, at the end of the 18th century, the manoeuvring of the French and British over colonisation of the Indian sub-continent highlighted the importance of Ceylon as a military naval base in maintaining overall control of this part of the contesting British and French empires.

In the Treaty of Amiens (1802), which comprised negotiations between Great Britain, the French Republic, Spain and the Batavian Republic (Netherlands) to bring an end to hostilities between the French and British – albeit temporary – during the French Revolutionary War, the transfer of Ceylon to British control was one point on which the British were never inclined to negotiate (V. L. B. Mendis, 1971). The European colonisation of Ceylon was officially transferred to Britain, whilst the Dutch retained control of the Cape of Good Hope. So acute were their concerns about the possibility of the French 'acquiring' the island before the signing of the treaty throughout the protracted negotiations, the British government convinced, or some might say, instructed, the East India Company to extend its administration of the Indian sub-continent to that of Ceylon from 1796. In exchange, the East India Company was granted a trade monopoly in Ceylon, which was centred on cinnamon. The significance of Ceylon was further punctuated when, well before the treaty was signed, administration of the island was shared by the East India Company with the appointment of Governor Frederick North in 1798, who operated under the Colonial Office in Whitehall (De Silva, 1973a).

In effect, Ceylon was being administered as a British Crown Colony well before its 'official' designation as such with the enactment of Treaty of Amiens on January 1, 1802, some 50 years before the conversion of the 'Jewel in the Crown' from a commercial entity to governed Crown Colony in 1857, and 60 years before the establishment and survival of Singapore as a British Colony. The sequence and dates of these events help to consolidate a view that the island of Ceylon was far more important to the British government as a strategic possession than for its resources. This perspective is further reinforced by contemporary correspondence and documentation relating to the Administration of Ceylon in the early 1800s, which indicated the precarious financial position of the island in terms of the cost of its administration compared to the income from its contribution to the spice trade (see, for example, Brownrigg, 1815a). The fact that the Colonial office was willing to subsidise the existence of the colonial administration on the island to the extent that it did, regardless of the continual imperatives to various governors to increase revenue from the island, is a measure of the political importance of the island beyond its own resource value. It also '. . . enabled the Colonial Office to exercise a control over the Governor . . . ' (Samaraweera, 1973b) to some degree, helping to produce an element of continuity in how the island was governed.

Part of the extensive cost of the colonial administration in Ceylon derived from the fact that, from the start, the various colonial administrations were focused on the colonising task of transforming Sri Lankan society into one that reflected the principles and actualities of British society itself. Unlike the Portuguese and the Dutch, there was an implementation of a British way of life, which went much deeper and was more integrated into every element of life in Sri Lanka than had been the case previously. Instead, the transformation, in large part, was not of an indigenous society, or societies, untouched by European or outside influences, but one that was arguably the result of the continual melding and absorption of different ethnic groups and cultural influences that had been interacting for over 5,000 years. Aside from the Kandyan Kingdom, which only became integrated into the British imperial administration in 1815 (see Godden & Casinader, 2013), the British were dealing with a society in the lowland coastal areas that had long been exposed to European influences. It comprised a myriad ethnic and cultural mix of peoples that included Sinhalese, Tamils, the emerging Dutch Burgher class and Muslims, along with a socio-economic and cultural set of structures that reflected a mix of Sinhalese, Tamil, Muslim, Portuguese and Dutch characteristics. To argue, then, that the British imperial period had such a negative effect on **traditional** Sri Lankan society is to ignore much of the nuances of Sri Lankan history.

## D Education in the British colonial period

### *An overview*

At the end of Chapter 4, I contended that one of the nuances of colonial education in Ceylon was that it was a positive and powerful force change for minority ethnic groups within the island, and, therefore, cannot be seen as a totally negative influence on pre-colonial ways of life. More specifically, it is my view that it was the British period of colonial education that facilitated the enabling and empowering of these groups, providing them with the means by which they were able to not only carve a distinct identity within Ceylonese society, but also to actualise their transnational capacity for self-development and improvement.

The major difference in the British approach to education lay, somewhat ironically, in the belief that, by disseminating the British way of life throughout the Empire, with its same principles of enlightenment and superiority, all peoples would have the ability to live a 'good life'. As discussed in Chapter 2, one of the main drivers of British imperialism was this unerring belief in the value and superiority of the British approach to society, one of the foundations of which was the British interpretation of Protestant Christianity. In one perspective, the principles of Jeremy Bentham had, at their heart, the notion of equity and equality of opportunity, which, in the case of Ceylon, translated into a far more inclusive notion of education that had existed previously, whether that was in pre-European, Portuguese or Dutch times. For the British administrators, there was no differentiation or prior conception of the class system between the various cultural and ethnic groups that were living on the island when they took over control. Consequently, Sinhalese, Tamils, the consolidating 'Dutch Burgher' class, as well as the small group of Muslims, were all seen to be of equal status in the British conception of Ceylonese society. Whether by accident or intent, there was no overt acceptance that the Sinhalese had a more inmate birthright to Ceylon than the Tamils, and both were treated in the same manner.

For those who see Empire as the substantiation of racism and prejudice, as represented in the postcolonial perspective, it has been suggested that such a tactic was a far more deliberate act; that is, the British were very aware of the divisions between different groups in their colonial territories, and used those points of differences to 'divide and conquer', with the rationale that groups that were competing with each other would not have the resources to contest the right of British rule. Furthermore,

> . . . in destroying the authority of indigenous cultures, and imposing its own, [British colonial practice] wrecked the self-confidence and creative capacity of local elites and drove a deep wage between a collaborative minority seduced by the charms of imported ideas and the rest of society.
>
> (Darwin, 2012, p. 5)

In my view, such cynicism as a broad brush across British imperial practice lends itself to oversimplification and a certain degree of obfuscation. In the case of Ceylon, the archival records in terms of Colonial office correspondence (see, for example, the *Ceylon Government Gazette*, 1815-onwards) tend to show, overall, that the majority of colonial administrations were more inclined to be responsive to the unique characteristics of Ceylonese society. Although overlain by the contemporary social and moral principles of 19th-century Britain, the attitudes and actions were, in general, more reflective of a policy of enlightenment than denigration. One general illustration of this difference in approach with previous practice was that the existing religions of Catholicism, Buddhism and Hinduism were not belittled to the point of abolition. The freedom to practise one's religion was continually reinforced throughout British colonial administration, and indeed, was the basis of the 1815 Kandyan Convention, under which the colonial administration under Governor Robert Brownrigg committed themselves to protecting the local people against the deprivations of the Kandyan King and enshrined the right for them to practise the Buddhist faith (Brownrigg, 1815b). In hindsight, whether this freedom was offered in a genuine expression of rights or was a medium-term strategic political device in the successful attempt to annex the Kandyan Kingdom remains contentious (Godden & Casinader, 2013), but it was a powerful restatement of British conceptions of enlightenment.

This argument notwithstanding, throughout the 19th century there was a certain degree of consistency in the way that British colonial administrations addressed education, but there were also distinct dichotomies that reflected the capacity of British administrators to nuance policy according to local conditions and needs, not all of which can be attributed to colonial imperatives. Educational practices that were introduced into the Ceylonese colonial context, whether intentional or fortuitous, can now be seen to be early precedents of policies later implemented in other parts of the British Empire such as Malaya.

In the context of this monograph, there were three distinct phases in the development of the educational system in Ceylon, leading to the point where it became the means of self -actualisation for certain cultural groups in colonial Sri Lanka. The first of these was in the early phases of the colony, up to the time of the Commission of Eastern Enquiry, commonly referred to as the Colebrooke-Cameron Reforms, in 1832. The second era is characterised by the rapid growth in schooling throughout all parts of the island, in which both government and religion-based private schools, working with government assistance, instigated the gradual development of a system of education that eventually led to the population of Sri Lanka being one of the most literate globally by of the time of independence in 1948. The beginnings of the third phase were marked by yet another review and restructure of island education in the late 1860s that saw the colonial administration move away finally from support of sectarian education as the primary base of the schooling system, a transition that resulted in the emergence of a dual sector school system, comprised of a government school sector and a private or independent school system that was controlled by various Christian churches.

### *The first phase*

To a degree, it is possible to argue that the policy of British enlightenment was introduced to the Ceylonese population more by accident than design, particularly in the early years of the colonial administration. The financial situation of the colony meant that there was little money to be spent on social provisions such as education. As discussed previously, the fact that British colonial acquisition and control of the island was based on strategic and political considerations, rather than that of commerce, resulted in the focus of the early colonial administrations being the consolidation of the financial and political stability of the colony. There was, however, consistent support for those who were willing and able to supply that education; that is, the various missionary societies that moved quickly into the Ceylonese space as soon as its colonial status was confirmed. The connection between education in the Christian base of British society and the values that were central to a 'civilised' existence was always a confirmed priority.

In this, the attitudes of the early governors of Ceylon were an important determinant of the official support for education through religion. In large part, this support, which was also confirmed by the Colonial Office in London, was due to utilitarian considerations as much as philosophical principles, and provided a contrast to the way in which the same situation was approached in other parts of the Empire, and in particular, India. The first governor, Frederick North (1798–1805), promoted the idea that providing a thorough English-language education for the Ceylonese provided local candidates who had the perceived 'appropriate' skills and attitudes – that is, they reflected the British idiom – to be employed in the Ceylon Civil Service. Economically, this was a logically sound decision, as it meant that the colonial administration did not have to incur the large expense of bringing out suitable young men from Britain to fulfil those roles. Consequently, one of the first government schools to be established in 1803 was the Colombo Academy, headed by another Reverend, James Cordiner, which aspired to '. . . prepare youths educated in English for the public service; especially the higher grades of the public service' (Ruberu, 1962, p. 67).

Even at this local scale, the contradictions between the principles behind social enlightenment and contemporary attitudes towards race of a different colour was reflected in the fact that, whilst race-derived opinions of hierarchy meant that there were separate buildings for the European boys, and another building for the Sinhalese and Tamil students – apartheid in its most basic form – the purpose of the English curriculum included a written acknowledgement of non-Western forms of knowledge, in that it should include '. . . oriental and native literatures to challenge and bring into life the best of minds' (Ruberu, 1962, p. 67). Such an early declaration of cultural equivalence does not sit easily with modern assertions as to the blanket cultural myopia attributed to the character and impact of colonial education. One of the colonial governors, Robert Brownrigg (1812–20), was even more overt in his encouragement of educational progress in both government and missionary schools. Although it was the missionary school system that remained the educational stalwart of his tenure as governor, it was Brownrigg who gave the government school system structure a more visible religious association by appointing the Archdeacon of Colombo as its head. After the British success in overcoming the Kandyan 'rebellion' or 'war of independence' in 1817–18, Brownrigg made the development of the educational system far more of a priority as the cessation of expensive military campaigns released some funds, and some of his time, for social infrastructure and concerns. His wife also became well-known for her efforts in assisting the development of both missionary and government schools, and in their farewell speeches in leaving Ceylon in 1820, both were specifically thanked for the attention that they had paid to this aspect of life in British Ceylon (Barnes, 1820). Robert Horton, who was governor in the early 1830s, established the first English-language government secondary school with the aim of giving young local Ceylonese men the opportunity to acquire the skills needed for civil service positions (Ludowyk, 1966).

Nevertheless, to add to the complexity of colonial attitudes, not all governors had such embedded convictions as to the righteousness of using education as a means of religious conversion. Brownrigg's successor as governor, Edward Barnes, believed that the system of parish-based government schools was thus far too inefficient and expensive given the financial situation of the Crown Colony, and severely cut educational expenditure. Interestingly, and quite uncharacteristic in this period of imperial history, he held great concerns about the morality of forcing Christianity onto others, as it negated the right of the individual to develop their own beliefs. Barnes thought that government-funded education should be based on learning how to read and write in a student's home or traditional language (de Silva, 2005, p. 323).

Whatever the reasons, the more concerted approach adopted by the missionary societies in the provision of educational opportunities led to increased substantial success on their part when compared to the reach of the government school system. As early as 1820, there were four missionary societies that had established themselves as non-government educational providers on the island: the Baptist Mission, that was centred on the Colombo region itself (1812); the American Mission, which was centred on the northern Jaffna peninsula and the areas of Tamil population (1813); the Wesleyan Society, which concentrated on the region from Colombo in the southwest through to Galle (1815); and the Church Missionary Society (1818), which focused on the southwest from Kandy in the centre of the island through to the coast (Ceylon Almanac and Compendium of Useful Information, 1833)

In line with the more inclusive approach of the British colonial authorities towards the various cultural groups within the local population, the strategies adopted by these various missionary societies were distinctly different to those employed in the educational campaigns of the Portuguese and Dutch clergy. From the beginning, unlike the Dutch all the missionary societies saw the value of conducting education in the vernacular languages, as well as English, and built their individual school systems on that basis. They were sufficiently realistic to appreciate that mass conversion was possible only through the languages of the people, first because of the inevitable difficulties that the masses would have in mastering an alien tongue and second, because teachers were not available in sufficient number to provide mass education in English (Jayasuriya, 1976, p. 531).

Second, education was for all, not just the elite, and for both genders. For the first time, girls were given the opportunity at primary level as an equal priority.

Progress in this area was slower, stifled to a degree because of the reluctance of Sinhalese and Tamil societies to encourage girls to be educated, a reflection of the Buddhist and Hindu practices of the pre-European era. Education was also free, opening up possibilities for children outside the traditional leadership elite that did not exist before the period of British colonisation. None of these schools were under any form of regulation or control by the colonial administration, the authority of which was restricted to the few English-language government schools that had been set up in major towns such as Colombo, Galle, Kandy (after 1815) and Jaffna. These government-run schools were designed to cater more for the children of the traditional leadership elite, and like the missionary schools, focused on primary education. In the initial stages, the British colonial administrations also maintained many of the educational structures that had been established by the Dutch. For instance, the Orphan Schools that had been established by the Dutch authorities for the education of children born to European fathers and Sinhalese mothers – the so-called Eurasians, and part of the emerging Dutch Burgher class – were maintained, being administered along with the Leper Hospital as charitable institutions.

These contestations about the role of missionary societies in the provision of imperial education and the value of using English or the vernacular language as the medium of instruction mirrored similar debates that were occurring at the same time in British India. By the beginning of the 19th century, the East India Company was being transformed from a purely mercantile operation into one of territorial governance, supported by the regular renewal of its Charter with the British government. It is no coincidence that the move of various missionary societies into the Ceylonese educational sphere occurred at the same time as the Company's 1813 Charter gave these groups official permission to proselytise through education in British India. Unlike Ceylon, the debate as to the language of instruction was far more heated and pointed, with a clear division between the Orientalists, who favoured the use of local vernacular languages, and the Anglicists, represented by the aforementioned Thomas Macaulay, who saw English as the only means by which a diverse and widespread English population could be unified (Levine, 2013), as well as providing a workforce suitable to support British and company interests across British India. One reason for the success of the Anglicists was that they were supported by the local elite, who, like their counterparts in Ceylon, wanted to cement their authority and status by becoming embedded in the ranks of colonial administrators (Ghosh, 1993). Nevertheless, the role of missionary societies as the instigators of educational provision and British notions of enlightenment in the vernacular became a standard feature of British imperialism, manifesting itself in other places such as Australia, Canada and East Africa (Elbourne, 2008).

One of the more distinctive features of British imperialism was its capacity to formalise the administration of its colonial territories, constructing an evolving set of administrative and governance structures that became the basis of government reports; it was the prime example of modernity reaching colonised society and the existential representation of the governmentality (Foucault, 1991) surrounding

British imperialism. In the case of Ceylon, the detail of that documentation illustrates well the principles of equity with which education was approached by the colonial administration in terms of the rights of the ethno-cultural groups that were part of the Ceylon that the British had acquired. For example, in the 1821 Ceylon Calendar, the government-run School of Colombo was listed under 'Ecclesiastical Establishments', a reminder of the religious context under which education was being conducted in the colony. More interestingly, however, was the staff list, which illustrated the importance placed by government on the importance of involving teachers from the different ethnic groups in the area of the school in question, as well as catering for all the vernacular languages of the region. The school of Colombo, led by a Scottish reverend as principal, had three English teachers, two locals as 'Cingalese' teachers (both of whom were Dutch Burgher), a teacher who taught Sinhalese to the Malabars (Tamils), and two schoolmasters for the Tamil students, both of whom were also Burgher (Ceylon Calendar, 1821).

The Colombo College or Academy, which had been established as early as 1803 by Frederick North, the governor at the beginning of Ceylon's official British colonial status, was an illustration of the early belief of the colony's administrators that there needed to be a pathway for local Ceylonese to be educated in the skills necessary that they could be employed in the lower ranks in the island's colonial administration. This was some 30 years before the emergence of a similar goal in the case of India, and was perhaps a joint consequence of both the earlier Crown Colony status of Ceylon, as well as the need to reduce the costs of operating a colony that, as argued previously, had more strategic value than economic to the Colonial Office. Whilst these aspects of policy do reinforce the postcolonial perspective that colonial education was very much concerned with the development and imposition of powerful and Really Useful Knowledge (Johnson, 1981; Popkewitz, 2002) in the British idiom, there were a number of additional facets that indicated a far more inclusive attitude to local traditions and capabilities in both knowledge and potential. For example, although the students were to be educated in English and its associated writings, there was a clear intention for these studies to include '. . . oriental and native literatures to challenge and bring into life the best of minds . . .' (Ruberu, 1962, p. 67), and that the opportunities for these Ceylonese students could extend to the higher levels of public service, and not just the lower ranks.

Regardless of these differences in historiography, the opportunities afforded by these new lines of education and employment that were generated by the onset of British imperial rule was seized upon by certain groups in Ceylonese society; specifically, the Goigama Mudaliyars, or the high-caste Sinhalese who comprised the traditional leadership elite; the Dutch Burghers; and the Ceylon Tamils (De Silva, 2005). For the Goigama, the learning of English was the '. . . most natural mode of maintaining their position' (Ludowyk, 1966, p. 115). In the case of the Dutch Burghers, their origins and location around the centres of European administration meant that they were aware of, and part of, the transitioning of the older Sinhalese kingdoms into multicultural regions that were being transformed in subtle ways into a governmentalised modern society.

For the Tamils, particularly those residing in the northern part of the island, their high capacity and willingness to be part of the new colonial administration can be attributed to a large part to the quality of the education work practised by the American Missionary Society (AMS) in the Jaffna peninsula and its surrounds. Unlike the other missionary societies, the AMS focus was highly localised in the northern tip of the island, and the effectiveness of their educational provision was only matched in size and extent by the Wesleyan missions mainly located in the southwestern part of the island. By 1833, within 30 years of their establishment, the American missionaries had established seven missionary centres, providing free education for 5,062 students across 18 parishes (Ceylon Calendar, 1833). At a time when education for girls did not seem to be a necessity even within Great Britain itself, nearly 17% of these day students were Tamil girls, with the addition of a girls' boarding school at Oodooville. The seminary at Batticotta (now known as Jaffna, the capital of the northern province), provided education up to high school and university equivalent standard for nearly 130 students, and was seen by a later governor, Sir James Emerson Tennent, to be providing an educational equivalent to a European university (Tennent, 1859).

It should be noted, however, that conclusions as these are in strong contrast to some of the views of some more recent Sinhalese historical researchers such as K.M. De Silva (2005), a comparison that may have been influenced by the pro-Sinhalese nationalist undercurrent in his work. Part of that ontology is the need to downplay the role of Tamils in Ceylonese society and to highlight any negative impacts of European colonisation. For example, de Silva argues that one feature of the Ceylon civil service was its rapid Europeanisation in comparison with the practices of the Dutch and Portuguese, and that it was not open to all. Appointment to the civil service in these early years was based on patronage, rather than merit, with a number of positions reserved for Europeans supported by the highest salary structure in the British Empire and a generous pension scheme. On the other hand, in the same comprehensive history of Ceylon, de Silva makes little reference to the educational success of the Tamils under the tutelage of the American Missionary Society, an organisation with a substantial presence in colonial Ceylon, but one that does not even warrant its own entry in the index.

### *The second phase*

The second phase of colonial education in Ceylon under British rule can be said to have started in 1831, with the Commission of Eastern Enquiry, under which the Colebrooke-Cameron Reforms into the future development of the colony were undertaken (Colebrooke, 1831). The establishment of the Commission was a direct result of the combination of the decreasing value of the island as a strategic colony after the end of the Napoleonic wars, and the decision that the financial drain of the Colony's administration needed to be staunched with a more proactive economic development policy. Across many areas of society, the resulting Colebrooke-Cameron Reforms are, in the eyes of many (De Silva, 2005; G. C. Mendis, 1956; Samaraweera, 1973a) seen as a time when the foundations for future liberal government along Benthamite lines of enlightenment were established, including those in terms of governmental and legislative structures. Such reforms, which recommended changes such as a restructuring of the authority of the governor so that it was to be held in tandem with an organ of representative government, and a comprehensive justice system, were far in advance of changes that would later occur in India and in other non-'white' colonies of the British Empire. Overall, the Commission's Report

> . . . marked the first systematic and successful attempt to break away from the Dutch pattern of colonial administration and to reject its basic assumptions in favour of a more enlightened form of government.
>
> (de Silva, 2005, p. 337)

The impact of the Report on education was no less substantial. Colebrooke was highly critical on the way in which the colonial administration had operated and administered the few schools under its control, and was highly praiseworthy of the quality and efficiency of the schools established by the various missionary societies. Aside from recommending that a Schools' Commission be formed to administer education under the Archdeacon of Colombo (the religious imperative was now very explicit in government policy), and reforms to manage and expand the system of governmental education, the Report represented a clear change in colonial administrative policy on the island as it was the first time that the colonial government accepted that there was a need for state supervision of education in a clear and transparent form.

In the context of this book, there are two specific aspects of the Colebrooke-Cameron Report that are of particular significance. First, in concert with past and persisting criticism of British colonial practice, the overriding intention of the recommended reforms was the construction of a Ceylonese society that reflected the 'superiority' of British societal mores. For instance, one major criticism expressed by Colebrooke was that, in contrast to the success of the missionary societies in using local Ceylonese as teachers in their schools the quality of teaching in government schools was very low, largely because teaching was entirely in the vernacular language, with no expectations of high English knowledge in the 'native' teachers or any inspectorate system to ensure that standards were being maintained. He did not mention, however, or appear to acknowledge, that the success of the missionary schools was partly due to their use of the vernacular in the teaching.

> Nothing is taught in the schools but reading in the native languages, and writing in the native character; and as the control exercised is insufficient to secure the attendance of either the masters or of the scholars, many abuses prevail . . .
>
> (Colebrooke, 1831, p. 31)

It was at the same time that the dichotomous debate as to which language should be the medium of instruction was taking place in India, but unlike that colony, the strength and success of the missionary schools in providing Christian-based education to regions away from the colonial centre in Colombo meant that the decree by Thomas Babington Macaulay that all mass education in India should be in English was not replicated in Ceylon.

The second relevant aspect of the Colebrooke report on education was that, as part of its reinforcement of contemporary British values, there was strong support for an education system that did not perpetuate existing class systems by favouring particular ethnic groups. The centrality of individual agency as a key feature of a British outlook on life, in combination with the maintenance of vernacular education as a major component of the educational system throughout the rest of the century, was to have a major impact on the awakening of the transnational spirit in the last 80 years of British colonial administration. In the early 1830s, the Ceylon Civil Service was being hindered in its operations by a shortage of British-born staff, with insufficient numbers able to be attracted to the colony. This opened up number of opportunities for those Ceylonese who could speak English, and these openings were being seized upon when they became available, especially in positions such as provincial magistrates and public office clerks (G. C. Mendis, 1956).

In his report, Colebrooke highlighted the fact that those Ceylonese who had already entered the lower ranks of the Ceylon Civil Service had tended to come from the existing leadership stratum of Ceylonese society – which was predominantly Sinhalese – and those of European descent; that is, the Dutch Burghers. As a result, he argued, such a system helped to '. . . foster the prejudices of the people in favour of a system from which the ascendancy of the privileged classes is derived . . .' (Colebrooke, 1831, p. 30). Instead, Colebrooke argued, appointment to positions in the civil service should be purely merit-based,

> . . . open to all classes of the inhabitants, without reference to caste or to other qualifications than respectability and fitness for employment. A competent knowledge of the English language should however be required in the principal native functionaries throughout the country. The prospect of future advancement to situations now exclusively held by Europeans will constitute a most powerful inducement with the natives of high caste to relinquish many absurd prejudices, and to qualify themselves for general employment.
> (Colebrooke, 1831, p. 30)

Although Colebrooke's opinion of some Ceylonese traditions was very much in sync with his times – for example, he had a very clear standpoint on the general superiority of British civilisation – the significance of such clear statements of equity of opportunity, regardless of culture or ethnic group, should not be underestimated by postcolonial critiques of British colonial education, particularly in the case of Ceylon. The multicultural mix that existed prior to European colonisation was based on contestation and right of existence, the Sinhalese claiming divine right to the island on the basis of belief, rather than evidence of Tamil migration and settlement. Regardless of the debate surrounding the colonial assumptions of rule, which were discussed in Chapters 2 and 3, the social and historical reality is that, under British imperial rule, the chance of advanced educational achievement not only became accessible equally to all ethnic and cultural groups, but also became the basis for self-improvement, for it created a far more equitable educational environment that had existed within pre-European Ceylonese societies. The suppression of pre-colonial educational practices had indeed taken place, but had been replaced by a modern system that opened up opportunities for all, rather than perpetuating custom that treated one particular group as being more deserving of opportunity than the rest of the population.

As was the case in India (Seth, 2007), some Ceylonese saw and accepted that education in the British idiom provided a pathway for life improvement, especially for minority groups such as the Tamils and Dutch Burghers, whose places in the pre-existing societal structures were very diminished. Education in English therefore ceased being just merely 'useful knowledge', and became the currency of 'Really Useful Knowledge' (Johnson, 1981). In some ways, this pre-empted the future situation in India that was the subject of much bewilderment on the part of the colonial administration, when they expressed dismay at the purely instrumental view that Indians had of education in English, seemingly ignoring its perceived enlightening qualities. Instead, it was seen as a pathway to a well-paying job, provision of a dowry and material success, and its transformative thinking qualities, acquired through a system of liberal education conducted in English, were not recognised (Seth, 2007, p. 32), except for a few of the upper elite.

It is on this point that the Ceylonese example pivots, however. Seth (2007) argues that, to a degree, such expressions show that the British colonial authorities could not see that Indians working in government jobs could operate in two spheres: one, based on the knowledge of English, that was directed at existence and the power that came with employability and confirmed income; and the other, founded on the use of local languages such as Bengali, that brought peace of the inner soul and heart. They possessed the capacity and self-belief to implement their own sense of agency. In Ceylon, groups such as the Ceylon Tamils and Dutch Burghers were able to enact their self-agency in a different way. Although knowledge of the English language and the British system was also seen as a path to self-empowerment, many of them were able to embrace its transformative elements in full, harvesting all that they could extract into their psyche, constructing a transnational sense that reconfigured their sense of the place in which they lived and worked. For groups such as these, colonial education was far from being a thief of a former identity; it enabled them to generate one in which **they** possessed the agency to act, and not those who ruled in the former pre-British society, combining both practicality and transformativity of the soul into an identity with a status and potentiality that they did not possess previously.

## *The third phase*

The advent of educational changes following the release of the Colebrooke-Cameron Report in 1832 did not lead to the immediate consolidation of educational provision in Ceylon. Colebrooke, in his report, was highly critical of the way in which the colonial administration was operating, commending the missionary schools for the standards that they employed and, in particular, the quality of their teachers. Government schools at this stage had no system for ensuring that the teachers employed were capable speakers of English. Colebrooke recommended that the government implement a national system of education, advocating the use of retired public service clerks and other European descendants, a move that opened up the field of education for the Dutch Burgher community to exploit in reconciling and consolidating a place for themselves in Ceylonese society.

After its release, the colonial administration followed the educational recommendations of the Colebrooke-Cameron Reforms by focusing on the development of government schools in the areas not well covered by the missionary societies; that is, the more inland areas, particularly in the centre and North. In that sense, implementation of education policy by the colonial administration throughout the rest of the 19th century can be characterised as a collaborative duopoly, with 'mass' education being provided largely by the independent church-based missionary school system in which the use of the vernacular languages was emphasised. It is important to note, however, that such educational expansion did not take place in a social vacuum. Other aspects of the Colebrooke-Cameron Report focused on the development of other systems of governmentality that was central to the British form of colonial governance, including a comprehensive justice system based on a court hierarchy administered through the provincial system of colonial administration.

Over the next 50 years, a number of organisational and government changes were implemented in order to find an effective and efficient means of delivering education in all parts of the country and community. The initial Schools' Commission established after Colebrooke-Cameron was dissolved in 1841, to be replaced by a more secular body (four of the seven commissioners were now lay people) that was more supportive of private educational ventures, in theory, at least. Unfortunately, this new body was also doomed to failure because it had '. . . vague aspirations and an undefined area of possible administration and organization. It had no central responsibility and therefore no central coherence. The labour was essentially volunteer and the results spasmodic' (Great Britain, 1901, pp. 770–771).

A further change in 1869 led to the secular centralisation of education under the Department of Public Instruction, headed by a director who was directly responsible to the governor, marking the end of direct church influence on the governance of colonial education. These changes were also reflected in the way in which governmentality was structured, with education now a general department under the heading of Civil Establishments in the Civil List (Ceylon Civil List, 1870). The Colonial Administration had paid for the supply of religious education textbooks to the schools of two missionary societies, with only completely secular schools being eligible for government aid. It was at this point many of the church-based schools became funded totally independently of government. The number of schools receiving government aid, however, increased markedly. Between 1869–97, the number of schools over which the Department had some form of control increased from 85 to 1,647. In the same period, the number of aided schools that were funded by the administration increased from 21 to 1,172, or 71% of the total (Great Britain, 1901, p. 771).

The further devolution of school administration continued to progress. In 1884, colonial administration withdrew from the operation of English-language schools, and it was left primarily to Independent, or missionary, sectors. Instead, government concerns were focused on vernacular schools and a small number of English-vernacular bilingual schools in designated key settlements around the island. By 1896, there was a new Board of Education, which included advisers from the Church of England, Catholic Church and the Wesleyan tradition, as well as a lay Buddhist. This gradual shift to a more laissez-faire form of educational administration also coincided with a noticeable restructuring of the cultural groups most concerned with the administration of schooling, with both Central Administration and schools being dominated by British appointments, particularly from Scotland, and the local Burgher community, with little overt evidence of participation at those levels by Tamil and Sinhalese. The education Director and principal inspectors were invariably British, but Burghers were now filling many of the middle management positions. Nevertheless, the government's acknowledgement of the cultural composition of the Colony's population still reflected in its administrative priorities, with specific Inspectorate roles concerned with the Sinhalese and Tamil-language establishments.

Throughout the early years of the 20th century, in the decades leading up to independence in 1948, the basic pattern of colonial educational administration established in the late 1800s persisted. The dominance of an educational system that was based on the British model, along with its associated curriculum and pedagogies, was maintained by several policy techniques. Up until the mid-1920s, the composition of the Board of Education remained constant in structure, origin and ideology, the majority of the Board being Christian and European. The introduction of a greater proportion of Ceylonese representation, including Buddhist and Hindu views (De Silva, 1973b, p. 465), in the years leading up to World War II did little to change educational policy direction, for the Ceylonese who held these positions were themselves members of the leadership group that had been educated under the British, and they had no wish to dilute their own power or sphere of influence. It is, of course, one of the great ironies of British colonial education that it created a leadership group from the local populace that was imbued with British liberal ideas about society and governance, and that it was this particular cadre of highly educated professionals who were inevitably the drivers of self-determination and independence from colonial rule.

The tripartite system schools based on language (English, English-vernacular and the vernacular) remained in existence until the end of colonial rule in 1948. The increasing value of an English language education as an employment advantage, fuelled by economic growth in the 1920s and 1930s, and the increasing wealth of an enlarged middle class that cut across ethnic and cultural lines, saw the emergence of a modern leadership group that extended beyond the traditional Sinhalese and Tamil leadership structures that were based on caste (De Silva, 1973b, p. 465–470). The wealthier upper class had the resources to send their offspring to acquire a university education in Britain, but for most of the English-educated minority, higher education was limited to the Medical and Law Schools in Colombo and external degrees of the University of London. Disquieted by the increasing intellectual rumble for self-government in India, the colonial administration was not keen to encourage the public cultural and political discussion that a local university would enable, but persistent pressure by various lobby groups from 1905 eventually resulted in the opening of University College in 1921, with 155 students enrolled in arts and science degrees administered by the University of London. It took until 1942 for the institution to be combined with the Ceylon Medical College to form the University of Ceylon, which awarded degrees in its own right.

## E In the wider colonial context: Ceylon and education

There were several ways in which the progressive development of educational provision in Ceylon mirrored certain aspects of events in other British colonies. In the first two decades of the 19th century, having taken over colonial control of Penang and Malacca from the Dutch in the last years of the 18th century, as was the case with Ceylon, it was the missionary schools that introduced British education into the Straits Settlement (Penang, Malacca and Singapore) as, once again, the colonial administration was more concerned with building up the mercantile base of the colony around the production and export of tin and rubber than spending limited funds on social infrastructure such as education. In conjunction with the colonial authorities, it was the religious societies that also oversaw the founding of the English-language medium schools (Ho Seng Ong, 1952), such as the Penang Free School (1821), Raffles (established as the Singapore Institution in 1823) and the Anglo-Chinese College (1818). On the other hand, it was not until the 1870s that government schooling in the vernacular language began, and the gradual emergence of a segregated school system that reflected the multi-ethnic character of Malaya meant that education became a symbol of division in colonial Malaya, and not the ameliorating force that it became in Ceylon. Consequently, it is another example of how the nuances of colonial experience make it unwise to generalise so pejoratively about the nature of colonialism as a holistic entity. The part that education played in creating a successful harmonious multicultural society in the Colony of Ceylon was not replicated necessarily in other outposts of the British Empire, the diversity of circumstances only serving to further illustrate the multiplicities of form under which the British colonial imaginary was practised and diffused, and underlining the dangers in oversimplifying patterns in postcolonial critique of colonial impact in the British context.

At the most fundamental level, there were a number of characteristics of the pre-colonial territories of what is now peninsular Malaysia and Singapore that inevitably meant that the colonial experience in these territories would be vastly different to that in Ceylon. The first was that they were disparate both geographically and in terms of governance, compared with the unity of Ceylon that flowed out of its geographical status as an island of reasonable size. The Straits

Settlements, largely composed of small islands and coastal outposts, were originally under the colonial oversight of the British East India Company from 1826, just as India and Ceylon had been. However, the military conflicts that emerged in India in the 1860s and led to the sub-continent being governed as a Crown Colony under the direct control of the British government, also saw the demise of the Company's authority in the Straits Settlements in 1867, some 65 years after the creation of the Colony of Ceylon. This meant that, for much of the 19th century, whilst Ceylon was being governed as a colonial society, the Straits Settlements were primarily a mercantile operation in which issues such as education remained lower in priorities.

Following its system of non-interventionism that was being practised simultaneously in India, the British (through the aegis of the East India Company), maintained a system of colonial administration based on cooperation with established local sultanates on the Malay Peninsula rather than the far more expensive system of territorial acquisition and direct rule (Chang Ming Phang, 1973). As was the case with the original Portuguese and Dutch colonial periods in Ceylon, the local leadership monarchies became increasingly integrated with the British mode of administration, and it was the children of the Malay elite who were largely the local clientele of the English-language schools established in places such as Penang in order to prepare them for access to the British civil service in Malaya. However, it was not until the early part of the 20th century that the British had negotiated treaties with all of the Malayan sultanates, offering the leadership families external security in exchange for economic and mercantile concessions, especially tin mining and rubber extraction (Yuen, 2010).

The most significant difference in educational terms, however, between the Malayan portion of the British Empire and Ceylon was the pre-existing unity of religion and schooling that existed prior to the colonial period. As is the case today, the indigenous Malays were Islamic, and a strong system of Islamic schooling based around the concept of *pondok* education – village-centred education guided by a religious teacher – was well established when the European waves of colonisation began.(Shuhaimi bin Haji Ishak & Abdullah, 2013) Unlike Ceylon, this embedded societal education system did not leave a vacuum for a British education to fill, even if the colonial administrators had been more proactive in their efforts. In the 1872, under the new British colonial structure, the provision of education for Malay children in their own language was introduced, which marked the beginning of the development of a multi-ethnic education system. In order to provide labour for the tin and rubber operations, as the Malays were more interested in maintaining their rural base and occupations, the British, as they had done previously the tea plantations in Ceylon, facilitated and encouraged the immigration of Chinese and Indians to the Malay Peninsula, the former largely because of their expertise in tin mining, and the latter predominantly for their grasp of English, which was becoming increasingly necessary for the conduct of business (Chang Ming Phang, 1973). The differences in governance between Ceylon and Malaya, with a much greater reliance on indirect means of colonial administration, meant that was little incentive for the British to develop the relevant educational system that would unite all the peoples in their zone of influence under the British imaginary. Their provision of English-language education was confined to the Crown Colonies themselves, and there was little political interest in providing education for the growing Chinese and Indian communities, although no barriers were put in the way of those communities developing their own educational facilities.

This educational form of apartheid can be seen as one of the major reasons why critiques of the British colonial period in Malaya tend to be very condemnatory of the power dynamics of the British authorities (for example, Joseph, 2008), describing their approaches being one of very much of 'divide and rule', and creating the foundations for post-independence system of education that has maintained the cultural divisions to a large degree. The alternative view, however, also has some traction, in that, whatever the reasons that underpinned the British approach to colonial rule, the result was that the different ethnic groups had the platform on which they could maintain the continuity of our own beliefs and systems. Unlike Ceylon, and other British colonies such as Australia, the belief that Christianity should be the basis of the British imaginary was a secondary, and even minor, consideration in the Malay context. In fact, it can be argued that the very reverse was true, with British colonial practices in the region reinforcing the rights of individual groups to maintain their own religious faiths, even if those practices in Malaya may have been more designed to enhance economic and trade interests than being derived out of a focus on human rights.

## F Colonial education in Sri Lanka: Constrainer or liberator?

As discussed in previous chapters, one of the dominant criticisms of colonisation, and of colonial systems of education, in particular, was that it privileged the knowledge and norms of the powerful, subjugating local systems of thinking, knowledge and societal behaviour. Education was the means by which that colonial imaginary was imposed and reinforced for future generations, guiding the local peoples into wants and desires that suited the needs of the colonised society rather than build on the established traditions and practices of the society that had been in place prior to the imperial age. The postcolonial perspective highlights the suppression of the subaltern history of the colonial period, and of the '. . . social and economic injustice sanctioned by Empire against those without access to political power' (Darwin, 2012, p. 4).

In the educational context, this negation of local desires and imperatives was both created and reinforced by an 'elite' structure of schooling, in which education in the colonial language and imaginary was targeted at a minority of the local population, focusing on the children of the upper section of the traditional leadership group and the offspring of the colonisers who were resident in the territory. The notion of an 'elite' school as being a highlighter and separator of class division in colonised societies, promoting the means and causes of the dominant or ruling class, has been generally influenced by the work of Pierre Bourdieu (Bourdieu, 1996; Kenway & Koh, 2013), and his work on the interactions between class, culture and power and education. In the context of the British Empire, such 'elite' schools, it has been argued, tend to follow the long established '. . . the traditional and prestigious British public school model . . .', very well resourced, designed to meet the needs of the colonising class and their local associates within the imperialised territory, and providing '. . . an avenue of social mobility for 'deserving' members of subaltern populations . . .' (Kenway & Fahey, 2014, pp. 177–178) who are '. . . colonial carriers of certain forms of eliteness' (Kenway & Fahey, 2014, p. 180).

The difficulty with such a focus on elitism, and the use of the word 'elite' to identify schools associated with the concept, is that it conveys prior assumptions and value standpoints about both the nature of independent schools generally, as well as the part that they are to have played and/or play in former colonial territories. The inconsistency in the logic of such approaches lies in the presumption that, because these schools in British colonial territories were usually designed in the mould of what were seen contemporarily as the pinnacle of 19th-century British education – that is, public schools such as Eton – the class system under which of these British original examples operated and maintained would be replicated in the colonial imaginary. What is not taken into account is the influence of local social and cultural parameters that shaped these outwardly public school replicants into a form that was compatible with each colony's particular context.

In the case of Ceylon, these generalisations are particularly inaccurate and inappropriate, largely because its assumptions regarding the nature of the leadership 'elite' prior to and as a result of British colonisation. The governance of Ceylonese people prior to European colonisation was not only fragmented, but also based on a feudal system that placed all power in the hands of one individual to the detriment of the bulk of a region's population. It reinforced the strong caste system that existed within the Sinhalese and Tamil communities, leaving little scope for self-improvement and socio-economic progression on the basis of individual merit. In contrast, the Ceylonese leadership group that was created and maintained by the introduced British colonial system of education was far more equitable in its cultural composition, with progress by individual merit providing minority groups with the opportunity to break out of previously established life pathways. The nature of an 'elite' is neither necessarily constant or consistent across space and time, and its automatic and unquestioned use in major postcolonial research perspectives is dependent ultimately on a modernist interpretation of privilege from a 'Western' or 'Euro-American viewpoint that effectively ignores the capacity of colonised subjects to make their own decisions and use their own circumstances to best advantage.

Operating in hindsight from the context of a 21st-century global community where notions of social justice and the universality of human rights are very much in play, I would argue that it is incongruous to condemn the introduction of an educational form into a historical territory that provided an improved sense of equity and opportunity for a greater number of people across ethnic lines. In the case of Ceylon, unlike the more stereotypical imperial approach taken in British

India, local languages were not downgraded and marginalised in the educational space, even if English was used as the means of national and global opportunity. The situation was far more complex and, to a large degree, contrary to the prevailing trope. The actuality was that, by 1931, 85% (1931) of children were being educated in government schools, which provided free primary education in the student's own vernacular language of Sinhalese or Tamil (de Silva, 1973b, p. 466). Aside from a few Anglo-vernacular schools that offered a bilingual education, the rest of the school population attended English-language schools that offered a pathway to secondary graduation, and if possible, higher education. Overall, it was these English-language schools that met the criteria now established by researchers as 'elite' schools, on the premise that the students who attended in these schools were socially and economically privileged, subjected to the '. . . transplantation of the metropolitan paradigm of British public school . . .' (McCarthy & Kenway, 2014, p. 166). Once again, though, the Colony of Ceylon exemplifies just how untempered such conclusions can be.

As discussed earlier in this chapter, the origins of English-language schools in colonial Ceylon lay primarily in the work of the various Christian missionary societies that operated on the island from the early days of British colonial rule. For much of the early part on the 19th century, the missionary schools operated independently from government, and it was not until after the 1831 Colebrooke-Cameron Reforms that the colonial administration began to both support such schools financially and emulate their educational provisions within government schools. This support stayed in place until the withdrawal of government grants and aid at the beginning of the 1870s forced the church-run schools to become fully independent once more.

Many of the English-language schools that emerged in colonial Ceylon after 1831 had their origins in either the existing missionary or church-operated schools or were instituted by various religious individuals to meet a perceived need. In structure and tone, these schools did follow the stereotype of the so-called 'elite' school and drew from the school experience of the founders, who were invariably graduates of British public schools in one form or another, and equally likely to be Scottish clergymen with an indefatigable spirit for human rights and justice. Such schools included current institutions such as Trinity College in Kandy and St Thomas's College in Mount Lavinia (Colombo), which date back to 1851 and 1872 respectively. There was, however, one English language government-operated school. Royal College, which is still in existence, which dates back to 1836, when it was established as Colombo Academy by then Governor Wilmot-Horton, and was also imagined as an Eton-style institution, but fee-free and culturally secular.

If the perception of schools such as these as being economically and culturally isolated is true, designed purely for the benefit of the upper strata of society, then it is logical to expect such schools to reflect these characteristics in their manner of operation, as well as in their interactions with the traditional leadership cohort in Ceylonese society. In some aspects, this was the case, for it is true to say that independent English-language schools such as these were designed specifically to prepare students to participate in colonial Ceylonese society in a manner that reflected the ideal British citizen, with all the values and attitudes contained therein. This was reflected in the predominance of British scholars, many of whom were also Christian clergy, as principals of these schools, a situation that did not really alter until either just before after Sri Lankan independence. For instance, Trinity College (Kandy), established by the Rev Richard Collins in 1872, had to wait for its 11th principal in 1941 for its 'first son of the soil' (Trinity College Kandy, 1972, p. 27), Mr C.E. Simiraaratchy, to be appointed. Even Royal College had to wait until 1948 and national independence for its first local leader. Curriculum, co-curriculum – particularly sports such as cricket, rugby and creative pursuits such as debating and drama – and pastoral care systems were based on the concept of vertically streamed Houses that reflected the traditions of the British public school system.

In many other respects, however, the English-language schools in Ceylon displayed characteristics that were far from 'elitist', and were more reflective of the principle of social even-handedness that seems to have underpinned much of the development of Ceylonese society during the British period of colonial rule. The sense of social justice and equity that was a part of the missionary school system from its very beginnings, particularly in relation to access to schooling by all cultural and social groups, was very much in evidence. There were two main ways in which this was apparent. First, English-language schooling offered by missionary societies was invariably low-fee or free, underwritten by the fundraising efforts of the missionary societies in either Britain or, as was the case with the American Missionary Society, in North America. In the latter part of the 19th century, when government aid to sectarian schools ceased, the emphasis on providing access to students of ability, regardless of economic circumstances, persisted. It was not until the years after independence, when national government priorities changed, that financial barriers began to be put into place. For example, St Thomas's College in Mount Lavinia, Colombo, and Trinity College Kandy did not start charging fees until the early 1950s, a decision made in order to maintain their neutrality and freedom at a time when independent schools were offered financial assistance by the post-independence Sinhalese government in exchange of the application of government educational policy, including the use of Sinhala as the language of instruction, rather than English. Whilst many have argued that the Christian basis of colonial British education was a negative for the local peoples, it was also as one of its main drivers of social justice in the modern vein. Principals of these schools, such as the Warden of St Thomas's College, Colombo often had the final say on admission to the school, and their own spiritual values were often played out in the admission of students from disadvantaged backgrounds.

Second, these church-based schools were not seen as discriminators against Ceylonese on the basis of cultural or ethnic grouping. Under the traditional leadership structures that operated prior to the European age, including the British, it was the Sinhalese who had the ascendancy. However, as described earlier, under the British system of equity of opportunity, all cultural groups, including those that had emerged under and as a result of European colonisation, such as the Burgher community, were treated equally on the basis of merit. Groups such as the Burghers – the definition of which was codified by the British to any person with European heritage, and not just Portuguese and Dutch – were astute enough to consciously target education in English and future government employment as a means to status and self- improvement; as a result, the Ceylon Civil Service was largely Burgher from its earlier transfigurations (de Silva, 1973b, p. 328).

In the end, however, it was the way in which education meshed into the structures of governmentality created by the British colonial administration that highlighted the positive aspects of the Ceylonese society created by the imperial imaginary. In strong contrast to the situation in India in the 1880s, a time that marks the midpoint of the British colonial experience in Ceylon, the island possessed a culturally and ethnically diverse community that, contrary to the tenets of postcolonial perspectives on imperialism, was characterised by the existence and encouragement of indigenous customs and practices, including that the freedom of religion. In contemporary writings, Ceylon was seen to be an example of innovative and successful colonial administration, where ideas being practised and implemented might then be transplanted into different colonial contexts. Moreover, Ceylonese society demonstrated few of the characteristics of imperial tyranny and subjugation that are identified so frequently in the postcolonial discourse.

In the record of various historical sources, the period of the early 1880s appears to mark a high point in the perception by the British themselves as to the exemplar presented by the Crown Colony of Ceylon. The census of 1881 (Lee, 1882) was only the second comprehensive formal assessment and evaluation of the nature of Ceylonese society that has been undertaken in the British period of rule, following on from the one conducted in 1871. The data presented in the census is not only significant because of its breadth, but also because of the acute depth of observation that it provides of Ceylonese society under the British imaginary. In 1881, the population of the island was just over 2.7 million, approximately 10% of its current 21st-century figure. Within that relatively small total, the British structures of colonialism had created an environment within which seven identifiable cultural and ethnic groups were living in relative harmony, collectively practising five main religions, including the two fundamental branches of Christianity. The 1881 census identified groups ranging from the Sinhalese (67% of the total population), the Tamils (25%) and the Moors to the 'Eurasians and Burghers', who numbered just under 40,000 people in all. Under the postcolonial perspective, the system of education that had been introduced should have resulted in the domination of Christianity and British modes of thinking across the population.

In reality, only 10% of the population of colonial Ceylon was Christian, although the success of the educational system in Ceylon was reflected in the fact that, at the same time, the Christian population of India was less than half a percent of the total population. The bulk of the Sinhalese remained Buddhist, the majority of the Tamils (who, even at this stage, were being separated into the Ceylon Tamil and the immigrant Tamil cohorts, the latter composed of those brought over to work on two plantations) were practising Hindus, and the majority of the Moors and Malays remained Muslim. Nevertheless, the intermarriage and intermixing between the different cultural and ethnic groups that had begun centuries before the beginning of the European colonial period was still having an impact on the increasingly integrated nature of Ceylonese society. The detail of the 1881 census was such that it pointed out that the religious adherences of the various cultural groups were far from fixed. Of the Sinhalese, 9% were Christian (mainly around the Western province centred on Colombo) and a few had converted to Islam through marriage to the Moors. Similarly, 16% of the Tamil population was Christian, with the small group of Moors and Malays being the ones who were less likely to have married out of their faith. By any measure, the destruction of indigenous Ceylonese society and customs had not taken place, and the instigation of a Christianised colonial entity that was dominated from the metropole had not come to pass (Lee, 1882).

In the context of a British colonial imaginary that promoted freedom of choice and opportunity, the 1881 Census showed equally that attempts to redress the more limiting aspects of traditional Sinhalese and Tamil society still had some way to go in achieving their long-term aims. Although all the missionary societies and government schools had provision for the education of girls, the Census noted that it was only the daughters of Christians, whatever their cultural and ethnic background, who were encouraged and allowed to attend school. The traditional attitudes of Sinhalese and Tamil society meant that they were '. . . always opposed to the education of their women, and the very early age at which girls are married renders it impossible that any real progress can be made until the habits of the people undergo a radical change' (Lee, 1882, p. xxiii). Overall, 12.6% of Christian girls and women were able to read and write, in comparison to the proportion of 1.7% for non-Christians (Lee, 1882, p. xxv).

The overall success of educational programmes from the official British perspective, however, was substantial, particularly when compared with the situation in India. As outlined in the 1881 Census, 15.7% of the population of Ceylon were now '. . . possessed of the rudiments of education . . . ' (Lee, 1882, p. xxiv), compared with only 5% in the 'Madras Presidency'. The importance placed by both missionary and government schools on using the relevant vernacular as the medium of mass education was showing itself to be of considerable long-term value, even if there was still considerable scope for further development.

Interestingly, the long-term impact of public instruction being largely conducted in the vernacular languages was to be seen later as not being without its divisive aspects by some members of the British community in colonial Ceylon. For example, in the years just after independence in 1948, observers such as Harry Williams, a long-time resident in pre-independence Ceylon with a scholarly interest in the life and history of the island, asserted that the insistence of the British administration on conducting all commercial and government business in English had created a yawning gulf between the English speakers and Ceylonese having been educated in their own languages. Although he acknowledged the great strides made in 'public instruction' since the late 1870s, creating an educated population, he argued that the result was an education being equated with a '. . . stubbornly uniform curriculum, a pursuit of knowledge without any particular search for wisdom . . .', and that the people were not prepared for the realities of independence, having been fed '. . . no political education whatever . . .' and an '. . . illusion of a democratic system of voting' (Williams, 1950, pp. 313–314)

The criticisms that have been made of the deleterious impacts of colonial education in subaltern societies, especially in the case of the British Empire, frequently have to confront a fundamental paradox, in which the reality of the past did not necessarily reflect the philosophical interpretations of the past. The condemnation of political and educational policy that, as is often argued, led to the sublimation of traditional lines of thought and practices, is often at odds with the reality of those indigenous ways of life. More often than not, as illustrated in colonial Ceylon, many aspects of those beliefs and practices would now be seen as being as unacceptable anomalies and a rejection of basic human rights. Issues such as educational access, regardless of gender, social standing and economic resources are now perceived to be fundamental facets of life that all should have access to, regardless of where they live, but which were not part of the pre-European imaginary of Ceylonese society.

Similarly, to condemn or criticise the moral of the imposition of Christianity as a religious practice on a colonised society, and to reject any possible value of an introduced Europeanised imaginary, is to assume that whatever societal structures were in place beforehand were not without fault and did not generate any imperative for change. In the case of Ceylon, it cannot be ignored that the British colonial period provided the people of the emerging modern State with strong foundations of education and language acuity, necessary building blocks that would enable Ceylon to transition more easily to participating in an increasingly globalised economy after independence in 1948. In particular, the liberal notions of equity that applied in the British colonial period enabled all cultural and ethnic groups, including previously marginalised cohorts such as the Dutch Burghers and Ceylon Tamils, to utilise colonially generated educational opportunities in ways that had previously not been possible. Retrospective analyses of colonialism often focus on the adverse rather than the progressive, with the consequence that, regardless of the actuality, any benefits to specific groups within the modernised state tend to be obscured and even lost within a framework that treats the original of the past as inviolable perfection, and not capable or worthy of change.

In some aspects, compared with the educational policies implemented in other parts of British colonies, the case study of Ceylon highlights distinct differences and a high degree of educational innovation, pre-empting some developments elsewhere by a number of years. In others, it illustrates some of the more dominant and recurring features of British colonial practice. More than anything, however, comparisons of different colonial sites merely serve to emphasise the multiplicities of reality that comprise the British Empire, and how the singularities surrounding any particular colonial encounter created a high degree of individuality in any location. Consequently, postcolonial critiques that make judgements about the overall nature of colonisation, and, in this context, colonial education, need to be approached with some caution. The peculiarities of the Ceylonese colonial experience, the features that emphasise the uniqueness of the case study's contribution to the overall analysis of the imperial venture, cannot be overridden in the search for general patterns about the colonising process, and the same will apply to any of the individual colonised territories in the British Empire. This is not to say that the postcolonial critique of imperial practice is not without some basis in truth, but the structure of that diassembling needs to be far more congruent of the individual characteristics of a particular place, and not attribute broader concepts of ideological approach that might be identified in British imperial policy as being self-evident in practice throughout all parts of the Empire as a whole.

The salient feature of the period of British colonial education in Ceylon was, in many ways, its underpinning principle of equity, which is not a characteristic normally associated with the practice of colonially directed learning under the postcolonial perspective. The primary reason for this more universal approach was the standards that were first set by the missionary school system from the early days of Ceylon being a Crown Colony. Ironically, of course, the reason for the influence of these church-based societies was that, for the first 30 years or so of colonial rule, the colonial administrators did not have the funds to focus on what was seen as a secondary consideration, but their practical sensibilities and spiritual affinity with Christianity as the foundation of British society meant that, to various degrees, these colonial leaders were very ready to support and encourage the actions of the missionary groups.

As a result, in law and in practice, the foundations established by the missionary school system became the foundation of public and private education throughout the colony over the next hundred years. For example, the success of the missionary school system in the early part of the 19th century was the stimulation for the Colebrooke-Cameron recommendation that the State – that is, the Colonial administration – should become actively involved in the funding and operation of schools. However, such a social commitment by a government body on a national scale was not to be seen in Britain itself for some decades. Although the concept of government-funded elementary education in Britain had its small beginnings in 1833, with the provision of a small amount of funding to two voluntary societies focused on the education of poor working-class children, it was not until 1870 that the British Parliament passed an Education Act that was committed to a nationally funded education provision for all children.

## References

Arasaratnam, S. (Ed.) (1978). *Francois Valentijn's Description of Ceylon*. London: The Hakluyt Society.

Barnes, Sir Edward (1820) Speech on the departure of Sir Robert Brownrigg. *Ceylon Government Gazette, No. 956*, January 15th 1820. The National Archives, United Kingdom. Series CO58/3.

Bourdieu, P. (1996). *The State Nobility: Elite Schools in the Field of Power*. Stanford, CA: Stanford University Press.

Brownrigg, Sir Robert. (1815a). Letters and Papers. The National Archives, United Kingdom. Series WO 133, November 19th 1819, No. 106.

Brownrigg, Sir Robert. (1815b). Proclamation (The Kandyan Convention). Ceylon Government Gazette Extraordinary. The National Archives, United Kingdom. Series CO58/1, January 10th 1815.

*Ceylon Almanac and Compendium of Useful Information* (1833). Colombo: Government Press. Department of National Archives, Sri Lanka, Series W/1/22.

*Ceylon Calendar* (1821). Colombo: Government Press. Department of National Archives, Sri Lanka, Series W/1/17.

*Ceylon Civil List* (1870). Colombo: Government Press. Department of National Archives, Sri Lanka.

*Ceylon Government Gazette* (1815–1850). Colombo: Government Press. The National Archives, United Kingdom. Series CO58.

Chang Ming Phang, P. (1973). *Education in a Plural Society: A Malaysian Case Study*. Singapore: Academia Publications.

Colebrooke, W. M. G. (1831). *Commission of Eastern Enquiry: Report upon the Administration of the Government of Ceylon: 24 December 1831*. The National Archives, United Kingdom, Series CO54, Folio 122.

Darwin, J. (2012). *Unfinished Empire: The Global Expansion of Britain*. London: Penguin.

De Silva, K. M. (1973a). The Coming of the British to Ceylon, 1762–1802. In K. M. De Silva (Ed.), *History of Ceylon* (Vol. 3, pp. 1–11). Colombo: University of Ceylon.

De Silva, K. M. (Ed.) (1973b). *History of Ceylon* (Vol. 3). Colombo: University of Ceylon.

De Silva, K. M. (2005). *A History of Sri Lanka*. Colombo: Vijitha Yapa /Penguin.

Elbourne, E. (2008). Religion in the British Empire. In S. Stockwell (Ed.), *The British Empire: Themes and Perspectives* (pp. 131–156). Carlton, Victoria: Blackwell Publishing.

Ferguson, N. (2003). *Empire: How Britain Made the Modern World*. London: Penguin.

Foucault, M. (1991). Governmentality. In G. Burchell, C. Gordon, & P. Miller (Eds.), *The Foucault Effect: Studies in Governmentality* (pp. 87–104). Chicago: University of Chicago Press.

Ghosh, S. C. (1993). 'English in Taste, in Opinion, in Words and Intellect': Indoctrinating the Indian through Textbook, Curriculum and Education. In J. A. Mangan (Ed.), *The Imperial Curriculum: Racial Images and Education in the British Colonial Experience* (pp. 175–193). London: Routledge.

Godden, L., & Casinader, N. (2013). The Kandyan Convention 1815: Consolidating the British Empire in Colonial Ceylon. *Comparative Legal History, 1*(2), 211–242. doi:10.5235/2049677X.1.2.211

Great Britain, Board of Education. (1901). *Special Reports on Educational Subjects. Volume 5. Educational Systems of the Chief Colonies of the British Empire. (Cape Colony: Natal: Commonwealth of Australia: New Zealand: Ceylon: Malta.)*. London: H.M.S.O.

Ho Seng Ong. (1952). *Education for Unity in Malaya*. Penang: Malayan Teachers' Union.

Hobsbawm, E. J. (1989). *The ge of Empire 1875–1914* (First Vintage Books ed.). New York: Vintage Books.
James, L. (1998). *The Rise and Fa of the British Empire*. London: Abacus.
Jayasuriya, J. E. (1969). *Educati n in Ceylon before and after independence*. Colombo: Associated Educational P ners.
Jayasuriya, J. E. (1976). *ational Policies and Progress during British Rule in Ceylon (Sri Lanka) 17 48*. Colombo: Associated Educational Publishers.
Johnson, R. (1981). ly Useful Knowledge': Radical Education and Working Class Culture 179 . In R. Dale, G. Esland, R. Furgusson, & M. Arnot (Eds.), *Education State Volume 2: Politics, Patriarchy and Practice* (pp. 3–19). Barcombe: almer Press.
Joseph . Difference, Subjectivities and Power: (De)Colonizing Practices in zing the Curriculum. *Intercultural Education, 19*(1), 29–39.
Fahey, J. (2014). Staying ahead of the Game: The Globalising Practices hools. *Globalisation, Societies and Education, 12*(2), 177–195. doi:10.10 67724.2014.890885
K J., & Koh, A. (2013). The Elite School as 'Cognitive Machine' and 'Social dise': Developing Transnational Capitals for the Mational 'Field of Power'. *rnal of Sociology, 49*(2–3), 272–290. doi:10.1177/1440783313481525
, L. (compiled by) (1882). *Census of Ceylon 1881*. Colombo: Government Printer.
evine, P. (2013). *The British Empire: Sunrise to Set* (Second ed.). Milton Park, Abingdon: Routledge.
Ludowyk, E. F. C. (1966). *The Modern History of Ceylon*. London: Weidenfield and Nicolson.
McCarthy, C., & Kenway, J. (2014). Introduction: Understanding the Re-Articulations of Privilege Over Time and Space. *Globalisation, Societies and Education, 12*(2), 165–176. doi:10.1080/14767724.2014.893188
Mendis, G. C. (Ed.) (1956). *The Colebrooke-Cameron Papers: Documents on British Colonial Policy in Ceylon 1796–1833* (Vol. 1). London: Geoffrey Cumberlege/Oxford University Press.
Mendis, V. L. B. (1971). *The Advent of the British to Ceylon: 1762–1803*. Dehiwala: Tissaro Prakasakayo.
Popkewitz, T. S. (2002). How the Alchemy Makes Inquiry, Evidence, and Exclusion. *Journal of Teacher Education, 53*(3), 262–267. doi:10.1177/0022487102053003011
Ruberu, T. R. (1962). *Education in Colonial Ceylon*. Kandy: The Kandy Printers.
Samaraweera, V. (1973a). The Colebrooke-Cameron Reforms. In K. M. De Silva (Ed.), *History of Ceylon* (Vol. 3, pp. 77–88). Colombo: University of Ceylon.
Samaraweera, V. (1973b). The Development of the Administrative System from 1802 to 1832. In K. M. De Silva (Ed.), *History of Ceylon* (Vol. 3, pp. 34–47). Colombo: University of Ceylon.
Seth, S. (2007). *Subject Lessons: The Western Education of Colonial India*. Durham and London: Duke University Press.
Shuhaimi bin Haji Ishak, M., & Abdullah, O. C. (2013). Islamic Education in Malaysia: A Study of History and Development. *Religious Education, 108*(3), 298–311. doi:10.1080/00344087.2013.783362
Tennent, J. E., Sir. (1859). *Ceylon: An Account of the Island Physical, Historical, and Topographical with Notices of Its Natural History, Antiquities and Productions* (Second ed., Vol. 1). London: Longman, Green, Longman, and Roberts.

Trinity College Kandy. (1972). *Centenary Number 1872–1972*. Kandy: Trinity College.

van Goor, J. (1978). *Jan Kompenie as Schoolmaster: Dutch Education in Ceylon 1690–1795*. Groningen: Wolters-Noordhoff.

Williams, H. (1950). *Ceylon: Pearl of the East* (Reprinted July 1956 ed.). London: Robert Hale Ltd.

Wyndham, H. A. (1933). *Native Education: Ceylon, Java, Formosa, the Philippines, French Indo-China, and British Malaya*. Oxford: Oxford University Press.

Yuen, C. Y. M. (2010). Dimensions of Diversity: Challenges to Secondary School Teachers with Implications for Intercultural Teacher Education. *Teaching and Teacher Education, 26*(3), 732–741. doi:http://dx.doi.org/10.1016/j.tate[illegible]009

# 6 Movements of mind and body

## A transnationalist story

### A The transnationalist imaginary redefined

As discussed in Chapter 1, the prevailing conception of transnationalism as being primarily centred on the movement of people from one sovereign State to another is highly problematic. In the first place, its conception of movement as being one of physical transference reflects a highly Euro-American, neoliberal emphasis on the visible, easily identifiable and quantifiable, a particular phenomenon to be counted, managed and addressed as an instrumental entity. It is a simplification of a far more complex imaginary, in which transnationalist thinking and behaviour are more accurately considered within a more opaque, multi-layered and yet equally organic, formulation that is founded on frames of mind and purpose, rather than the actuality of existence in one location or another.

Second, the prevailing interpretation of transnationalism relies on the conception of 'place' as a definable phenomenon, actualised by the existence of national boundaries that have themselves been established as legal constructs that may, or may not, be replicated within the mindset of the transnational individual. In modern transnationalism, movement of people, whether permanent or temporary, is defined by the crossing of sovereign borders, the existence and maintenance of which have come to be seen as the primary focus of sovereign governments, regardless of their socio-political direction. The period of 18th- and 19th-century European colonialism, which in the context of this monograph is referred to as the period of historical globalisation, has been criticised in the postcolonial meme for its imposition of colonial sovereign borders over existing territorial mindsets that had been held by different groups of people and societies in the times prior to European colonisation.

As the previous three chapters have explored, such critiques are simplifications of the pre-colonial reality, and tend to assume an automatic or self-evident homogeneity, righteousness and equity on the part of those who had been colonised. In addition, they are conceptualised on the basis of seeing colonial administration as an inevitable oppressor of the local, with little possibility of acknowledgement and respect for what had existed prior. However, within the British Empire, whilst there were commonalities in the intention and practice of colonial policy across locations, deeper insights into localised examples of colonial administration reveal a range of nuances in the interactions between the coloniser and colonised that make such generalisations as to the all-encompassing negativity of the colonial experience difficult to sustain as a broad theme. For instance, in the case of colonial Ceylon, the creation of hybrid identities through colonisation did not always occur at the borders of pre-existing society, but instead emanated from the deconstruction of internal sociocultural boundaries as a consequence of British colonial practice. As a result, pre-existing local cultural minorities were able to actualise and maintain a transnational identity derived from the creation of a self-defined character that was *built* on the notion of 'place', but not *defined* by 'place'.

One of the more commonly accepted features of British colonial practice was the use of rationality and order as the basis of management and administration of territory and people's lives. The institution of social, political, economic and legal structures, both in the physicality of buildings and other resources and the policies and practices that targeted the behaviour of human beings, has been commonly regarded as an indication of the modernisation of the colonised territories and a precursor to the integration of the colonised regions into the modern family of nation-States once political independence was achieved in the 20th century. In Ceylon, major historical researchers such as V.L.B. Mendis (1971), G. C. Mendis (1956) and De Silva (2005) have tended to see such progression as representing a positive impact of the colonial period, laying the foundations for modern Ceylon, or Sri Lanka, to participate effectively in the contemporary global imaginary. The creation and existence of a working, sophisticated political, judicial and economic system that reflected the mores and guiding principles of British Enlightenment is seen to be a hallmark of the colonial success story of modern Ceylon; it gave the country the ability to participate in 21st century global affairs from the moment of independence, a natural step forward that carried Sri Lanka into the community of nations.

For other researchers such as Scott (1995), however, this focus on governmental structures in colonial rule, both physical and psychological, only serves to highlight the conception of colonialism as being based on sovereignty of government over territory. What is more important and relevant is the Foucauldian principle of governmentality, or

> . . . the arts and rationalities of governing, where the conduct of conduct is the key activity. It is an attempt to reformulate the governor-governed relationship, one that does not make the relation dependent upon administrative machines, judicial institutions, or other apparatuses that usually get grouped under the rubric of work of the State.
>
> (Bratich, Packer, & McCarthy, 2003, p. 4)

Consequently, what is more significant and interesting about British colonial practice is the variation in the nature and history of governmentality, a point at which colonial administration shifts from being concerned with the structures that comprise and support society as a whole, to a concern that is more focused deliberately on the transformation of individual lives: '. . . the systematic redefinition and transformation of the terrain on which the life of the colonised was lived' (Scott, 2005, p. 25).

Nevertheless, for minority groups such as the Ceylon Tamil and Burgher communities in colonised Ceylon, such distinctions were effectively irrelevant. For them, it was the combination of British government structures and their associated policy foci that became a conduit and enabler for self-empowerment and advancement, rather than being mere visible definers and representations of the British colonial experience.

## B Embedded transnationality: A family case study

One of the common oversimplifications and, therefore, one of the falser assumptions, about Sri Lankan colonialism from the postcolonial perspective is that the European period of imperialism displaced an indigenous society that was both cohesive and composed of a long-established endemic cultural imaginary and practice. However, as examined in Chapters 2 and 3 and demonstrated by more intensive historical accounts such as De Silva (2005, 1973), Ludowyk (1966) and Tennent (1859a, 1859b), the world into which the Europeans entered was far from settled and coherent. To a large degree, the pattern of migration between the island, India and the historical trading centres of the Arab world had been both continuous and in some cases reciprocal. Far from being a territory that was uniquely Sinhalese, with a specific 'Ceylonese' culture, the island that the Dutch called 'Zeylan', and had been known to Arab traders as 'Taprobane', had long been a transnationalised space, both externally and internally, as the continuous waves of migration from India to Ceylon, and the shifting locations and positioning of local kingdoms reflect so clearly (see Chapter 3). The introduction of the Portuguese and Dutch colonial administrations, it can be argued, merely accentuated an existing situation of demographic flux, a positioning that was made even more complex by the time the British period of colonial administration began at the end of the 18th century.

As such, the history of my own family within the *Ceylonese* context is, in some ways, a misnomer, for their very presence in Ceylon at the start of the British colonial period was the consequence of prior transnational activity, mirroring the migratory fluidity that was so evident in pre-European Sri Lanka. My ancestry emanates from a bifurcated cultural and ethnic network, with one branch seemingly embedded within longstanding Ceylon Tamil society, and the other apparently derived from the more recent emergence of the Dutch Burgher community. As with all family histories in which migration plays a major part, however, the transnational aspects of both branches run deep (see Figure 6.1). The complexities and nuances of this family exposition serve as an illustration of how colonial practice could be utilised by the subaltern voice as a deliberate strategy of self-empowerment, with education acting as the pivot.

### *1 The paternal imaginary*

My father's side of the family are Ceylon Tamils, an ancestry that can be traced back to an Indian Hindu merchant/trader called Udayappa Chetty in the mid to late 17th century. The Chettys had been trading out of the Coromandel Coast on

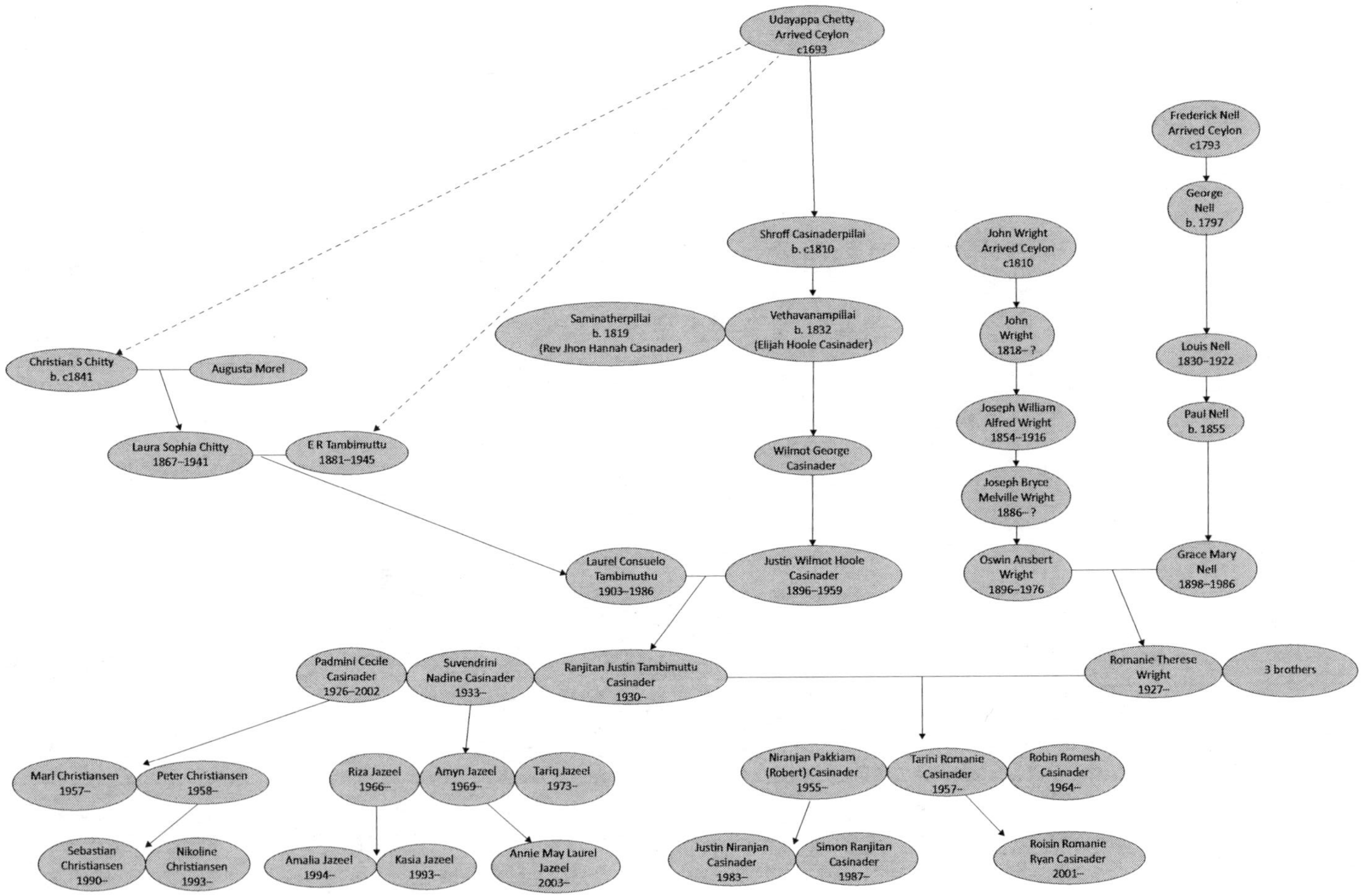


*Figure 6.1* The Casinader-Wright family: A selected family tree

the southeastern Indian margins for some centuries, and so the family was already essentially transnational in action, if not mind. Although Ceylon was already under European colonial rule, the continuing independence of the Kandyan Kingdom – which was located in the central highlands centred on the town of Kandy (see Figure 6.2) – against Portuguese incursions meant that control of the northern coasts and the area around the northeastern port of Trincomalee remained in the hands of the Kandyan King. As colonial rulers, the Portuguese were also less inclined to interfere in existing, longstanding trade relations and networks within the Indian

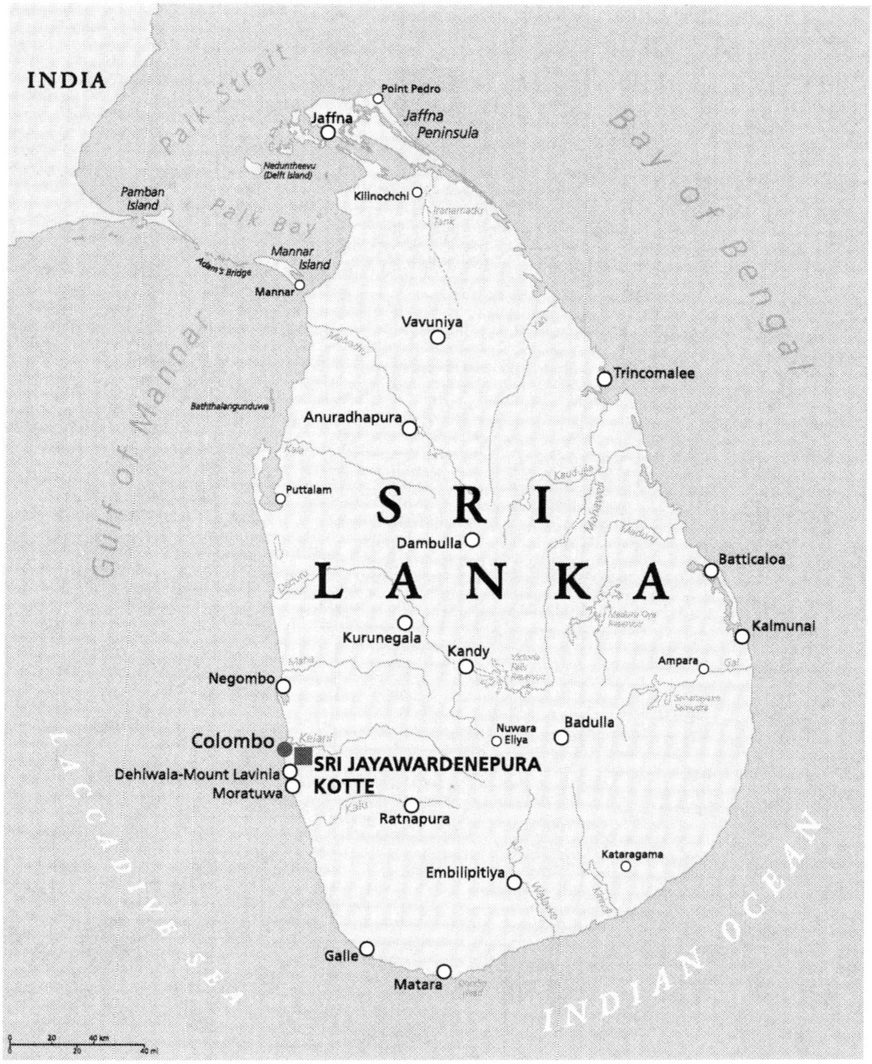


*Figure 6.2* Sri Lanka in the modern age

Ocean, which became a highly globalised territory in the contemporary sense, with participants including Indians, Southeast Asians, Chinese, Persians, Armenians, Arabs and Jewish merchants. Given the value of Ceylon to the spice trade, it can be argued that the coastal regions of the island had long been a transnationalised space, and that to consider pre-European Ceylonese society as a singular Sinhalese entity that had not been exposed to outside influences is highly implausible.

Under the protection of the Kandyan King of the time, Rajasingha II, Udayappa Chetty settled in Kottiyar, near modern-day Trincomalee, on the northeastern coast, in 1693. However, the greater determination of the Dutch, as the next wave of European colonisers, to acquire and maintain monopolistic control of island trade appears to have encouraged a further family shift. By the early to mid-18th century, Chetty and some of his descendants had moved south and settled in the area around Batticaloa on the central eastern coast, redefining themselves as internally focused traders. One of these descendants, Shroff Casinaderpillai (the suffix is a denotation of caste), became the originator of the Casinader clan that now lives across countries as diverse as Sri Lanka (Batticaloa and Colombo), Australia, Canada, New Zealand, the United Kingdom and the United States. At this stage, the family was still Hindu, and the original spelling of the surname (Kasinather or Kasinathan) reflects that.

Augmented by more migrants from the wider Chetty family resident on the Coromandel Coast, where trading had also diminished as the British in India began to trade directly with local producers, bypassing merchants entirely, the Casinaderpillais became part of the dominant clan or local ruling group in the Batticaloa region. The Anglicisation of the name occurred when two of Casinaderpillai's sons converted to Christianity, predominantly in response to the work of the Anglican Church in the Batticaloa region through the London Missionary Society in the early years of British colonial rule. The second son of Shroff Casinaderpillai converted to Christianity and took the name of Elijah Hoole Casinader (see Figure 6.1), and it was his grandson, Justin Wilmot Hoole Casinader, who became my family branch's generational grandfather.

To a degree, it is logical to assume that the extended Casinader family had some advantages in developing a role as intermediaries between the local population and the British colonial authorities, as their experience as traders would have provided them with the confidence and communication skills necessary for them to move easily between the two communities. It is also likely that, just as was the case later in India in the mid-19th century (Seth, 2007), the choice of some (but not all) Casinaders to convert to Christianity was seen as a practical move, for it improved their chances of becoming a member of the local officialdom class and highlighted their willingness to co-operate with the colonial regime. Nonetheless, in these earlier years of British colonial rule, when the vast majority of the island population spoke either Tamil or Sinhalese, opportunities for the Hindu, Tamil-speaking Casinaderpillai clan were limited on the eastern coast around Batticaloa. Since the colonial capital was in Colombo, located on the southwestern coast, where the population was predominantly Sinhalese, the opportunities for local intermediary officials in that part of the island were much higher. This is where the majority of opportunities for further promotion in government employment existed, but they were predominantly available to those who could speak Sinhalese and English, in line with the composition of the local Ceylonese population. In addition, as outlined in Chapter 3, the missionary schools outside Colombo taught in the vernacular languages, and the main English-language schools that provided a pathway to higher education and/or government employment were located in the area around Colombo. Consequently, as Hindu, Tamil-speaking people, the Casinader extended clan around Batticaloa were unable to see government service at the higher levels around the capital as an attainable goal, and focused instead on regional involvement.

The postcolonial perspective would interpret such a situation as representing an example of how British colonial rule was selective in its treatment of local populations, but as was discussed in Chapter 3, educational policy in colonial Ceylon was characterised more by its accessibility to all groups than any pattern of deliberate exclusion. The wider Casinader clan placed their focus on entering the professions and building up their status within the eastern coast communities around Batticaloa, as well as continuing to seek positions in the lower levels of government service. For example, by the end of the 19th century, the number of doctors, lawyers, accountants and engineers throughout my immediate set of family ancestors had increased markedly.

It would be incorrect, however, see all of the Chetty clan taking up leadership positions within the local Tamil communities. The sheer size and complexity of the various arms of the family meant that there would be an inevitable internal hierarchy of success and relative poverty. Although my great-grandfather, Wilmot George Casinader, had a good position in government service as Customs Officer, he died when my grandfather, Justin Wilmot Hoole (JWH) Casinader was about 12 years old. The sudden lack of family income meant that JWH had to sell matches on the street after school in order to help his mother make ends meet, but this only served to intensify his drive to succeed; a determination to improve the life of his mother became a major driver for self-improvement for him. One of the enduring family stories involves the house of the District Engineer in Batticaloa, which arguably can be seen to symbolise the impact that JWH's transnational disposition would have on his life:

> . . . when he was a little boy he was walking past the house with his mother and sister and his mother (Ammah to us), admired the house as it was so beautiful. My father then said to his mother that when he grew up he would buy that house for her to live in. He didn't buy the house, but he certainly brought her to live in it. She came to stay with us and, in fact, died there.
>
> (Suvendrini Jazeel, personal communication, January 17, 2016)

## 2 *The maternal imaginary*

As outlined previously, the family connections on the paternal side of my ancestral family tree had their origins firmly located in the middle of the European colonial period in Ceylon, and the same temporal pattern is evident on the maternal line (see Figure 6.1), with both threads of my mother's forebears arriving in Ceylon in the years straddling the dawn of the 19th century. However, the complexities of that side of the family history have been characterised by a constant dichotomy based largely on religion.

My maternal grandfather, Oswin Ansbert Wright, was a Catholic who was excommunicated by the Jesuit church in Ceylon for marrying my grandmother, a Protestant, and choosing to teach in a Protestant school (Trinity College in Kandy). It was his great-great-grandfather, John Wright, who had arrived in Ceylon, early in the 19th century, as Bombardier in the 207th Regiment of Artillery. John Wright the Elder was Protestant, and it was not until his son, also named John, married the daughter of the Portuguese Consul-General in 1843 that the line of Catholicism became established. It was the successive progeny of this marriage, including my grandfather, which maintained the Catholic faith. It is interesting to note that other members of the Wright family stayed staunchly Protestant throughout multiple marriages and births, with a number of weddings taking place in the main Dutch Reformed Church as the Wrights married into the existing Dutch Burgher community.

In contrast, the ancestry on the side of Grace Nell, my maternal grandmother, was classically Protestant, with the Nells descended from French Huguenots who had emigrated initially to the Cape Colony in what is now South Africa. Frederick August Nell arrived from the Cape Colony in 1793, on the cusp of the transition from Dutch to British colonial rule. He was Major-Domo to the leader of a Swiss mercenary regiment that was, at that time, providing its services to the VOC (Vereenigde Oost-Indische Compagnie). This United East Indian Company (or, as the British referred to it, the Dutch East Indies Company) controlled and administered the Dutch administration on the island (Wright Mulvaney, 2006). Frederick Nell married into the Dutch Burgher community, which, at that time, was firmly domiciled in the region surrounding Colombo, extending southwards to the port of Galle, as well as in the northern Jaffna Peninsula (see Figure 6.2)

The European connections that fostered collaborative relationships between the Dutch Burgher community and the new British administration meant there was little reason or incentive for this emerging cultural group on the island to move beyond the European colonial heartland in the early years of British administration. When the Dutch relinquished control of the island officially in 1802 after the Treaty of Amiens, a number of the Dutch Burgher community members chose to leave rather than stay in Ceylon under the British. However, approximately 900 families remained, required to swear allegiance to the British administration in order to do so. Since English was now the language of governance, the Burgher community was quick to move away from Dutch as their language of choice, leading them well-placed to take up positions within the developing and growing colonial British administration. When the island's colonial authorities under Governor Robert Brownrigg were able to acquire control over the Kandyan Kingdom in 1815, thereby bringing the island under a single administration for the first time, the Burgher community was able to move into the region within and around the hill capital of Kandy, taking advantage of the new opportunities that arose within the provincial civil service and the professions serving the diffused leadership elite, and it was in Kandy that my mother was born and raised.

It should be noted here that the Dutch Burgher community is not strictly an ethnic group, like the Ceylon Tamils or Sinhalese, but more of a cultural grouping with the mindset of a people that saw themselves closely allied with the European, and more specifically, the British, way of life. The influx of British people over the 19th century, whether for military, administrative or commercial reasons, helped to reinforce that identity as the two groups coalesced in terms of perspective and intermarriage. The term 'Burgher', which in its original form, applied only to descendants of Dutch citizens who had intermarried with local Sinhalese, or those that descended from earlier Portuguese colonialists, came to include all those Europeans from Great Britain, France and Germany who had strong Protestant convictions, particularly those of John Calvin, and who had consequently married into the existing Burgher population. Indeed, it was not until 1883 that the British administration formulated a legal definition of the group. Under the census conducted in that year, Burghers were legally defined as those who had fathers born in Sri Lanka who had at least one direct European ancestor. The ethnic origin of the mother was of no consequence (Lee, 1882), and meant that virtually all Burghers have surnames that are European, not only Portuguese, Dutch and British, but also French, German and even Russian.

## C Embedded transnationality: The family experience

In searching for patterns of transnational behaviour and experience throughout this family history, two distinct yet interdependent patterns emerge: the willingness and desire (however subconscious) to negate the value of place as part of one's identity if an action leads to the improvement of one's life and the circumstances; and the ways in which the character of British colonial administration in Ceylon created the conditions of governmentality that were necessary for those aims to be created and enacted, especially in the context of religion and education. Binding these two threads of transnationality together was the centrality of education as the main determinant of the strategy to be adopted to attain those improvements, whatever the context.

### *1 The ambiguity of place*

The frequency, speed and diverse spatiality of this family story of migration over the generations exemplifies the contention, as outlined in Chapter 1, that transnationalism is far from a modern phenomenon that has emerged out of the contemporary phase of globalisation. One of the key principles underpinning the revised concept of an embedded transnationality is the disaggregation of the concept and meaning of 'place', both geographically and emotionally, in the construction of an individual's identity. On that score, the history of both sides of my ancestry suggest strong indications that they possessed a strong internal sense of embedded transnationality, a mind-centred approach to self-improvement that was not tied umbilically to any sense of location.

Between the beginning of the 17th century, when the progenitor of this particular branch of the Casinader family found a more permanent foothold in northern Ceylon, and the latter part of the 20th century, the diverse and widespread branches of the clan have shifted from localised origins in Europe (specifically Derbyshire and France) and the southeastern coast of India to a diffused presence across the United Kingdom, continental Europe, Southern Africa, and Australasia. In addition, from the time of the originator of the extended paternal clan in Ceylon, Udayappa Chetty, who was ready to move from long-established family surroundings in Southeast India to take advantage of the commercial opportunities offered by association with the monarchy of Kandyan Kingdom, that movement appears to have been guided as much as by utilitarianism and the opportunities generated in new locations as by any push factors; it was a relocation founded more on intent than rejection. Throughout these shifts, the primary driving forces have been the improvement of life and living standards, and the capacity to sustain a higher quality of life. In the years prior to British colonial rule, the avenue to this improvement followed a largely mercantile pattern, reinforced by the advantages of gaining positions in the intermediary levels of government service, as seen during the British administration. The major shift, however, that came with the introduction of British colonial administration and its accompanying governmentality, was a centralised realisation and focus that education, particularly in the English language, would be more fruitful and long-lasting as a pathway to follow. Contrary to the dominant postcolonial critique, whether subaltern or not, the opportunity to displace the existing education system was not perceived as one of cultural loss, or negation of identity, but more as a utilitarian acceptance of reality combined with the greater primacy of the wish to create and essentialise a higher quality of life.

In the case of the Casinader family, the sequence of fundamental movements illustrates this contention clearly. The shift of the original Chetty group from the Trincomalee region on the northeast coast further south to the area on the central eastern coastline around Batticaloa in the mid-18th century was largely necessitated by the Dutch introduction of a highly restrictive policy on island trade, one which limited the opportunities of non-Dutch traders considerably. In this region outside the direct gaze of Dutch rule, which was more focused on other parts of the island such as the western and northern coasts, the Chetty clan was able to reinvent itself as an internal trading force. By the time that Great Britain became the ruling colonial power, various branches of the family had established themselves throughout the local leadership group, with positions such as '. . . Adigars, Mudilyars, Vanniahs, Shroffs, Kanakepulles . . . ' (R. A. Casinader, circa 2003, p. 5). As a result, they were ideally placed to take advantage of lower-level intermediary positions in the Dutch and British colonial administrations. Government employment was not only a symbol of status, but was also a source of stability of employment and income that further consolidated the leadership status of the family members involved.

Although the larger family contingent remained centred around Batticaloa, more recent generations have also demonstrated a sense of that embedded transnationality. My paternal grandfather, Justin Willmot Hoole Casinader (JWH) enlisted in the Ceylon Light Infantry at the start of World War I, and two years later transferred to the Ceylon Artillery Volunteers. At that stage, he was an indentured engineering apprentice working in various workshops in Colombo, in addition to attending Government Technical College (R.J.T. Casinader, 2006) In May 1917, however, JWH wrote to the Director of Public Works asking for permission to enlist for war service in the British Army and active combat in Europe. His sole motivation for this determination and a willingness to travel across the world was not imperial glory, as was the case for some in white settler British colonies such as Australia and Canada, but the knowledge that, unlike the Ceylon armed services, service in the British Army would guarantee him the offer of a tertiary education in civil engineering at war's end. From all accounts, the possibility that he might have died before the fighting ended does not seem to have entered his calculations. The possibility of education as a means of transformation into another future better life was enough motivation. Later on, when he was a district engineer for the Public Works Department of Ceylon, JWH and my grandmother, Laurel Tambimuttu, maintained the principle of embedded transnationality as they moved from town to town across Ceylon as my grandfather moved up the engineering ladder.

On the matrilineal line, a similar combination of push and pull factors appears regarding transnational movement of the family strands towards their coalescence in Ceylon in the late 1800s. There was, nevertheless, a lesser emphasis on spatial movement as a means of life development beyond the initial arrival of the Nells and Wrights in Ceylon. The greater localisation of the two families in central and southwest Ceylon, as discussed earlier, was more a reflection of their historical synergy as a Burgher (originally Dutch Burgher) community that was innately connected to the existence of the Dutch and British colonial cohort. Although the first two arrivals – John Wright and Frederick Nell – had military positions that brought them to the island, the succession of generations highlights a very close relationship between the family and positions in governance or the professions that worked so closely with the colonial administrators. Amongst the Nells was the mid-19th century Crown counsel of Ceylon, Louis Nell, as well as lawyers, doctors, eye surgeons, engineers, customs officers and politicians. A similar range can be found amongst the Wrights, a list of professions that included surgeons, medical practitioners, coffee planters, surveyors, police inspectors and teachers. Consequently, there was no perceived need for them to shift location in the search for more life opportunities within the context of British colonial rule. Local opportunities existed, and a more privileged position as a cultural group that was highly educated in English and European traditions gave natural advantages that did not exist to the same extent for Tamil or Sinhalese families elsewhere on the island.

## 2 *The centrality of education and Church: Governmentality as facilitator*

The two lines of lineage described in the first part of this chapter present a comparison that highlights a particular dichotomy; that is, two sociocultural groups that, in terms of the cultural mix of colonial Sri Lanka, formed two key minorities for whom education became a means for building a life profile with more opportunity for improved quality of life within the context of colonial rule. For the Ceylon Tamils on the eastern coast, however, access to the particular form of education that had cachet in the British context – English language education – was, for the majority, only accessible through translocation, and was therefore more difficult to enact. Ceylon Tamils who lived in the Colombo or Jaffna regions had, access to resources aside, a pathway to the system of English language schools that had been established by the British (both government and missionary) to educate local Ceylonese for lower-level governmental positions. These schools were firmly centred on Colombo, and later on, Kandy and Jaffna in the central highlands and north, respectively, but this was not the case in Batticaloa.

The willingness of 19th-century members of my immediate Batticaloa ancestors to move to wherever was needed in order to obtain that educational edge suggests a highly developed embedded transnationality, one that was independent of any practical, emotional or spiritual links to place, regardless of how deep the roots that the family might have to a particular location. As addressed earlier, the determination of my grandfather to go to war in Europe with the aim of getting a free tertiary education was one example. Nevertheless, there were earlier illustrations. My paternal grandmother, Laurel Consuelo Tambimuttu (see Figure 6.1), came from a family that was also connected to the Casinaderpillai tree, albeit very distant from the Casinaders themselves. Her father, E. R. Tambimuttu, was a lawyer and national politician who was well-known and respected amongst the East Coast Tamil community. However, he was born into a poor, if devoutly Anglican, family and was well aware that, if he was to advance in life to any significant extent, he would have to find a way to gain an English language education. As a child, he was determined to find a way of achieving that educational Nirvana, and in this, showed a significant degree of innovation and determination. In the late 1880s, he became aware that the Anglican Bishop was making one of his regular tours through eastern Ceylon, and contrived to meet him. Having asked for assistance, the family story outlines how E. R. was told to be in Colombo at a certain time and place, which appears to have been – if true – some form of device to test the young boy's commitment. E. R. was at the appointed place at the appropriate time, and ending up having his schooling sponsored by the Bishop throughout.

> There's an interesting story about E.R. because he went to school in Batticaloa . . . and he knew that to get anywhere he had to come to Colombo where the English speaking schools were. The story is that the Bishop did a tour of the country every so often. He came to Batticaloa and he stayed

> in a town or a village quite close to the city. My grandfather – that's E.R. – explained that he walked all the way, 10 or 15 miles, to go and see the Bishop, who was so impressed by the fact that his interest in education was such that he would travel all that way to come and see him, that he then helped my grandfather to get a better education in Colombo.
>
> (R.J.T. Casinader, personal communication, March 28, 2015)

As a result of his education in Colombo, which was sponsored by the Bishop, E. R. was able to begin his rise through the legal profession, and eventually entered national politics on the State Council of Ceylon as a representative of the Batticaloa and East Coast Tamil communities, establishing himself as a member of the local and national Ceylonese social, political and economic leadership. It was an example of how the drive for an education displaced any feelings of attachment to 'place' that might have prevented others from making a similar move, an exposition of intra-transnationality.

Perhaps the most forceful indication of how education was seen by many Ceylon Tamils as an empowering force in the Ceylonese context at this time was indicated by the unusually progressive attitudes of E. R. Tambimuttu towards his children's education. As discussed in Chapter 3, the conservatism of traditional Tamil and Sinhalese society had long placed the education of women as a very low priority. Despite the fact that one of the major achievements of British education in Ceylon was the development of educational structures for girls (see Chapter 3), such elements of British governmentality, which were aligned with social attitudes in Britain itself, focused on the provision of primary education for girls, with secondary opportunities limited to the major colonial administrative centres. However, as my grandmother reflected, 'My father believed in a liberal education for girls and boys and [as a young girl] encouraged me to use the [Batticaloa] library which was at that time the most well equipped in Ceylon barring Jaffna . . .' (Casinader, L., 1986, p. 5). Later, towards the end of the first World War, these priorities were reinforced when she and her brother were sent to board at two of the English-language schools in Colombo (Bishop's and Royal Colleges). The educational imprimatur was echoed later on when Laurel and her husband (JWH) chose to place my father, Ranjitan Justin Tambimuttu, in boarding school at St Thomas' College in Colombo at the age of four, accompanied by his ayah, or nanny, at the time when my grandfather was being moved regularly in his job as a District Engineer.

The singularity of E. R.'s attitudes towards education in contemporary Ceylon Tamil circles was emphasised by the comparative way in which the education of young women was addressed by other members of the Casinader family. Three of my grandmother's female cousins were taken out of school and home-schooled by governesses because of their father's displeasure in the fact that they were attracting too much male attention, even though my grandmother thought them to be more intelligent than she (Casinader, L., 1986). The contrast was highlighted even further when, in the early 1920s, Laurel was encouraged by her father to become one of the first group of six women to be educated at the newly-formed University of Ceylon, which was, at that time, affiliated with the University of London. She was one of two who finally graduated, majoring in the then-new science of Economics. This educational focus itself was highly contentious in the context of a society where women, whatever their ethnicity or background, were not seen as being capable in the areas of finance and business. E. R. was not without some affinity with social convention, though, as Laurel could only attend university if she was being chaperoned by her '. . . ayah [nanny], appu or brother' (Casinader, L., 1986, p. 7). In education, however, E. R. was immune to gender-based traditions, ignoring the entreaties of his friends that Laurel would '. . . become a blue stocking and no-one would marry [her]' (Casinader, L., 1986, p. 7).

A similar determination to emphasise the practicalities of educational success can later be observed in the actions of my own father, who, having done well in the final secondary school examinations overseen by the University of London, was offered a future engineering place at the new local university in two years' time, once the Department had been formed, or else a place at Cambridge University the very next year. In the environment of the day, making the move to live and study in a different country was not as straightforward as it is in the modern era. Quite apart from the cost of living overseas, my father had only been outside Ceylon once in his life, when his parents had taken the family for a holiday to Bangalore in India. When he accepted the Cambridge offer for 1949, a string of family events confluenced in the decision by my grandparents to accompany all three of their children to England, as the two eldest (my father and his elder sister) would be both undertaking tertiary degrees (R.J.T. Casinader, personal communication, March 28, 2015; Suvendrini Jazeel, personal communication, January 17, 2016). Any apprehensions about living and working in England were, to some extent, mollified by my grandfather's previous experience as an apprentice engineer in Sheffield, but whether this readiness was also inspired by the imperial connection to Britain, as postcolonial historical critiques might suggest, is a moot point, and will be discussed later in this chapter.

On the Burgher side of my ancestry, such transportability of desire in terms of education is less obvious to see, partly for reasons already discussed. Nevertheless, the very nature of the family occupations and positions in government are very clear statements that education was central to their lives and existence, especially that which was offered by the religious schools, both Catholic and Protestant. The stronghold of the original Dutch Reformed Church in Colombo, Wolvendaal, along with others such as Holy Trinity Church, had become one of the favoured sites of Buddhist ceremonies such as marriage for the Burgher community, and the Nells were no exception. Trinity College in Kandy, at which my grandfather taught, became the focal point of the Burgher community in central Ceylon, and even today, is a rallying point for sections of the Burgher diaspora, especially those who emigrated after Independence in 1948. However, whilst a unifier of the Burgher communities, education in the colonial era was not the transformative avenue that it was for those in the Ceylon Tamil community who were able to utilise it. Education was the connecting sinew between Burgher and the British way of life, and in that context, it can be seen more as the last bastion of community unity and advantage between the Burghers and Sri Lankan society. Consequently, the nationalist push that saw English replaced by Sinhalese and Tamil as the first language of instruction in schools and universities from 1955, except for the teaching of Science, Mathematics and Western languages (Sumathipala, 1968, p. 401), eradicated the fundamental raison d'être for the Burgher community in modern Sri Lanka, and produced a major wave of diasporic emigration to countries such as Australia, Canada and the United Kingdom.

One aspect that perhaps defines the embedded transnationality of both lines of my ancestry more than any other, however, is more a mirrored reflection of that de-spatialised perspective than a direct consequence of it. The inherent cultural and ethnic mix that characterises both families, particularly in my mother's familial connections, further highlight the social complexities that were in place by the time British colonialism arrived on the island. It also further exemplifies the argument that many of the peoples who became incorporated into British imperialism were far from being defined local entities whose lives and positions were upended by British colonial practice. The plurality of pre-British Ceylonese society was more complex and diverse that the trope of Sinhalese nationalism allows. For example, there is a strong French and central European influence on both ancestral lines of the family that extends well beyond the axis group of French and German Huguenots that were the origin of one side of my matrilineal line. My great-grandfather, Paul Nell, married an Englishwoman, and one of his daughters married a Sinhalese lawyer, George de Silva, who was later elected to the Ceylon State Council and became a Minister in the country's first post-independence cabinet. The eponymously-named son of the original John Wright married the daughter of the Consul-General of Portugal, bringing in the thread of Catholicism. Ceylonese society was very much in flux and undergoing change well before the onset of British colonial rule.

With the Tamil family network, it would be logical to assume that there was a greater sense of ethnic insularity, given that the relative isolation of the family on the Batticaloa Coast, removed from the centre of socio-political power in the southwest, did not expose the wider family to a great variety of influences. For those who either moved to the Colombo-Kandy colonial axis, or who were descendants of the same, similar signs of ethnic and cultural diversity did become evident, reinforcing the family's European ancestry and connection to European – if not British – ideas in ways independent of any place: It was the people themselves who were important. For example, my father's maternal great-grandfather, Suppramanian Chetty, was a wealthy Ceylon Hindu Tamil in early-19th century Colombo who converted to Christianity in order to marry Augusta Morel, a Frenchwoman whose blue eyes were a topic of interest amongst her grandchildren (Casinader, L., 1986). The Morels were descendants of another wave of French émigrés, loyalists who were exiled to French colonies such as Mauritius during the Napoleonic era. Following the Battle of Waterloo, the loyalists were forced to emigrate in a bid to rebuild their lives. Augusta (or 'Mitzie') was one of those who came to Ceylon with her father and the rest of her family, encouraged by a fellow French émigré from Mauritius who had already made a successful journey to Ceylon (Casinader, L., 1986).

With Tamils, Burghers and Sinhalese marrying into this complex cultural and ethnic mix, the more visible aspects of the family's transnational character had been firmly established by the early 20th century. With the modern phase of globalisation that emerged after World War II, however, the eclectic ethnic nature of these supposedly essentialised Tamil and Burgher families became even more actualised after Independence in 1948. The implications and impact of these more modern manifestations of embedded transnationality are evident in the creation of the cultural identity, or perceived identity, of the more recent generations, and it is in this aspect that the notion of place as an identifier of self becomes even more obtuse. By the early 1950s, my father, aunts and grandparents were living in London, a move at first initiated by the combination of the desire by my paternal grandparents to monitor the tertiary education of their eldest daughter, Padmini, whilst my father attended university. It was also at this time that my mother was travelling around Europe, inspired by the ideas that had come principally from her father, a teacher of Latin and Greek, about European – and predominantly British – centres of learning. From that time forward, the rate of de-spatialisation and intensification of ethnic and cultural diversity exploded, facilitated and encouraged by the opportunities emerging through the new world order in the 1960s, but nevertheless, I would argue, nurtured by that embedded transnational sensibility.

During the 1960s, my eldest aunt married a Dane and moved to Copenhagen, and nearly all my mother's immediate and wider Burgher family had emigrated to Australia, following on from the footsteps of a great-uncle on my mother's side who had moved to the area around Goulburn, New South Wales, in the early 1900s. This large-scale migration was part of the diasporic Burgher leaving of Sri Lanka as Sinhalese nationalism and ideology came to dominate island life in a direct response to the perceived imposition of Britishness during the colonial period. By the 1970s, the immediate branches of my own family were spread across Australia, the United Kingdom and Denmark, and the ethnic-cultural constancy that had remained essentially consolidated prior to World War II was now beginning to meander across the globe into far more pluralistic contexts.

In reality, this plurality of identity, which I would posit is inextricably linked to an increasingly de-emphasised identity of place, began with my parents' generation, freed up by the combination of the evolving internationalisation of global society after World War II and the possibilities of life outside Ceylon that had been generated progressively throughout the British colonial period. In an ironic contrast to the family history prior to World War II, this diversification of identity is more directly evident on the Tamil side of my family than the Burgher. Aside from my aunt who married a Dane and, as a result, made her life in Denmark – highly unusual for the late 1950s – my father's younger sister (an Anglican) married a Muslim Sri Lankan who was living in England. In an interesting contrast to possible reactions in a contemporary world that is having difficulty responding to the existence of ISIL (the Islamic State), a relationship between a Christian and a

Muslim in 1960s Sri Lanka was far more of an issue than differences in ethnicity. My father's second marriage is to an Australian of English descent, whilst my mother continued to exemplify her own embedded transnationality in her unique style. Having been initially married to a Frenchman, her future marriages were to Australians of German and English/Irish descent.

The pattern becomes even more acute in my own generation, born in the period from the mid-1950s to the mid-1960s. What is perhaps particularly noticeable, is that, except for one instance, none of the eight members of this generation has married or had longstanding relationships with anyone of Sri Lankan heritage or background, even though, for the most part, we have all lived in regions of the world with very strongly defined Sri Lankan communities. Between us, the siblings and cousins who live in Australia, United Kingdom and Denmark currently have partnered up with European Australians of Irish, Dutch, English and German descent, as well as those with French Canadian, Polish English, Danish and Spanish heritage. As one cousin in the United Kingdom explains it,

> We all grew up in neighbourhoods that were . . . quite ethnically homogenous, quite white, so it's not like we grew up in big South-Asian communities, or big Sri Lankan communities. Most of my friends growing up were white. There was that experience of growing up in very nice, well-to-do, middle class suburbs. We were fitting in, that's what our parents wanted us to do, was fit in, to be British, in some senses. Maybe that has something to do with the fact that we didn't couple up with other Sri Lankans.
>
> (Tariq Jazeel, personal communication, October 31, 2015)

More particularly, his brother highlights the connections that inevitably exist between people of hybrid origins:

> I've always thought it's quite interesting that my ex-wife and Rik's current wife are both children or immigrants, albeit not Sri Lankans. My current girlfriend, who although Sri Lankan, has spent most of the 24 years of her life in the UK. I do feel that there's a sort of commonality between children of immigrants. I think they're called – what are they called? Third culture kids.
>
> (Riza Jazeel, personal communication, October 12, 2015)

In many respects, this greater ethnic and cultural plurality is a localised manifestation of the hybridity of cultural identity that has been long identified as a consequence of intensified globalisation of human activity and behaviour (Bhabha, 1994), and in that sense, is not unexpected. However, some commentators have argued that this hybridity or diffusion of identity has not come at the expense of personal de-association with a sense of original place, similar to the prevailing definition of transnationalism as embodying a deep connection with the place of origin after migration (see Chapter 1). In the case of embedded transnationality, however, any connection with place tends to be diluted, with association or identification with place being more symbiotic with connections to people and relationships in that place, rather than the geographical space itself. Identity, cultural or otherwise, is constructed on the notion of place, but not defined by place.

## D De-spatialised identities

### *1 Early years*

If the family disposition towards transnationality was activated by the onset of the modern phase of globalisation and its ultimate beginnings in the context of British colonial rule, one of the more interesting contrasts can be seen in the comparison of the concepts of identity as expressed by the three 20th-century generations of the family on both sides: the colonial generation (my grandparents); the post-war generation (that of my parents) and the current adult generation to which I belong. Contrary to the strand of postcolonial discourse that argues that British imperialism imposed sets of values and ways of being that were inherently British, superseding indigenous cognitive and societal frameworks, the dominant theme in the colonial and post-war generations is that their initial cultural identities were firmly located in the Ceylon island context, but not the British. For Justin and Laurel Casinader, as well as Oswin and Grace Wright (see Figure 6.2), their self-identification as Ceylonese within the extended British imaginary was acute; they did not see themselves as British, but more as 'reflections of the Raj' (Wright Mulvaney, 2006).

For my paternal grandfather, that connection was accentuated by the ties that he developed as a result of his army service in Europe and the years spent in Sheffield during his engineering apprenticeship, and was a distinct consideration in the family's move to Britain in the 1950s as support for their two eldest children obtaining a tertiary degree in Britain. The identification of themselves as Ceylonese, and not British, can be seen in other facets of the family story. Despite being very much part of what imperial historians would call the local leadership 'elite', E. R. Tambimuttu did not have total acceptance of all aspects of British cultural identity, reiterating the deliberate distance that he placed between his background and British societal principles. As young women, my grandmother and her friends were often invited to '. . . all the invitations to the Governor's functions and all upper strata society activities . . . ' because the '. . . wives of the upper echelons of the English administrative service began to take an interest in the indigenous educated Ceylonese . . . ' (Casinader, L., 1986, p. 6). However, my great-grandfather displayed a disdain for the arts as defined by the colonial power, refusing to allow his daughter to dance with young men:

> You see my dear, I understand Tamil music – it has rhythm and rhyme. English music to me is only cacophony of sound and noise with no meaning. So when I hear this and see a young man pull my daughter to her feet, hug her to his bosom and run around the room, I feel like thrashing him.
>
> (Casinader, L., 1986, p. 7)

This dichotomous and selective attitude towards 'Britishness' existed despite, or in spite of, the psychological reach of the colonial imaginary, suggesting that there was, to some extent, a sense of separation, but no conflict, between the Ceylonese and British identity. The view that this disposition was a reflection of the Tamils being a minority ethnic group that had gained traction from being part of the British imperial period was brought into sharper relief later on, when my grandparents and their children went to live more permanently in Britain in the 1950s. As a cultural geographer, my cousin Tariq has published on the work and social context of our grandmother (Jazeel, 2006) and his evaluation as to the impact of the family shift on their sense of self is clear; opposing notions of Britishness as perceived in the 'homeland' and colony came into stark contrast:

> The point is that it was one space. And the British worked hard at making it one space, forcibly and ideologically. . . . I do get the sense that there was this ambivalence, I think you're right, an ambivalence about place for people like Pati (Laurel) until they came up against the real difficulties of buying a loaf of bread in the neighbourhood, when they were so obviously very culturally different. These were people who enjoyed a lot of privilege in Ceylon, who had come to the UK and then they're marked out . . .
>
> (Tariq Jazeel, personal communication, October 30, 2015)

What is also evident from her unpublished memoirs is that our grandmother, who went to 'work' for the first time in her life when she went to London, became far more acutely aware of the class and social divisions within British society as a result. Working in the account frauds backroom at Harrods, '. . . the cross-questioning of people [she] met – from a Colonel's wife to the bricklayer's daughter . . . ' meant that she '. . . really began to understand the problems of working women and the frustrations of youth . . . ', whilst ignoring those '. . . among the men some retired colonels who were very obnoxious . . . much to their chagrin' (Casinader, L., 1986, p. 14)

Her later work with the Commonwealth Institute in London as a lecturer to school groups and organisations '. . . gave [her] an insight into British family life from those of aristocrats to building workers, all of which were interesting, amusing sometimes and also enab[ling her] to give most of them a different idea of Easterners' (Casinader, L., 1986, p. 14). The sense of being distinctly Ceylonese, as opposed to being British, was still pronounced. It was not until she was confronted personally with the reality of the worst of communal violence whilst on a visit to Sri Lanka in 1983 that her sense of Britishness superseded any Ceylonese affiliation, and she gave up her Sri Lankan passport. The Ceylon that she had known, in which the cohesion and equity within a diverse community had been maintained by British governmentality, was now non-existent, replaced by a more strident, violent form of Sinhalese Sri Lankan nationalism.

As might expected from the historical symbiosis between the Dutch Burghers and European colonialism, the centrality of the British consciousness within the Wrights and Nells in the 1914–18 generation was more explicitly defined than in the Tamil, but the dichotomy between celebration and rejection of different aspects of the British imaginary was still evident. It was not a case of unthinking acceptance of an imposed perspective and rationale of life, but more of a critical evaluation of all aspects of Ceylonese society, utilising the principle of reasoned exploration of ideas that was inevitably embedded in the British-influenced education system that all had experienced.

For example, my great-grandfather, Paul Nell, was a '. . . liberal and cultivated man who had little time for the false distinctions of Victorian society . . . [and] affirmed his independent spirit by befriending those who were marginalized by the conventions of the time' (Wright Mulvaney, 2006, p. 5) One of the least attractive characteristics of 19th-century British society that the Burghers had adopted was a sense of class difference, although this was, in many ways, not too divorced from the traditional caste structures at the heart of the Sinhalese and Tamil societies that existed prior to European colonisation. Paul Nell, in a rejection of such attitudes, supported the marriage of his eldest daughter, Agnes, to an up-and-coming Sinhalese lawyer, George de Silva, who later became an important political figure in the government of the newly independent Ceylon. My grandfather Oswin was a classics scholar, a teacher who was fluent in Latin and ancient Greek and a lover of English literature, as well as being a well- known cricketer who broke national batting records in the 1913–15 era. But he was also a breaker of convention, a Roman Catholic who married a Protestant and was excommunicated for his sense of independence. Obedience to the societal conventions of a colonial society formed within the bubble of British intellectual ideas was not, therefore, a unilateral characteristic of the Burgher community.

## *2 Post-war transnationality*

The transnationality of the Great War family generation was reflected more in their determination to use education as a means of improvement rather than any desire to detach themselves from British colonial identity. Nevertheless, it might be expected that their children, the post-World War I family group, all of whom were born in the last 20 years of British rule in Ceylon and witnessed the transition to independence as adults, would show a deeper attachment to the British imaginary, but this is not the case. Instead, despite having lived their lives embedded within a bubble of British colonialism, they maintained a far more *distinct* identification with being *Ceylonese*, an identity that persisted alongside other feelings related to any 'British' mindset.

Such a perspective, on the face of it, contradicts the probability that the cumulative effect of over 100 years of British colonial education might have created am almost seamless British imaginary within the last generation of colonisation. Instead, it was more the reality of the evolution of their lives, and the relationships established, that generated any gradual shift in identity. Consequently, when he left the place of his birth to go to university in Great Britain, my father

> . . . just felt like I was Ceylonese in Britain. [As a child], I was more aware that I was Ceylonese. I didn't for a moment think I was English, or – anyways,

> it was not relevant to think I was British. I was – although I was obviously aware that Sri Lanka, Ceylon, was part of the British Empire.
>
> (R.J.T. Casinader, personal communication, March 28, 2015)

Alongside this sureness of self is also another facet of an embedded transnationality, a confidence to be oneself and not dependent upon an artificial construction for the sake of others: 'What is British? I don't feel the need to define myself, in a way' (R.J.T. Casinader, personal communication, March 28, 2015). Even now, in his later years, he sees himself as being '. . . Sri Lankan-British-Australian, because it seems irrelevant to me whether you're one or the other . . . ' (R.J.T. Casinader, personal communication, March 28, 2015). The order of identities – in a classic reflection of a civil engineer's mind, all his ideas are arranged sequentially, not emotionally – is simply governed by no more than the chronology of his life. In hindsight, it is this the same sense of grounded identity of 'place-less-ness' that has enabled my father to treat any sign of prejudice towards him on the basis of colour or race with total disdain:

> I don't think that [he] has ever seen anybody as having some sort of racist thing towards him. He has the ability to override anything like that in an amazing way. A person is not worth it – what they said isn't worth worrying about. It's like a total blindness, and it's as if you're sure of yourself, you don't see it. That's their sad problem, not his. There are things that I've thought, "That person's being racist," but he just ignores it.
>
> (Jennifer Casinader, personal communication, March 28, 2015)

In contrast to her brother, however, my paternal aunt developed a more place-focused transnationality, in line with the term's current prevailing associations with the maintenance of links between locations of origin and destination (see Chapter 1). Throughout her schooldays and early adulthood in Britain, she

> . . . remained Ceylonese. I was proud of being a Ceylonese . . . Never thought of [the British Empire]. You think differently. At that stage, the fact is the British Empire and all that didn't actually affect me at all, you know, because all of my personal life and what I was going to do.
>
> (Suvendrini Jazeel, personal communication, January 17, 2016)

For both my father and his sister, the concept or existence of the British Empire, or its legacy, had little impact on their eventual decisions to define themselves other than Ceylonese much later in their lives. For my aunt, it is more a matter of liking where she is living, the life that she is leading and being close to the people who are important to her:

> I started working in hospitals and I liked it very much, and it was a gradual process of thinking "well this is my life, this is my country", you know. I can't tell you when it happened, but I think I gradually considered myself British. British of Sri Lankan origin.
>
> (Suvendrini Jazeel, personal communication, January 17, 2016)

Even so, she and my late uncle maintained a constant connection with Sri Lanka by going back to visit his family and their friends on a regular basis, and her identification with being Ceylonese remains undiminished, if specifically place-based:

> I remember Batticaloa so well. Throughout my later life, I seem to have always considered Batticaloa as "where I came from" – my hometown. I'm not quite certain why. My father was from Batticaloa. My mother's father was from Batticaloa, although my grandmother was a Colombo Chetty. I lived in Batticaloa only for about 3 years, I think, from the age of 7 to 9 or 10. But somehow I keep telling people that I'm from Batticaloa. Perhaps it was because of the ethnic conflict going on in Sri lanka, and my desire to be identified as a Tamil from Batticaloa, and the pride that my father had in his hometown. Also, because I was older, I remember so much more about Batticaloa – the house we lived in, the friends who came there, the people we knew. I was a person in my own right by then.
>
> (Suvendrini Jazeel, personal communication, January 17, 2016)

Similar ambivalences, reflecting a more critical evaluation towards British colonialism, whilst acknowledging and identifying very clearly with its perceived benefits, can be found within my mother's Burgher family. Like their father, her brothers were successful scholars in the classics tradition, one gaining a scholarship to Oxford, following the colonial path to higher education, as well as being high achievers in the classic British sports of cricket and rugby. However, my mother, in particular, was highly critical of what she perceived to be the divisive aspects of British administration. She saw herself as a Burgher living in a British-influenced society, and the essence of rational thought that was the foundation of British societal attitudes and educational curriculum was activated within her to a high degree:

> An independent spirit grew within me which in a strange way set me apart. I never wanted to be part of the herd – and the herd was happy to exclude me.
>
> (Wright Mulvaney, 2006, p. 22)

The school in Kandy in which my grandfather taught, and the community in which my mother and her siblings grew up, was '. . . a faithful echo of an English public school . . . ' (Wright Mulvaney, 2006, p. 24), and as such embodied some of the contemporary morals and practices of such institutions, such as calling all male servants, regardless of age, 'Boy'. Despite the fact that she abhorred such class distinctions –

> To me it reeked of patronage, but such a term was common across the British colonised world . . .
>
> (Wright Mulvaney, 2006, p. 35)

– our mother still accepted it as an inevitable aspect of the British colonial life that, in fact, created the school community in which she believes she was happiest.

The school's principal during her childhood was an Oxford-educated, Scottish clergyman, the Rev J. McLeod Campbell, whom she remembers as a very humble man who '. . . had the gift of inspiring others to excellence and extended his friendship to everyone in the school' (Wright Mulvaney, 2006, p. 24). Far from being entirely Anglo-centric in its conceptions, the College, in common with many schools that had missionary origins (see Chapter 3), had a history of being led by Scottish educational theologians with a great respect for local Ceylonese cultures and diversity of ideas. Campbell himself supported an openness to new philosophies, illustrated by events such as when my mother's family hosted Michael Kagwa, the son of a Ugandan old boy of the school, whilst he attended the College in the early 1930s. Campbell's predecessor, the Rev Andrew Fraser, was noted for his introduction of Sinhalese and Tamil languages into the curriculum and encouraging greater engagement with the local Kandyan community. He believed that fluency in the mother tongue, as well as English, would better place his school's graduates as future national leaders, as they would not be then isolated from the majority of the population (Daniel, 1992).

Within such diverse contexts, replicated in other English-language schools that were also seen to be the schools of the future national leadership such as St Thomas' College in Colombo (Daniel, 1992), it is difficult to sustain an argument that colonial education under the British in Ceylon was a universal homogeniser of local thought and an unblinking advocate for British superiority over local ideas and traditions. Instead, it was seen by some Ceylonese such as those in my two family branches as being both an enabler and facilitator of personal identity:

> Immersed in the English language, British history and tradition for most of my life, I was inevitably a reflection of the Raj. But I had grown up in the East with a mixed heritage and had ancestral roots in other lands. I have lived in India at a time of historic change and learned about different religions and cultures. It seemed to me as singular privilege to be part of East and West. The English language would soon become the lingua franca of the world. So, for me, dispossessed of its attitudes of superiority, the Raj had left an enlightened legacy, and I was content with my inheritance.
>
> (Wright Mulvaney, 2006, p. 79)

### 3 *Modern transnationalities*

When these conceptualisations of place and identity are compared with that of the current generation, the saliences that emerge are more striking in the similarities than the differences. As with the older generations, identity and cultural identification is, from one perspective, defined on the basis of where the person happens to live. At the same time, there are differing degrees of nebulousness evident in the conception and significance attributed to 'place' as an element in their personal identity. For example, two cousins living in the United Kingdom see themselves as being British-Sri Lankan, but from divergent perspectives. On the one hand, ambiguity of identity in terms of complexity can become a signifier of self-awareness and identity in itself, in which 'place' is moderated by a sense of personal connection. Riza, as the eldest of the siblings, found the Sri Lankan facets of his identity (his choice of terminology marks a clear separation from the use of 'Ceylon' in our parents' generation) catalysed by the same personal experience of Sri Lankan communal violence in 1983 that had the contrary effect on my father, our grandmother and one of our Danish cousins:

> Since then, my feeling of connection or attachment to Sri Lanka has just increased considerably to the extent that I feel both Sri Lankan and British now rather than one or the other.
>
> (Riza Jazeel, personal communication, October 12, 2015)

Ultimately, though, Riza sees himself as British –

> I feel more British than Sri Lankan largely because of language, because I don't, unfortunately, speak either Tamil or Sinhalese. So that makes me a little bit of an outsider there. Also, realistically, I feel more British. If I had to choose one place . . . well I do. I've chosen one place to live and currently that's the UK and it's more my home than Sri Lanka and I've lived all my life here.
>
> (Riza Jazeel, personal communication, October 12, 2015)

He emphasises the fluidity, and therefore the lack of fixedness, in his self-perceived identity by highlighting overlapping nature:

> Instead of thinking of identity as a scarce commodity, in which our identity is 100 per cent, and that might consist of 70 per cent British and 30 per cent Sri Lankan or whatever the mixture is adding to 100 per cent, I decided the way I'd approach it is it can be any number of a percent (which I know doesn't work mathematically). So therefore I thought, in theory, I could think of myself as a hundred per cent British and a hundred per cent Sri Lankan . . . but, using that sort of frame of reference, I consider myself about 90 per cent British and about 70 per cent Sri Lankan. I think that makes sense to most people when I tell them, but at first they're a bit weirded out by it.
>
> (Riza Jazeel, personal communication, October 12, 2015)

In contrast, Tariq, as an academic geographer, has concerns about tying oneself down to an identity, believing that nomination of identity is itself performative, encouraging stasis rather than evolution.

> I think [talking about identity] can too easily fix and essentialise one's sense of self, or people's sense of self. It gives an illusionary sense that there's some connect, some permanent native roots to one's make-up, to what makes one's self . . . As long as we keep using it[identity] as a category and deploying it as a category, it becomes real, right. Actually, I think our identities are

relationally and dynamically constructed in everyday situations and spaces. If you ask someone what their identity is, they're going to verbalise what they think their identity is, and then they're going to perform that identity as well, and not change.

(Tariq Jazeel, personal communication, October 31, 2015)

Consequently, he sees Sri Lanka more of an external connection that reflects circumstance and reality –

> That is just a symptom of being born in a diaspora. I was never born there – I was not born there, I never lived there, so "going back" doesn't make sense. I don't have any claims to native belonging, so to speak, my belonging to Sri Lanka is different.
>
> (Tariq Jazeel, personal communication, October 31, 2015)

The importance of generational embedded transnationality, or, more specifically, the ways in which it is or is not manifested, can be observed in the comparison of the attitudes of my generational cousins in Britain, Denmark and Australia towards notions of identity. Significantly, my aunt and uncle, the parents of Riza, Amyn and Tariq (see Figure 6.2), always made the conscious effort to maintain a regular and meaningful connection with Sri Lankan society through visits to my uncle's family:

> [We] were determined that the boys should know about where they are from – their parents' heritage.
>
> (Suvendrini Jazeel, personal communication, January 17, 2016)

In contrast, the Danish connection had very limited exposure to Sri Lankan ideas whilst they were growing up, beyond the occasional food. As Marl – who further compounded the transnational complexity by emigrating to Australia as an adult – comments, his mother Padmini appeared to be more focused on ensuring that she built a successful life as a Ceylonese in Denmark (a highly unusual relationship in the 1950s) than retaining her cultural roots beyond immediate family connections.

> I do feel maybe she didn't have the same connection herself with her Ceylonese background, as in Tamil background . . . that is why that we never got the Sri Lankan, Ceylonese background, as my mother herself was slightly removed from the actual original Tamil background that her family came from
>
> (Marl Christiansen, personal communication, January 3, 2016)

What is perhaps more interesting is Marl's greater attachment to the Sri Lanka of memory – that is, Ceylon, or the colonial state – or the one that was more closely associated to the heritage in which his mother grew up, especially in light of the recognition that, under British governance, Ceylon Tamils had more equality of citizenship than in the post-independence era.

> I feel annoyed that that's a loss of identity in some ways, but that was my mother's homeland when she left in the '40's, that it was called Ceylon and we were brought up to say 'Ceylon'. I can slightly remember that we went for a ceremony where they changed the flag, or put up the flag celebrating that it was now called Sri Lanka. But I sort of felt that did not belong to a Tamil background . . . it's mostly Sinhalese that wanted to be more independent and give the name "Sri Lanka" to Ceylon. And I understand that, but at the same time, I felt a bit of loss there, in some ways because I felt an affinity with my mother's background as 'Ceylon'.
>
> (Marl Christiansen, personal communication, January 3, 2016)

Notwithstanding a certain degree of hybridity of identity in the two family branches in the Northern Hemisphere, there is still a partial identification that is based distinctly on the specification of geographical places or regions. In contrast, the particular Australian branch of the Casinader family that is descended from Justin Wilmot Hoole has a much more comprehensive embedded transnationalism, perhaps a transparent reflection of the attitudes of both our parents. Of the three children of Justin and Laurel, our father, as discussed earlier in this chapter, was the one more inclined to follow his patrilineal willingness to move location, country and continent for life and work opportunities. From his earlier determination to attend Cambridge University across the other side of the world rather than wait for local engineering degree opportunities at the University of Ceylon, to his movement around the British Empire during our childhood, and later on, the wider globe in the course of his work as a hydro engineer, he continually demonstrated the capacity to look beyond 'place' as the definer of his own personal and professional identity.

Similarly, our mother has always proclaimed her determination to be herself, no matter what others thought, an attitude that she put down largely to the negative impact of her convent education experiences in Kandy and Colombo:

> It's coloured my whole life. It fostered a feeling of inner independence, like I never wanted to be part of the outside crowd, and I wasn't, I was myself and I still am.
>
> (Romany Wright Mulvaney, personal communication, March 22, 2015)

It was that same sense of independence and detachment from the physicalities of 'place' that led to her to leave Ceylon to go to India as one of the first air stewardesses for Air India in 1949, and then later to the United Kingdom and Europe as she set out to explore the world, always seeking new horizons (Romany Wright Mulvaney, 2006).

Given this dual ancestral disposition for creating identity through movement, rather than spatial identification through stasis, it is unsurprising that my siblings and I have emerged with a highly developed sense of embedded transnationality. I have written elsewhere the ways in which my own sense of self has been created and modified by transnational forces (Casinader, N., 2014; Casinader, N., Parr, Joseph, & Seddon, 2014), but whereas my own journey towards identity has been numbed and numbing due to an initial confusion that my understanding of self was, in fact, disaggregated from the notion of place, instead of being woven into it, my sister and brother are far more assertive in knowing and declaring a lack of an umbilical link to place. From my sister's perspective, she does not

> . . . have a link to a particular place, a geographic place or like a single one. I've got equally strong links still to England where we mostly grew up, and to Australia where I live, but I feel more like a mixture of things. In terms of Western/Eastern, I don't feel at all Eastern; I feel completely Western. I feel like a total visitor if I go to the East and I don't relate to anything, except the food, probably, as if it's mine or anything like that. In fact, it's a bit strange. I feel much more at home in North-West Europe, the North-Western edge of Europe, West Coast of Ireland, Scotland and it's not just because I was born there because I didn't live there for very long. It just seems to be a sort of place that I like.
>
> (Tarini Casinader, personal communication, August 23, 2015)

More significantly, unlike our British cousins, for us, Sri Lanka is a place of temporary destination, where all the various threads of our ancestry met and came together, before moving on to places around the globe; in short, the island was, and is, a staging post, just another node on the family's transnational journey:

> I don't feel entirely Sri Lankan because there seem to be links to all sorts of other countries. Yes, that's where Mum and Dad came from, and it's sort of a core place, but it's really just a place where all sorts of other things coalesced . . . So it's like all these different strands from different parts of the world happen to coalesce in Sri Lanka, and that's why we're there. So I'm interested in it. I don't mind being Sri Lankan. It's very interesting but it's more interesting in that it's not really Sri Lankan. It's all these other threads that have gathered in this place and that's how I feel it.
>
> (Tarini Casinader, personal communication, August 23, 2015)

As a consequence, individual places in the world have little significance in themselves; it is the people who live in those places that have more importance:

> I guess I don't have that real connection to a single piece of land: "It has to be this piece of land. It can't be any other piece of land." I've got a connection to lots of pieces of land all over the whole country, and I own the whole

> world, so I don't get why it has to be that particular piece of land. I understand it intellectually, but. . .
>
> (Tarini Casinader, personal communication, August 23, 2015)

For our brother, the sense of place is, in some ways, much stronger, perhaps the function or consequence of having spent his entire formative years in either England or Australia, with relatively little of the diverse trans-spatial life experiences that my sister and I experienced. Consequently, he has

> . . . realised that I have a foot in both places. I think maybe that initial impression of the landscape and everything in England was very strong, strong enough to provoke this almost surreal feeling – it was like watching a movie going back there.
>
> (Robin Casinader, personal communication, August 5, 2015)

Ultimately, however, in a strong echo and mirror of our father's expression of identity, Robin has a far more succinct interpretation:

> My identity is in terms of where I choose to live. That's it there.
>
> (Robin Casinader, personal communication, August 5, 2015)

## E Place-lessness in identity: A review

If this selected Casinader-Wright family genealogy is seen as an example of a transnationalised family evolution, then the pathway to that position was founded on an inherent disposition to move geographical location in search of life improvement. It is aligned with the capability of being able to choose those elements of place to be retained as a cultural identifier, whilst not being constrained or paralysed by an 'over connection' to a place in and of the past. Education in the British colonial period of Sri Lanka became the catalyst and the conduit for that embedded transnationality to be actualised, enabled by the existence of Empire both as geographical entity and conceptual space, facilitated, but not defined, by colonial experience. As a collective, the world of British imperialism created within pre-independent Ceylon provided the intellectual and practical mindset for them to enact their inherent disposition for geographical and psychological transference, if they perceived the need, with the increased ethnic plurality and complexity of the more recent generations being echoed in an increasingly de-spatialised sense of personal identity. Partly, this ambivalence of place-related identity, most noticeable in the modern generation, is aligned with the similar incongruities present in the Great War generation of our grandparents, and is therefore another example of

> the ambivalence of identity specific to the generation of' coloured' children in multicultural Britain contains deep complexities during the conceptualization

of their identities, which inevitably lack fixity compared to those of their diasporic parents.

(Toplu, 2011, p. 162)

It is the same 'place-less' transnationality that my sister sees as key to the next generation, that of her daughter, Róisín and my youngest son, Simon:

> I think Mum used to call us hybrids, or "Citizens of the World"? I want [Róisín] to be free to connect herself to whatever things in the world she wants to, without feeling that she has to do something because she can't get away from doing something, because she's tied to the place she was born, or the place that we were born, or where she lives. I want her to feel that she can get away.
>
> (Tarini Casinader, personal communication, August 23, 2015)

Such hopes are a direct reflection of an embedded transnationality, in which the individual is empowered to see identity as not only self-drawn, but self-maintained.

> If people go, "Who am I?", I say, "Simon" . . . I very much identify as Australian. [But] I don't travel to see things; I travel to more experience things. I think I drove past where you used to live [in Malaysia] the last time I was there, but that didn't intrigue me at all. I've seen your school in Malaysia, and you enjoyed it. But I got more out of eating the food, I got more in London through taking the tube, seeing things and walking around . . . to see people, family, and see what their life is like.
>
> (Simon Casinader, personal communication, August 9, 2015)

'Place', for the most recent Casinader generations, is more of a transnational guide to the present and future through their connections with people, and not so much the specific geographical imaginary of the past.

## References


Bhabha, H. (1994). *The Location of Culture*. London: Routledge.

Bratich, J. Z., Packer, J., & McCarthy, C. (Eds.) (2003). *Foucault, Cultural Studies, and Governmentality*. Albany: State University of New York.

Casinader, L. (1986). *Memoirs: 1903–1986*. London: Unpublished.

Casinader, N. (2014). *Culture, Transnational Education and Thinking: Case Studies in Global Schooling*. Milton Park, Abingdon: Routledge.

Casinader, N., Parr, G., Joseph, C., & Seddon, T. (2014). Adult Educators and 'Really Useful Knowledge': Navigating Democratic Politics in Mobile and Transitional Times. In B. Käpplinger & S. Robak (Eds.), *Changing Configurations in Adult Education in Transitional Times – Perspectives in Different Countries* (pp. 223–242). Frankfurt am Main: Peter Lang.

Casinader, R. A. (c. 2003). *An Abridged Casinader Genealogy: Extract from an Extended Genealogy of Select Batticaloa Families – Circa late 16th Century to Late 20th Century*. Vancouver,Canada: Unpublished.

Casinader, R. A. (c. 2005). *A Preamble to the Casinader Genealogical Chart*. Vancouver, Canada: Unpublished.
Casinader, R. J. T. (2006). *Justin Wilmot Hoole (Pakkiathurai) Casinader: A Humble Achiever – Major Events in the Story of His Life*. Melbourne, Australia: Unpublished.
Daniel, L. K. (1992). *Privilege and Policy: The Indigenous Elite and the Colonial Education System in Ceylon: 1912–1948*. (Doctor of Philosophy), Oxford University.
De Silva, K. M. (Ed.) (1973). *History of Ceylon* (Vol. 3). Colombo: University of Ceylon.
De Silva, K. M. (2005). *A History of Sri Lanka*. Colombo: Vijitha Yapa/Penguin.
Jazeel, T. (2006). Postcolonial Geographies of Privilege: Diaspora Space, the Politics of Personhood and the 'Sri Lankan Women's Association in the UK'. *Transactions of the Institute of British Geographers, 31*(1), 19–33. doi:10.1111/j.1475-5661.2006.00192.x
Lee, L. (compiled by) (1882). *Census of Ceylon 1881*. Colombo: Government Printer.
Ludowyk, E. F. C. (1966). *The Modern History of Ceylon*. London: Weidenfield and Nicolson.
Mendis, G. C. (Ed.) (1956). *The Colebrooke-Cameron Papers: Documents on British Colonial Policy in Ceylon 1796–1833* (Vol. 1). London: Geoffrey Cumberlege/Oxford University Press.
Mendis, V. L. B. (1971). *The Advent of the British to Ceylon: 1762–1803*. Dehiwala: Tissaro Prakasakayo.
Scott, D. (2005). Colonial Governmentality. In J. X. Inda (Ed.), *Anthropologies of Modernity: Foucault, Governmentality, and Life Politics* (pp. 23–49). Oxford: Blackwell.
Seth, S. (2007). *Subject Lessons: The Western Education of Colonial India*. Durham and London: Duke University Press.
Sumathipala, K. H. M. (1968). *History of Education in Ceylon: 1796–1965*. Dehiwala, Sri Lanka: Tisara Prakasakayo.
Tennent, J. E., Sir. (1859a). *Ceylon: An Account of the Island Physical, Historical, and Topographical with Notices of Its Natural History, Antiquities and Productions* (Second ed., Vol. 1). London: Longman, Green, Longman, and Roberts.
Tennent, J. E., Sir. (1859b). *Ceylon: An Account of the Island Physical, Historical, and Topographical with Notices of Its Natural History, Antiquities and Productions* (Second ed., Vol. 2). London: Longman, Green, Longman, and Roberts.
Toplu, S. (2011). Transnational Identity Mappings in Andrea Levy's Fiction. In M. Friedman & S. Schultermandl (Eds.), *Growing Up Transnational: Identity and Kinship in a Global Era* (pp. 160–178). Toronto: University of Toronto Press.
Wright Mulvaney, R. (2006). *Reflections of the Raj: An Early Memoir*. Blackburn, Victoria: Penfolk Publishing.

# 7 Re-imagining transnationalism

## Trans-spatiality and implications for teaching, learning and beyond

### A Area-construction of transnationalism: Towards trans-spatiality

In Chapter 1, it was argued that the conception of transnationalism in the contemporary discourse was lacking in both scope and character, being largely constructed in the broader context of the movement of phenomena, and particularly that of people, from place to place around the globe across the boundaries of sovereign States. A concomitance of this tunnelled vision of transnationalism is that it has become associated primarily with the nexus between personal and cultural identification and a defined territory, delineated by borders that are intrinsically co-existent with those of a nation-State. For a person to be defined as transnational, therefore, is to be identified as an individual whose migratory movements, whether temporary or permanent, have moved across the parameters of a nation- or sovereign State. Inherent within this transnational character is a continued deep and interactive connection with both the territory of origin and the region of destination, one that persists regardless of the level of permanence embodied in the movement. Also embedded within this conception of transnationalism is the assumption that there is a certain degree of cultural homogeneity within that defined political space, one that is strong enough to generate the line of connection and regular interaction back and forth between the place or territory of origin and the destination of movement, covering all facets of societal life. The intensity and essentiality of mutual interdependence between place of origin and place of destination – what Yang & Qiu (2010) refer to as 'homeland' and 'hostland' – is reflected in the nature of the connection: the maintenance of language and lingual connectivity; the frequency and duration of familial journeys between the two locations; and knowledge and understanding of the cultural drivers of both regions and how to operate in each environment:

> The language of diaspora not only advocates the importance of homeland, but also entails fluidity, transnationality and economic-driven characteristics that emphasise the equal importance of hostland and the social transactions between homeland and hostland.
>
> (Yang & Qiu, 2010, p. 22)

The first section of this book also examined the argument that, in addition to its transactional core, the contemporary notion and use of transnationalism has tended to be implanted within the context of the modern phase of globalisation. As a result, it has been associated with the same primary drivers and impacts of the globalisation process, and, in particular, the ever-increasing complex webs of global trade and its constant companions, trade liberalisation and the integration of national economies into regional trade associations. The semi-unification of groups of sovereign States into numerous regional trading co-operatives such as ASEAN, the EU, APEC, TPP and COMESA for economic purposes has evolved into the encouragement of transnational, 'transactional' movements in multiple other fields, including that of people migrating to work, whether permanently or temporarily, in an expanded employment field of opportunities.

Paradoxically, however, the process of globalisation has created a context in which the 'transactional' mode of transnationalism – the exchange of phenomena across national borders – has been difficult to sustain as its primary form. One of the other consequences of contemporary globalisation is that it has hastened the process of creating culturally diverse communities within a greater number of sovereign States, although the transition has been more evident in some States than others. In other words, many societies are now evolving more inevitably, more continuously and at a greater speed through the addition of new cultural identities, principally through acquired migration. Events such as BREXIT in 2016 notwithstanding, the increasing complexity of this cultural mix, and the speed and fluidity with which it can change, has heightened the wider sociological implications of transnationalism to the point that they challenge the relevance of its own nomenclature in the modern context. The implications of transnationalism extend far beyond locational shifts of people between sovereign or nation-States. Thus, the contention on which this book has been based is that transnationalism is a far more wide-ranging, dynamic and mind-centred entity than the one reflected in current iterations, echoing a state of mind and attitude towards life or disposition that is not aligned with the delineations of political spatial entities in the form of sovereign States. Instead, boundaries of difference between peoples, especially when imposed by human decision, are being seen increasingly as being of lesser importance and relevance in a world where the complexity of human character and existence is now the dominant feature.

Also contrary to current assumptions, transnationalism is not a phenomenon that can be limited to the contemporary era of the 21st century. As Chapters 3 and 4 explored, using the context of Ceylon – or, as it is identified in its modern conceptualisation, Sri Lanka – the degree of cultural complexity within any region, whether demarcated by the mutually accepted borders of a sovereign State or not, has been essentially dynamic through historical time. The perception of a region as a geographically associated cultural monolith that is in never-ending stasis, cannot be sustained when the finer points of history are explored. As Iriye illustrates, in an extension of Said, there has been an extensive and ongoing interaction between Europe, North America and the Islamic world as a result of contemporary globalisation (Iriye, 2004), highlighting the hidden reality that a transnational global history is more of a temporal constant than a defined event. Consequently, to see transnationalism being treated in the context of cultural geographical specifics is a *non sequitur*, in which the transference of personal identity is coupled to a permanent connection and interaction with a cultural space – a sovereign or nation-State – that is itself evolving. This makes it difficult to sustain the degree of cultural homogeneity and stability in a region that the current definitional interpretation of transnationalism demands.

In previous works (see Casinader, 2014, 2016a, 2016b), I have argued that the notion of culture needs to be reconfigured in the 21st-century imaginary as being essentially mind-centred, rather than being solely associated with the anthropological and more visible considerations such as language, customs, religion and artefacts. In the same vein, I would like to propose that transnationalism – which, by its very name, is associated with the physical movement of phenomena across national boundaries that are constructed by human thought, not reality – should be transformed into a similar mind-centred formation, defined by the existence of the capacity and disposition to transcend or ignore the existence of territorial or nation-State borders in the creation of personal and/or cultural identity. This distinctiveness is created by the self, and is not associated necessarily by a connection with the existence or delineation of a geographical space.

This evolved notion of transnationalism, which is better articulated as the posited concept of *trans-spatiality* (see Figure 7.1) is inherently incorporated into,

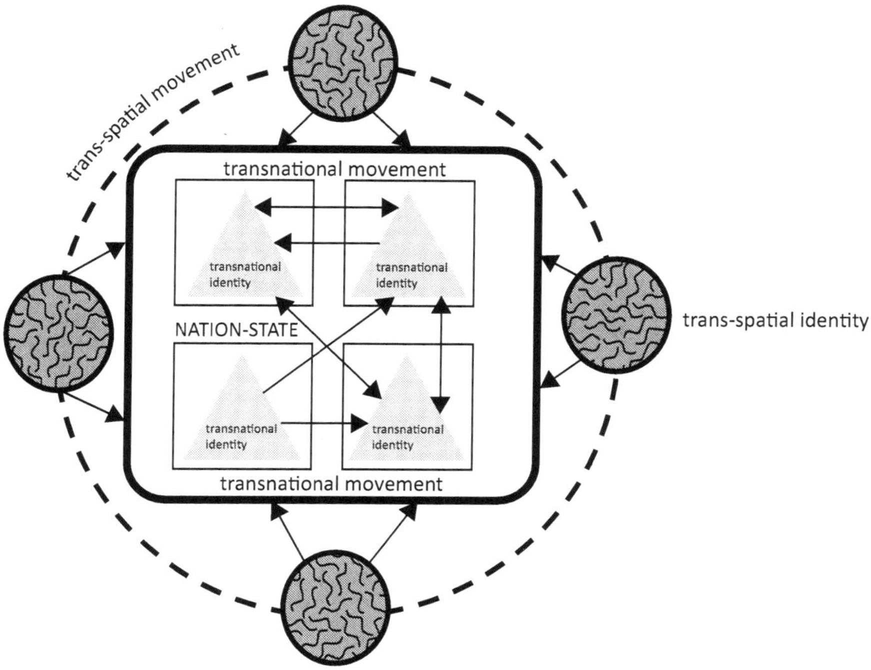


*Figure 7.1* The creation of a trans-spatial identity

as well as being symbiotically associated with, the notion of transculturalism; that is, the capacity to work within, amongst and across differing cultural dispositions of thought. Although transculturalism has certain commonalities with other mindsets such as cosmopolitanism and global mindedness in its inclusive attitude towards diverse cultures, it differs from other mindsets in that it sees this global variation of cultures as being the norm or observable natural societal state. Cultural variance is seen as the natural societal condition in a globalised and globalising world, and not as an anomaly that needs to isolated and addressed as an issue of concern. It is an attitude, aptitude and capability that emerges with, and is enhanced by, more complex patterns of globalised experience on the part of the individual or group of people concerned.

The multifarious nature of this globalised experience is crucial to the development of a fully-formed transcultural disposition. The essence of transculturalism is the capacity to engage with and work between cultural dispositions of thinking that are quite diverse in their formulations and starting points (Casinader, 2014). To stay within, for instance, any single societal sphere of influence, such as the Euro-American, or 'Western', does expose an individual to certain specific conceptions and approaches about thinking. Engagement and absorption of the contrasting principles in different cultural environments creates the internalised debate of ideas and processes in the individual that, once resolved, leads to a greater depth of knowledge and understanding about different cultural approaches to societal constructions and how to live and operate within them. The notion of trans-spatiality, therefore, looks beyond the notion of cultural differences to one that is constructed upon the acceptance of the existence of diverse cultural realities as the fundamental norm in global society, transcending those realities that are geographically fixed, which is not the case in the prevailing iteration of transnationalism.

The notion of trans-spatiality does not assume that the current iteration of transnationalism, as a form of demographic transaction between sovereign States, needs to be overridden, but sees it as a building block on which trans-spatiality is conceived. As illustrated by Figure 7.1, it acknowledges the existence of transnational cultural identities, ones that have been formed and continually moulded by individuals or groups continuing to interact regularly through flows between their 'home' and 'host regions'. These transnational identities are aligned with the delineated territories associated with existing sovereign of nation-States, and so transnational movement in the contemporary transactional sense occurs across these borders. In concert with Bhabha's articulation of liminality of existence, the hybridity of these entities is essentially one formed out of tensions between the competing identities that need to be mollified; it is a complexity, perceived as a problem that requires resolution of some form on the part of the individual, rather than the State.

The essence of trans-spatiality is that it sees these multiple transnational identities as creating a holistic perception of the world that leads to some people developing a more evolved and heightened level of transcultural understanding. Whilst acknowledging the individuality and singularity of multiple cultural identities, trans-spatiality does not see them as so much creating unresolvable tensions as merely reflecting the reality of the world as it exists. Those who have developed a trans-spatial mindset (see Figure 7.1) embody the capabilities reflected in transculturalism, particularly the capacity to see beyond the cultural differences that might exist within or between sovereign States, and to treat them as more a symbol of the embedded cultural diversity that is the natural state of societies that are exposed to the processes of contemporary globalisation. Consequently, transcultural people have the capability of relating to and working within multiple societies that may or may not have a national or territorial base, continually modifying and regenerating their own identities in response to movements and shifts at that more defined level. They have the capacity to transcend the cultural variations that exist on the level of the sovereign or nation-state (see Figure 7.1), with the ability to move into and between any of these regions, and yet operate productively and collaboratively, whatever the nature of the cultural milieux. The result is a notion of transculturalism in which identity is defined not so much by attachment to place, but more by the attitudinal capacity to look beyond difference and the confines of culture and space.

To be trans-spatial, therefore, is to disrupt the false assumptions that cultural and societal homogeneity is the ultimate representation of an evolved human society. Instead, difference, whether cultural or otherwise, is perceived as a catalyst of potential advantage, and not a problem phenomenon that requires isolation and treatment of the 'Other'. A *trans-spatial* identity is formed from the varying interactions of the self with other cultural iterations (Figure 7.1), continually adapting to and being formed by those interactions, not all of which may be geographically confined, and in the process creating a capacity to transcend or override the imposed barriers that such boundaries might create.

For the remainder of this chapter, the term '*transnational*' will be used to refer to the movement of people and other phenomena across national borders, whereas the term '*trans-spatiality*' will be employed in the context of the posited mindset that is founded on transculturalism.

## B Education, transnationalism and trans-spatiality

In educational terms, the reconfigured notion of *trans-spatiality* has the potential to have a major impact on teacher education, the development and utilisation of pedagogy and the construction and implementation of educational policy. Under the principle that the globalisation of human activity will become even more acute and intense over the forthcoming years, there will be three main areas in which *trans-spatiality* will become evident in the educational sphere.

The first two of these areas can be seen as mirror images of each other. First of all, student cohorts in many parts of the world, but especially those that are still perceived as the preferred destination of transnational movements, such as Europe, North America and Australasia, will become increasingly diverse in the degree and nature of their trans-spatiality. Second, the same is likely to occur in the composition of teacher workforces in each sovereign State, even though current trends in educational research in regions such as Australia tend to ignore the trans-spatial diversity of current teacher workforces (Casinader & Walsh, 2015) It appears that there is a great deal of educational research to be conducted in order to determine the true trans-spatial nature of teacher workforces. However, despite the increasing cultural diversity of Australia's population between 2001–15 to the point where approximately 50% of the population had a parent who was born overseas (Australian Bureau of Statistics, 2016), governments and educational interests tend to ignore the wider cultural background of teachers completely, focusing only on languages spoken and country of birth in recent major national studies of Australian school teachers (McKenzie, Kos, Walker, & Hong, 2008; McKenzie, Rowley, Weldon, & Murphy, 2011; McKenzie, Weldon, Rowley, Murphy, & McMillan, 2014). Such a trend implies that Australian educational stakeholders do not see a need for the Australian teacher workforce to reflect the cultural diversity of its population, or – and arguably more of a concern – that such considerations are irrelevant. Consequently, it is likely that there will be growing pressure on teacher education to prepare future educators in ways so that they can position themselves with the full range of transcultural capabilities necessary to teach student cohorts that are characterised by ever more complex patterns of cultural identity, including the trans-spatial.

Indications of some strategies that might engender such trans-spatial capabilities within school educators are becoming evident through current research projects within Australian school education. These projects include investigations of the transcultural capacities of pre-service teachers, as well as those of established teachers working within schools, building upon the foundations of earlier research (Casinader, 2014). Although in the early stages at the time of writing, preliminary analyses are revealing that teachers who have engaged with and immersed themselves in the philosophies, practicalities and conceptualisations of life in regions that are far removed from their own place of origin are more likely to develop transcultural dispositions of thought. Those who place a priority on deeply engaging visits to countries and ways of life outside the mainstream of their experience in their personal lives, as well as the professional, tend to have a far more developed transcultural sensibility (Casinader, 2016a). Moreover, regardless of teaching experience or area of expertise, these same educators showed an increased capacity to both perceive and enact positive changes to a number of aspects in teacher practice, including the building of student relationships and more individualised, diversified systems of pedagogy to reflect the learning needs of an increasingly trans-spatial generation of students. Such patterns are aligned with other global research, which argues that '[i]nternational teacher exchange programmes are another method to expose educators to other countries, cultures and societies as well as to new pedagogical methods and competencies' (UNESCO, 2014, p. 32).

The third area of educational trans-spatiality where the potential for more significant change exists at the systemic level, both within national parameters and across the international sphere. If education itself is to become more transformational and trans-spatial at the global level, then the sources of knowledge and conceptual input themselves need to become more diverse and transcultural. At present, the structure of educational provision and intent on the global scale is, to a very large degree, determined by the predilections and conceptual frameworks of the Euro-American axis. Despite the arguments being put to the contrary, the benchmarking of international educational practice as defined by international measures such as PISA is not culturally neutral, let alone transcultural. Instead, such systems of educational priority are based on 'Western' conceptualisations of culture and societal improvement, where the notion of individualisation of achievement holds priority over principles of contribution to community engagement as a primary measure of individual educational attainment (Casinader, 2015).

In many ways, the power that the former metropolitan colonial powers exert over national systems of education through pathways as diverse as conditions placed on aid programmes, the export of curricula and pedagogies to countries outside the Euro-American context, and control of global media outlets, is far more insidious and disempowering than the structures of colonial education that were implemented in places such as Sri Lanka during the historical period of European colonisation. In the British imperial context, the implementation of guided educational systems of education were, nevertheless, modified by emerging and emerged local considerations, to the point that, as discussed specifically throughout Chapters 5 and 6, certain groups were able to both acquire and utilise powers of individual self-determination that had previously not been existent, or not accessible to them. In the era of the 21st century, however, the hidden intentions of educational neo-colonialism do not appear to have been countered effectively in the construction of global or national educational policy. It is not a case of ignoring the contributions and ideas of the 'Western' context, but ensuring that they are better integrated with ideas and principles evident in 'Other' traditions of educational culture to form a more cohesive, inclusive and transcultural approach to the aims and objectives of teaching and learning.

In national terms, a trans-spatial approach to curriculum and pedagogical provision would enable educational programmes to be more effectively geared around the notion and inherent innovation of cultural dynamism, constructed around conceptions of diversity as positive opportunities, rather than being constrained by the perception of cultural variants as anomalies that require extraordinary solutions devised and implemented. A further difficulty arises in this particular space because educational systems, when dealing with the issues of cultural education, invariably base their ideas and policies on conceptualisations of culture and cultural education that are founded on notions of separateness, rather than inclusion, the situation further hindered by the variance in definition of cultural education across different national systems (Casinader, 2016a). In Australia, for instance, the historical pattern of cultural education between different state educational administrations demonstrates differences in the interpretation of the concepts of multiculturalism and intercultural learning, with both being used interchangeably. In North America, the conception of multiculturalism is seen to apply to a much more diverse range of variations in student characteristics than is the case in either Europe or Australasia. Regimes in places such as East Asia, Southeast Asia, and South America, in their bids to emulate the perceived economic success of the Euro-American sphere, have adopted some of the similar underlying principles of thinking about education that are culturally embedded in 'Western' systems of education (Casinader, 2015; Kumar, 2013; Ministry of Education Malaysia, 2012). To implement a more trans-spatial, transcultural educational approach would require, therefore, a concerted international programme in the consolidation of ideas, as well as a more exploratory examination of educational concepts and principles.

To work towards this particular goal, utopian or not, however, raises wider issues of individual rights and the determination of self. If, for instance, it is deemed that a trans-spatial or transcultural capacity is a compulsory graduate attribute in teacher education, the moral question arises as to whether this means that educators whose personal beliefs, whether social, political philosophical, are not aligned with that of trans-spatiality, should be able to receive accreditation to teach students of the modern trans-spatial generation. Ultimately, the Benthamite principle of the utilitarian good becomes the focus of debate, competing on the inalienable right of a student to be educated for a modern transnational, trans-spatial future against the equally foundational right of an individual teacher to be allowed to practise according to the parameters of their socio-political conscience. Ironically, of course, the same principle of utilitarian benefit has been employed by those who have adopted attitudes that are essentially anti-trans-spatial. Groups and organisations, including current and recent Australian governments of contrasting political persuasion, the US administration, European states such as Greece, and the BREXIT campaigners of the United Kingdom have all argued that the security of their populations as a whole relies on stringent 'border protection' measures that are, in effect, anti-transnationalist and anti-trans-spatial.

## C Trans-spatiality: Wider implications

One of the consistent fundamental debates about the contemporary era of globalisation has focused on the impact of the phenomenon on the viability and relevance of the nation-State as the foundation of global governance. Since World War II, the creation of international collaborative organisations such as the United Nations, along with its subsequent and/or complementary derivatives such as the World Trade Organisation (WTO) and UNESCO, and the various treaties that govern the international use and management of aspects of human activity and the physical environment, has been constructed on the basis of the sovereign State as being the basis for the organisation of societies.

However, in an environment that continues to see the growth of global corporations, the economic activities and political power of which often outstrip the capacities of individual sovereign States, the status of the modern nation-State has been reduced to that of a service provider; they have been reconstructed into the effective role of local governments or councils, effectively only responsible to and for the daily lives and welfare of its citizens. The proportion of the world's economic workforce that operates on a transnational basis, functioning between location of home and place of work within timeframes that range from a few days to a year or more, continues to grow as the reality of the global economy's demands for an equivalent workforce become more in focus. As argued by Fazal Rizvi (for example, 2009a, 2009b), the true essence of transnationalism in the modern age is global mobility, which in itself diminishes the need for acknowledgement of difference as a visible feature of global society.

The degree to which these globally mobile workers have genuine trans-spatial capacity is moot, however. For those leaving a region out of the desperation of absolute poverty, moving from the homelands in sovereign States such as Bangladesh and Sri Lanka to take advantage of construction jobs being generated in locations such as the United Arab Emirates, the capacity to be mobile is highly constrained. The restrictions placed on their movement and activities at the point of destination inevitably affect their capacity to develop and maintain those lines of reverse communication. They are unable to use their transnational activity to transform their trans-spatial capacity, and remain as unempowered as they were in their home location. Although the economic activity that requires their presence is born out of globalisation and transnational economic corporatisation, the constraints and restrictions upon their individual capacity for economic and social liberation are very much implemented and applied through the infrastructures developed and maintained by individual sovereign States, whether by themselves or in collaboration with others. Trans-spatial activity that is the vehicle of self-empowerment remains the province of those with the existing economic, social and cultural capital to mobilise that activity towards their own benefit, rather than that of the nation-State in which they might live or work. Consequently, trans-spatiality in the modern age is not an inevitability for all, but more a capacity that is reserved for the few – the new, if expanding, group of the globalised society, created and managed by the primary actors, the sovereign State (albeit in a reconfigured form) and the transnational corporation.

This reduced capacity for individualised trans-spatial agency makes the current global situation different from the power dynamics generated during the period of European colonialism, and specifically, those that existed within the context of British imperialism. In regions such as Ceylon (Sri Lanka), the introduction of an education system that reflected the principles of Enlightenment in the British mould, and which was characterised by equitable access founded on merit, regardless of ethnic or cultural background, provided the conduit through which individuals could actualise their trans-spatial dispositions whilst attaining some degree of self-determination in their life progression. The creation of such a system of governmentality was possible because, at that stage of global history, the hierarchy of international power was founded very much on the capacities and policies of individual States, or sovereign territories. Governance of geographical space was the underlying principle of international activity, and agreements between nation-States were the means by which international collaborations were actualised, largely because the state of technology in both communications and the application of military force was such that the fledgling global corporations of the era, such as the British East India company, were still subject to and able to be controlled by the activities and policies of the governments in sovereign States. The decreasing power base of the British East India Company in the mid-19th century, with its eventual removal by the British government as the administrator of the Indian colony, as well as its limited, defined role in the establishment of the Crown Colony of Ceylon, was a classic exemplar of the global situation at the time.

Within the contemporary phase of globalisation, however, the power base of international dominants has shifted more from the activities of sovereign States towards that of transnational globalised corporations. Operations and philosophies occur independently of governance of geographical space, and are, instead, constructed on control of mind-framed and financial space, both of which are not constrained by the principle of geographical jurisdiction that remains the heart of the raison d'être of the sovereign State. Whereas the function of a sovereign State is the management of individual human activity, employing the framework of attaching a personal identity to residence and attachment to a particular geographical space, global corporations are essentially constructed behemoths that downgrade the importance of the individual, replacing it with the deification of corporate activity. In essence, they have usurped the capacity of trans-spatiality for themselves, removing the capacity of individuals to activate their own innate trans-spatial dispositions, unless they attach themselves to the 21st-century global power structures that are managed or influenced by the same global corporations.

Further, the global systems that do exist, such as those that operate within the auspices of organisations such as the United Nations, are themselves increasingly divorced from the reality of contemporary trans-spatialities because they are founded on collaborations between sovereign States, and not the global corporations that have potentially greater power. These economic colossuses have little interest in the *direct* control of the entirety of geographical space and human populations governed by sovereign States; instead, their focus is on influencing and using the power of the sovereign State to gain access to and control of those geographical spaces and human contingents within the State that are central to their own corporate interests, often at the cost of the economic and political capital possessed by local people and institutions. Clear illustrations of this can be seen in the operations of global mining corporations such as BHP Billiton, with its mining assets in sovereign states throughout regions ranging from South America, North America, Australia, the Caribbean and Europe (BHP Billiton, 2016a), as well as in the ways that global companies such as McDonald's are able to mould consumer buying habits through worldwide advertising strategies (Ritzer, 2006), themselves facilitated by globalised communication technologies. The philosophy of such corporations is essentially trans-spatial because they are not concerned with the development of human society within a particular sovereign state *per se*, even if, as in the case of BHP Billiton, they profess a deep commitment to sustainable welfare by:

> [making] a broader contribution to the communities, regions and nations in which we operate, thereby strengthening society. We are committed to

achieving this through engagement and advocacy on important issues and by supporting targeted development areas to benefit the communities where we operate.

(BHP Billiton, 2016b)

The difficulty with such public declarations is that they are often at odds with real events. In the case of BHP Billiton, the environmental and human disasters caused by the collapse of mining dams at Ok Tedi, Papua New Guinea in 1984 (Low & Gleeson, 1998) and Bento Rodriguez, Brazil in 2015 (Moulton, 2016) were both characterised by environmental management failures and inadequate communications with local communities. Instead, the national political entities – that is, the sovereign States – along with the geographical and human assets located or resident within them, are resources to be utilised for the benefit of the corporation itself. The capacity of global corporations to, at the least, equal, and at the most, surpass, the power of sovereign States is reflected in the fact that many corporations have annual revenue that far exceeds that of most States. On this measure, in 2014, sovereign States comprised only 37% of the top hundred governments and corporations. (Freudenberg, 2015). Consequently, national-based conduits such as educational systems that might enable individuals to develop and employ their own capacities for trans-spatial advancement tend to be irrelevant to global corporations, unless it is to their own, corporate advantage. Instead, trans-spatiality has been commandeered by global corporations for selective purposes that may not necessarily coincide with the interests of global, national or local communities.

The widening gap between the perceptions of trans-spatial considerations that are held by sovereign States in comparison with global corporations can also provide some insight into one aspect of the dominant transnational feature impacting upon human society at this stage of the 21st century – that of growing ideological conflicts, as represented by the tension between the existence of Daesh, also known as ISIL or Islamic State, and the loose coalition of the 'West' and its allies (that is, those who wish to remove Daesh). The ways in which the Euro-American grouping, which includes regional partners such as Turkey, have attempted to meet the challenges posed to global stability have continued to be limited by their reliance on the outdated notion of transnationalism; that is, the significance placed upon the existence and employment of the borders of sovereign States in managing the flows of people around the world. The continuing military operations in locations such as Afghanistan, Iraq and Syria are all underpinned by the persistent conception of the 'enemy' or 'Other' being defined by their existence and control of a geographical space; that is, that the State – sovereign or otherwise – and its associated boundaries remains the ultimate foundation in the application of regional or global power. However, if we take the view that the prospective sources of global power and dominance can now be framed within trans-spatiality, not transnationalism, it is possible to break this unproductive nexus between the physicality of space and globalised activity in the modern era.

However it is identified and whatever name is attached to it, the phenomenon of Daesh is essentially the symptom of an ideological psychological imaginary that does not have to be intrinsically defined by the occupation of a demarcated geographical space, regardless of the call of its proponents for the existence of a caliphate. This is not to argue that the 'Western' coalition, nor Daesh itself, do not acknowledge the existence, or importance, of an ideological mindset that reflects a 'Western' point of view; the difference is primarily one of emphasis and priority. The success that Daesh has had, and is having, with its own programme of enculturation across different parts of the world, using social media in particular to attract people born in the 'West' to their cause suggests that, as an organisation, it has a more highly developed understanding of trans-spatiality, or at least their variation of it, than that evidenced by the efforts of the Euro-American coalition. The ISIL use of trans-spatiality is not, however, transcultural in the sense that it is accepting and incorporative of cultural variation; instead, it focuses on creating an ideological imaginary that transcends location, an imaginary that is 'place-less' in the sense that it is not attached so much to the actuality of an associated territory, as to the ideal of one; that is, a caliphate.

To meet the challenges posed by Daesh, the 'Western' coalition needs to develop and actively promote a unified and powerful trans-spatial imaginary of its own. Ironically, the success of the British vote to leave the European Union (BREXIT) in June 2016, promoted as both a step towards a reinforcement of national identity and more effective management of the impact of Daesh in Europe, was another example of the inability of 'Western' communities to move beyond the confines of transnationalism as 'transaction', and acknowledge the more effective impact of developing a wider trans-spatial, more inclusive imaginary as a means of counteracting the ISIL equivalent. Instead, the reverse is occurring, as the fears generated by Daesh are actualised into heightened anxiety about transnational movement, and sovereign States fall back behind the supposed safety of their defended national borders. Ironically, however, such reinforcement of supposed control is likely to fail, because the success of Daesh in its appropriation of its version of trans-spatiality is reliant fundamentally on its control of the very transnational movement that 'secure borders' cannot control – the use of the internet and social media as tractor-beams to radicalise and mobilise new supporters and adherents. As it is, it is likely that the ultimate consequences of the partial splintering of whatever unified anti-Daesh imaginary that did exist will not be known for some time.

As it exists in the first quarter of the 21st century, trans-spatiality, as an expanded reconfiguration of transnationalism, remains an attitudinal entity that has the potential to be utilised by all, whether they be individuals, states or organisations. It is a disposition or frame of mind that is not tied to an unalterable sense of place and cultural identity. More significantly, it encapsulates an understanding of how contemporary 21st-century globalisation is facilitating more prevalent transcultural perspectives on global thoughts, events and actions. Whether such transculturalism can be employed to move towards a more peaceful coexistence between ideologically disparate elements of human society, or whether it will be manipulated as an instrument of suppression and eradication, remains to be seen.

## References

Australian Bureau of Statistics. (2016). Migration, Australia, 2014-15 Cat. No. 3412.0. Retrieved from http://www.abs.gov.au/AUSSTATS/abs@.nsf/Lookup/3412.0Main+Features12014-15?OpenDocument

BHP Billiton. (2016a). Global Locations. Retrieved from http://www.bhpbilliton.com/businesses/globaloperationsmap

BHP Billiton. (2016b). Our Contribution. Retrieved from http://www.bhpbilliton.com/society/ourcontribution

Casinader, N. (2014). *Culture, Transnational Education and Thinking: Case Studies in Global Schooling*. Milton Park, Abingdon: Routledge.

Casinader, N. (2015). Culture and Thinking in Comparative Education: The Globalism of an Empirical Mutual Identity. In J. Zajda (Ed.), *Second International Handbook on Globalisation, Education and Policy Research* (pp. 337–352). Dordrecht, The Netherlands: Springer.

Casinader, N. (2016a). A Lost Conduit for Intercultural Education: School Geography and the Potential for Transformation in the Australian Curriculum. *Intercultural Education, 27*(3), 257–273. doi:10.1080/14675986.2016.1150650 [Early Online June 30 2016].

Casinader, N. (2016b) Transnationalism in the Australian Curriculum: new horizons or destinations of the past?. *Discourse: Studies in the Cultural Politics of Education, 37(3)*, 327-340, doi: 10.1080/01596306.2015.1023701 [Early Online March 25 2015].

Casinader, N., & Walsh, L. (2015). Teacher Transculturalism and Cultural Difference: Addressing Racism in Australian Schools. *International Education Journal: Comparative Perspectives, Special Edition: ANZCIES Conference Proceedings, 14*(2), 51–62.

Freudenberg, N. (2015). The 100 largest Governments and Corporations by Revenue. Retrieved from http://www.corporationsandhealth.org/2015/08/27/the-100-largest-governments-and-corporations-by-revenue/

Iriye, A. (2004). Transnational History. *Contemporary European History, 13*(2), 211–222.

Kumar, P. (2013). Bridging East and West Educational Divides in Singapore. *Comparative Education, 49*(1), 72–87. doi:10.1080/03050068.2012.740221

Low, N., & Gleeson, B. (1998). Situating Justice in the Environment: The Case of BHP at the Ok Tedi Copper Mine. *Antipode, 30*(3), 201–226.

McKenzie, P., Kos, J., Walker, M., & Hong, J. (2008). *Staff in Australia's Schools 2007*. Retrieved from Canberra: http://docs.education.gov.au/system/files/doc/other/sias2010_main_report_final_nov11_2.pdf

McKenzie, P., Rowley, G., Weldon, P., & Murphy, M. (2011). *Staff in Australia's Schools 2010: Main Report on the Survey*. Retrieved from Melbourne: http://docs.education.gov.au/system/files/doc/other/sias2010_main_report_final_nov11_2.pdf

McKenzie, P., Weldon, P., Rowley, G., Murphy, M., & McMillan, J. (2014). *Staff in Australia's Schools 2013: Main Report on the Survey*. Melbourne: Australian Council for Educational Research. Retrieved from http://docs.education.gov.au/system/files/doc/other/sias2010_main_report_final_nov11_2.pdf.

Ministry of Education Malaysia. (2012). *Malaysia Education Blueprint 2013–25: Preliminary Report*. Retrieved from Kuala Lumpur: http://www.moe.gov.my/userfiles/file/PPP/Preliminary-Blueprint-ExecSummary-Eng.pdf

Moulton, E. (2016). BHP Billiton, Vale Facing $7 Billion Fine for Brazil's Biggest Environmental Disaster. *news.com.au*. Retrieved from http://www.news.com.au/technology/environment/bhp-billiton-vale-facing-7-billion-fine-for-brazils-biggest-environmental-disaster/news-story/60c8e007d64f98fd701cbfb75ec23621

Ritzer, G. (2006). *Mcdonaldization: The Reader*. Thousand Oaks, CA: Pine Forge Press.

Rizvi, F. (2009a). Global Mobility and the Challenges of Educational Research and Policy. *Yearbook of the National Society for the Study of Education, 108*(2), 268–289. doi:10.1111/j.1744-7984.2009.01172.x

Rizvi, F. (2009b). Towards Cosmopolitan Learning. *Discourse: Studies in the Cultural Politics of Education, 30*(3), 253–268. doi:10.1080/01596300903036863

UNESCO. (2014). *Global Citizenship Education – Preparing Learners for the Challenges of the Twenty-First Century*. Paris: UNESCO.

Yang, R., & Qiu, F.-F. (2010). Globalisation and Chinese Knowledge Diaspora: An Australian Case Study. *Australian Educational Researcher, 37*(3), 19–37.

# Index

Note: figures and tables are denoted with italicized page numbers.